CHRISTOPHER MARLOWE AND THE FAILURE TO UNIFY

In this sustained full length study of Marlowe's plays, Andrew Duxfield argues that Marlovian drama exhibits a marked interest in unity and unification, and that in doing so it engages with a discourse of anxiety over social discord that was prominent in the 1580s and 1590s. In combination with the ambiguity of the plays, he suggests, this focus produces a tension that both heightens dramatic effect and facilitates a cynical response to contemporary evocations of and pleas for unity.

This book has three main aims. Firstly, it establishes that Marlowe's tragedies exhibit a profound interest in the process of reduction and the ideal of unity. Duxfield shows this interest to manifest itself in different ways in each of the plays. Secondly, it identifies this interest in unity and unification as an engagement in a cultural discourse that was particularly prevalent in England during Marlowe's writing career; during the late 1580s and early 1590s heightened inter-confessional tension, the threat and reality of foreign invasion and public puritan dissent in the form of the Marprelate controversy provoked considerable public anxiety about social discord. Thirdly, the book considers the plays' focus on unity in relation to their marked ambiguity; throughout all of the plays, unifying ideals and reductive processes are consistently subject to renegotiation with, or undercut entirely by, the complexity and ambiguity of the dramas in which they feature.

Duxfield's focus on unity as a theme throughout the plays provides a new lens through which to examine the place of Marlowe's work in its cultural moment.

Andrew Duxfield is Lecturer in English Literature at Coventry University, UK.

Studies in Performance and Early Modern Drama

General Editor's Preface
Helen Ostovich, McMaster University

Performance assumes a string of creative, analytical, and collaborative acts that, in defiance of theatrical ephemerality, live on through records, manuscripts, and printed books. The monographs and essay collections in this series offer original research which addresses theatre histories and performance histories in the context of the sixteenth and seventeenth century life. Of especial interest are studies in which women's activities are a central feature of discussion as financial or technical supporters (patrons, musicians, dancers, seamstresses, wigmakers, or 'gatherers'), if not authors or performers per se. Welcome too are critiques of early modern drama that not only take into account the production values of the plays, but also speculate on how intellectual advances or popular culture affect the theatre.

The series logo, selected by my colleague Mary V. Silcox, derives from Thomas Combe's duodecimo volume, *The Theater of Fine Devices* (London, 1592), Emblem VI, sig. B. The emblem of four masks has a verse which makes claims for the increasing complexity of early modern experience, a complexity that makes interpretation difficult. Hence the corresponding perhaps uneasy rise in sophistication:

> Masks will be more hereafter in request,
> And grow more deare than they did heretofore.

No longer simply signs of performance 'in play and jest', the mask has become the 'double face' worn 'in earnest' even by 'the best' of people, in order to manipulate or profit from the world around them. The books stamped with this design attempt to understand the complications of performance produced on stage and interpreted by the audience, whose experiences outside the theatre may reflect the emblem's argument:

> Most men do use some colour'd shift
> For to conceal their craftie drift.

Centuries after their first presentations, the possible performance choices and meanings they engender still stir the imaginations of actors, audiences, and readers of early plays. The products of scholarly creativity in this series, I hope, will also stir imaginations to new ways of thinking about performance.

Christopher Marlowe and the Failure to Unify

ANDREW DUXFIELD
Coventry University, UK

ASHGATE

© Andrew Duxfield 2015

All rights reserved. No part of this publication may be reproduced, stored in a retrieval system or transmitted in any form or by any means, electronic, mechanical, photocopying, recording or otherwise without the prior permission of the publisher.

Andrew Duxfield has asserted his right under the Copyright, Designs and Patents Act, 1988, to be identified as the author of this work.

Published by
Ashgate Publishing Limited
Wey Court East
Union Road
Farnham
Surrey, GU9 7PT
England

Ashgate Publishing Company
110 Cherry Street
Suite 3-1
Burlington, VT 05401-3818
USA

www.ashgate.com

British Library Cataloguing in Publication Data
A catalogue record for this book is available from the British Library

The Library of Congress has cataloged the printed edition as follows:
Duxfield, Andrew.
  Christopher Marlowe and the failure to unify / by Andrew Duxfield.
   pages cm. — (Studies in performance and early modern drama)
  Includes bibliographical references and index.
   ISBN 978-1-4724-3951-2 (hardcover) — ISBN 978-1-4724-3952-9 (ebook) — ISBN 978-1-4724-3953-6 (epub)
  1. Marlowe, Christopher, 1564–1593—Criticism and interpretation. I. Title.
  PR2674.D79 2015
  822'.3—dc23
                                                                    2014045102
ISBN: 9781472439512 (hbk)
ISBN: 9781472439529 (ebk – PDF)
ISBN: 9781472439536 (ebk – ePUB)

Printed in the United Kingdom by Henry Ling Limited, at the Dorset Press, Dorchester, DT1 1HD

Contents

Acknowledgements	*vii*
Introduction	1
1 Building a Statelier Troy: *Dido, Queen of Carthage*	13
2 Reduced to a Map: *Tamburlaine the Great*, Parts One and Two	39
3 "Resolve me of all ambiguities": *Doctor Faustus*	65
4 Individual and Multitude: *The Jew of Malta* and *The Massacre at Paris*	89
5 True Contraries: *Edward II*	117
Afterword	147
Bibliography	*149*
Index	*161*

Acknowledgements

Throughout the preparation and completion of this project I have been lucky enough to receive advice and support from a range of talented and generous people from inside and outside of the academic community. My former colleagues at Sheffield Hallam University have all played a part in getting the project to this final stage, whether by offering practical advice, sharing ideas or providing the good company necessary to keep things in perspective. Special thanks, though, are due to a few colleagues from SHU and further afield: my PhD supervisor Lisa Hopkins, under whose astute guidance and kind support I produced what turned out to be the initial version of this book; Matthew Steggle, Tom Rutter and Mark Burnett, who each read the MS in its early form and provided invaluable feedback; Annaliese Connolly, who offered insight on Marlowe's dramatic relationship to George Peele; Dan Cadman, who as well as offering a reservoir of moral support also read the final draft; and, finally, Ashgate's anonymous reviewer, whose comments were both erudite and constructive. Each of these individuals has made this a better book than it would have been without their help, but any flaws which remain are, of course, entirely of my own making. Many thanks are due also to Erika Gaffney and Stephanie Peake, whose patience and professionalism have made this first foray into monograph publication considerably less stressful than it might have been.

I would like to thank my friends and family, whose confidence in me is always a great tonic. Mum and Helen, this book is for you.

Some material in this book has been published elsewhere. A small section of the Introduction and part of Chapter 4 appeared in "The Uses of Unity: Individual and Multitude in *The Jew of Malta*," *Marlowe Studies: An Annual* 3 (2013): 63–82, while work from Chapter 3 has formed the basis of two publications: "'Resolve me of all ambiguities': *Doctor Faustus* and the Failure to Unify," *EMLS* Special Issue 17 (2007): n.p., and "New Directions: *Doctor Faustus* and Renaissance Hermeticism," in *Doctor Faustus: A Critical Guide*, edited by Sara Munson Deats (London: Continuum, 2010), 96–110.

Introduction

Critical tradition has often associated the work of Christopher Marlowe with grandness of scale. The motivating spirit of the plays, this tradition suggests, is an overreaching ambition which always longs for expansion; Marlowe's protagonists crave more knowledge, more power and more territory, and are ultimately destroyed by the limitlessness of their desires. This book does not seek to overturn this entirely reasonable conception of Marlowe's plays, but nonetheless aims to examine a tendency within the plays which ostensibly runs counter to a preoccupation with expansion and aggrandizement. That is, this book will suggest that Marlowe's tragedies exhibit a profound interest in the process of reduction and the ideal of unity. This interest is manifested in different ways in each of the plays: in some cases unifying projects are pursued by individual protagonists, while in others the application of unifying logic or rhetoric by representatives of state power is foregrounded. Throughout all of the plays, though, this focus on reduction and unity helps to produce a tension: unifying ideals and reductive processes are consistently subject to renegotiation with or undercut entirely by the complexity and ambiguity of the dramas in which they feature.

Why might a playwright of the late 1580s and early 1590s be particularly interested in the idea of unity? In approaching the concept, I argue, Marlowe engages in a discourse that was particularly prevalent in the cultural consciousness during his short writing career. In a sense, much of Elizabeth I's reign had been devoted to establishing and maintaining a degree of unity amongst a religiously bifurcated populace, a task that she and her Privy Council approached pragmatically by offering a *via media* and refusing to open windows into men's souls. In the latter part of her reign, from the time at which Marlowe was probably writing *Dido, Queen of Carthage* at Cambridge, that unity becomes a particularly urgent topic. John Guy has argued persuasively for the consideration of Elizabeth's reign as consisting of two distinct phases, the second of which began in 1585. This second phase, opening with the deployment of English troops to the Low Countries, was characterized by the reversal of a previously non-interventionist foreign policy and subsequently by the threat of both invasion from foreign Catholic enemies and usurpation by recusant plotters at home. The "physical and emotional strains" of these aspects of Elizabeth's "second reign," Guy suggests, were exacerbated by an unstable economic climate, bad harvests and outbreaks of disease, and manifested themselves in increased factionalism at court and insubordination in the country.[1]

---

[1] John Guy, "Introduction: The 1590s: The Second Reign of Elizabeth I?" in *The Reign of Elizabeth I: Court and Culture in the Last Decade*, ed. John Guy (Cambridge: Cambridge University Press, 1995), 1. On factionalism at court, see Paul E. J. Hammer, *The Polarisation of Elizabethan Politics: The Political Career of Robert Devereux, 2nd Earl of Essex, 1585–1597* (Cambridge: Cambridge University Press, 1999). Hammer writes that "Compared to the glories of the 'high Elizabethan' age of the 1570s and early 1580s,

In the years from the first performances of *Tamburlaine* in 1587 to Marlowe's death in 1593, the execution of Mary, Queen of Scots, the Spanish Armada, the papal bull renewing the excommunication of Elizabeth and the Marprelate controversy all contributed to this acute sense of dissolution.

In this atmosphere of political and societal discord, England's cultural output exhibits an intensified interest in the idea of political and civil unity, as a number of clergymen, polemicists and cultural commentators exhorted their readers and auditors to understand the dangers of discord and the virtues of a unified society. Robert Hitchcock, in a pamphlet published in 1590, warned that "Euen as discord in a cittie doth discouer and giues occasion to those that lye in waite to betray, to perform their practises well: so vnitie doth knit together the diuersities of opinions, and of many making one body alone keepe gouernments and States vncorrupted."[2]

Hitchcock's point, that unity makes a commonwealth strong while discord presents opportunities to its enemies, is made in a variety of ways by a range of writers in the latter half of the 1580s. William Averell argues in 1588 that "if wee liue together in unitie … wee shall bée more sure and safe than if wee were enclosed about with the strongest bulwarkes, or enuironed rounde with inuincible rampiers."[3] Contemporary calls for unity often made use of theological reasoning. Unity had previously tended to be a barb thrown by Catholic polemicists keen to demonstrate the illegitimacy of Reformation theology by virtue of its separation from the true unified church, but the increasingly vocal presence of nonconformist Protestantism in England, manifested most famously in the Marprelate controversy, meant that unity began to become a watchword of Anglican sympathizers too.[4] A commonly occurring trope is that presented by the clergyman George Wither in 1585, who argues that "The *body* compacted of many members, setteth before vs the vnity that ought to be amongst all true Christians, who are the misticall *body*

---

the 1590s seem bleak and dark," and notes that this gloomy decade was "characterized by war and the heavy burdens which it imposed on the realm, the growing senescence of the queen and her councillors, and bitter factional discord which tore at the very heart of the regime" (1). Patrick Collinson also demonstrates the extent to which governance in the late Elizabethan period was multivocal; see "The Monarchical Republic of Queen Elizabeth I" in *Elizabethan Essays* (London: The Hambledon Press, 1994).

[2] Robert Hitchcock, *The quintesence of wit being a corrant comfort of conceites, maximies, and poleticke deuises* (London: 1590), STC (2nd ed.) / 21744, Sig. D4v–E.

[3] William Averell, *A mervailous combat of contrarieties* (London: 1588). STC (2nd ed.) / 981, Sig. D3.

[4] An example of the Catholic characterization of Protestants as disunifiers of the true church can be seen in an account of the defence of Robert Anderton, a Jesuit seminarist who had been arrested and faced interrogation by members of the Privy Council. Anderton, the account goes, justified his proselytizing on the grounds that "he taketh such as be out of the unitie of the Church of Rome, to stand in state of damnation, and that therefore he is bounde in conscience to doe what he can to reclaime them." Anon., *A Declaration of the Queenes Maiesties most gratious dealing with William Marsden and Robert Anderton, seminarie priests sithence the time of their iust condemnation, being conuicted according to the lawes, and of their obstinacie in refusing to acknowledge their duetie and allegeance to her Maiestie, 1586* (London: 1586), STC (2nd ed.) / 8157.

of Iesus Christ."[5] The notion of the body politic, or of its oneness with Christ, is not a new one in the 1580s, but the period does see it begin to be invoked as an urgent plea to potentially schismatic members of the commonweal to remember the importance of unity. As William James preaches in a sermon of 1589:

> If therfore one spirit haue fashioned vs all, and haue made vs all one body, and fed vs with one & the same heauenly table, haue watred vs all with one heauenly deaw from aboue, which all are to haue drunke of the same spirit: If it haue vnited vs who were before so farre different one from another: If the members then make one body, when they all as it were do grow and knit themselues together: why dreame we of any the least dissention, the least difference?[6]

These public expressions of concerns over discord were reflective of what Guy terms an "obsessional" emphasis on addressing social revolt and religious nonconformity increasingly adopted by privy councillors and magistrates from 1585 onwards.[7] This atmosphere of concern over the discordance of society and desire for a move towards unity provides an illuminating context for a number of Marlowe's plays. Depictions of civil unrest in *Edward II* and *The Massacre at Paris* register the 1590s climate of anxiety, while *Dido, Queen of Carthage* and *The Jew of Malta* undertake caustic interrogations of unifying narratives imposed from above by self-interested powers.

More broadly speaking, the sixteenth-century schism in European Christianity prompted new philosophical and theological developments amongst the intellectual community that proposed syncretic solutions to the ongoing religious strife. Hermeticism, a quasi-religious blend of Christianity and neoplatonism, was prominent among these pan-European irenic visions in the 1580s and 1590s, with proponents including the English magus John Dee and the itinerant cleric Giordano Bruno. The central focus of Hermeticism, put forward in works such as Dee's *Monas Hieroglyphica*, was oneness achieved through knowledge: since the world and all of its inhabitants are the products of the intellect of God, a complete understanding of the world and the self could provide the spiritually wise with knowledge of – and oneness with – God. With its focus on unity and its potential for human ascension, Hermeticism provided a spiritual world view that was both a tonic for post-Reformation religious discord and a good fit for the Renaissance mood of secular aspiration. In *Doctor Faustus*, Marlowe engages with the unifying drive of this esoteric philosophy, depicting in the process a protagonist whose frustration with disparate, compartmentalized knowledge leads him to seek to be resolved "of all ambiguities" (1. 1. 82).[8] Faustus's ambitions are grand, but the end

---

[5] George Wither, *An A. B. C. for Layemen* (London: 1585), STC (2nd ed.) / 25888, Sig. B4.

[6] William James, *A sermon preached at Paules Crosse the IX. of Nouember, 1589* (London: 1590), STC (2nd ed.) / 14464, Sig. C.

[7] Guy, "The Second Reign," 1.

[8] Christopher Marlowe, *Doctor Faustus: A- and B-Texts (1604, 1616)*, ed. David Bevington and Eric Rasmussen (Manchester: Manchester University Press, 1993). A-Text.

to which they are aimed is essentially one which reduces and unites. The same can be said of Marlowe's other famously self-aggrandizing protagonist, Tamburlaine, who labours to conquer vast expanses of land only in order to "reduce them to a map" (4. 4. 80).[9]

Marlowe's interest in reduction and unity is not unique in the literature of the period. In the first years of Elizabeth's reign, as England was emerging from a volatile period of successive regime changes, the preface to Sackville and Norton's political tragedy *Gorboduc* employed a dumb show to demonstrate the virtues of a unified society:

> First the music of the violins began to play, during which came in upon the stage six wild men, clothed in leaves. Of whom the first bare in his neck a fagot of small sticks, which they all, both severally and together, assayed with all their strengths to break, but it could not be broken by them. At the length one of them plucked out one of the sticks and brake it: and the rest plucking out all the other sticks one after another did easily break them, the same being severed, which being conjoined they had before attempted in vain. After they had this done, they departed the stage, and the music ceased. Hereby was signified, that a state knit in unity doth continue strong against all force, but being divided, is easily destroyed.[10]

The point of the dumb show – that unity is the soundest form of defence while discord invites defeat to external enemies – anticipates those made by many pamphlet writers during Marlowe's writing career, but it is also one which resurfaces in a number of guises in the work of the dramatist's literary contemporaries. It can be seen in Shakespeare's *Henry VI*, which dramatizes the disintegration of an empire brought about by the disunity of its nobility; the point is made explicit by Sir William Lucy in Part One, when he reprimands the squabbling Somerset and York for their failure to come to the aid of the captured Talbot. "The fraud of England, not the force of France," he says, is responsible for the demise of Talbot, who "dies betray'd to fortune by your strife" (4. 4. 36, 39).[11]

England need fear no enemy, the prevailing impression seems to be, if only it could unite itself. But along with that notion seems to come a deep-rooted sense

---

[9] Christopher Marlowe, *Tamburlaine*, ed. J. S. Cunningham (Manchester: Manchester University Press, 1981).

[10] A. K. McIlwraith, ed., *Five Elizabethan Tragedies* (Oxford: Oxford University Press, 1938), 73.

[11] William Shakespeare, *The First Part of King Henry VI* (The Arden Shakespeare), ed. Andrew S. Cairncross (London: Methuen, 1962). For a discussion on the debate over the authorship of the play, in which Marlowe's contribution has been suggested, see introduction, xxviii–xxxvii. Cairncross concludes that "there seems no sufficient reason to doubt Shakespeare's authorship of the whole play" (xxxvi). This view is supported by C. G. Harlow in "A Source for Nashe's Terrors of the Night, and the Authorship of *1 Henry VI*," *Studies in English Literature, 1500–1900* 5, no. 1 (1965), and "The Authorship of *1 Henry VI* (Continued)," *Studies in English Literature, 1500–1900* 5, no. 2 (1965).

Introduction 5

of English division. Carol Weiner has noted that English anti-Catholic sentiment was informed by the often mistaken notion that the Roman Church was a wholly harmonious body, united under an admired and unilaterally obeyed spiritual leader.[12] That the Catholic other was popularly constructed in this way suggests that the disunity of the self against which it was constructed was keenly felt in Elizabethan England, particularly at times of intensified religious conflict such as the years during which Marlowe wrote.

Thus far this discussion has focused on the conception of unity as a source of strength at the level of the state, but late Elizabethan writers employed the trope when examining personal and spiritual concerns also. In *Arden of Faversham*, Mosbie characterizes inconstant love as "Like to a pillar built of many stones, / Yet neither with good mortar well compact / Nor with cement to fasten it at the joints" (4. 1. 91–3). Just as the discordant state is vulnerable to calamity, so inconstant love, composed precariously from numerous disparate parts, shakes in the wind and "being touched, straight falls unto the earth" (4. 1. 96).[13] Perhaps a more striking equation of unity with constancy occurs in Book One of Spenser's *The Faerie Queene*, which offers an extended exposition of the singularity of faith, loyalty and truth, in opposition to the duplicity of ambition, greed and lies. The book deals with the spiritual maturation of the Redcrosse Knight, who must eschew the company of the false Duessa in favour of that of the faithful Una, whose names are cognates of "two" and "one" respectively. Beyond the implications of the names given to his characters, Spenser drives home his point by presenting the book's corrupting characters as possessing multiple identities. Archimago appears in a number of guises to gull his victims, and Duessa, "the daughter of deceit and shame" (1. 5. 26. 9), adopts the persona of Fidessa. By contrast, Una, "the only daughter of a king and queen" (1. 7. 5. 43), is Una throughout.[14] Spenser's epic clearly equates unity with virtue.

As this volume will show, Marlowe interrogates the notion of unity in an altogether different way to Spenser, and in a way which engages sceptically with the kinds of calls to unity that were appearing in the pamphlet culture of the late 1580s and early 1590s. Crucial to understanding Marlowe's treatment of unity, and central to the argument of this book, is the marked ambiguity of his plays. The moral ambiguity, in particular, of Marlowe's work has been the subject of some critical attention over the years. Christopher Fanta's extended essay *Marlowe's "Agonists"* considers at length the "perplexing ambiguity" of the moral content of the plays, suggesting that only certain minor characters (virtuous if one-dimensional figures such as Abigail in *The Jew of Malta* or the old man in *Faustus*, whom he terms "agonists") offer a moral compass to the audience

---

[12] See Carol Z. Weiner, "The Beleaguered Isle: A Study of Elizabethan and Early Jacobean Anti-Catholicism," *Past and Present* 51 (1971).

[13] Anon., *Arden of Feversham*, in *Minor Elizabethan Drama (1): Pre-Shakespearean Tragedies* (London: J. M. Dent & Sons, 1929).

[14] Edmund Spenser, *The Faerie Queene*, ed. Thomas P. Roche Jr. and C. Patrick O'Donnell Jr. (London: Penguin, 1987).

in what is otherwise a morass of repugnant alternatives.[15] Fanta sees Marlowe's drama as uniquely ambiguous even by the standards of the dense and complex literary output of the age; for him, even Shakespeare's drama, nuanced as it is, tends ultimately towards a sense of order that is eschewed by Marlowe. Fanta is astute in his observation of the plays' ambiguity, but, as with many twentieth-century Marlowe critics, the rationale of his project is to extrapolate from the indeterminacy of the texts an impression of the author's psyche: "ambiguity in the creation," he suggests, "may ... result from ambivalence in the creator," and accordingly "the plays give expression to a duality of outlook, and equally to a gradually developed pessimism, that characterized Marlowe's mind."[16] I am more cautious than Fanta about claiming a uniqueness for Marlowe's ambiguity and I read the texts as cultural products rather than as conduits to the mind of an artist (more on this shortly), but Fanta's central observation – that Marlowe's plays exhibit a moral ambiguity that is at the very least striking – forms one of the key premises of this book. More recently, Sara Munson Deats has argued that Marlowe's plays can be conceived of as "interrogative drama," that is, drama which poses but does not resolve questions.[17] Deats cites the work of critics who have theorized ambiguity in Shakespeare's plays as providing paradigms that might garner a fuller understanding of Marlowe's work. These critics include Annabel Patterson, who coins the term "functional ambiguity" to denote the tactical deployment of indeterminacy by dramatists who sought to avoid the scrutiny of the censor; Joel Altman, who suggests that drama in the period mimicked the dialectical rhetoric of the kind practised in the universities; and Ernest B. Gilman, who sees in the drama an echo of the fashion for anamorphic paintings which reveal different content depending on the perspective of the viewer.[18] Deats applies these lines

---

[15] Christopher G. Fanta, *Marlowe's "Agonists": An Approach to the Ambiguity of His Plays* (Cambridge, MA: Harvard University Press, 1970).

[16] Ibid., 7.

[17] Sara Munson Deats, "Marlowe's Interrogative Drama: *Dido, Tamburlaine, Faustus*, and *Edward II*," in *Marlowe's Empery: Expanding His Critical Contexts*, ed. Sara Munson Deats and Robert A. Logan (London: Associated University Presses, 2002). For other discussions that foreground the ambiguity of Marlowe's work see, for example, William French, "Double View in *Doctor Faustus*," *West Virginia University Philological Papers* 17 (1970); John F. McElroy, "Repetition, Contrariety, and Individualization in *Edward II*," *Studies in English Literature, 1500–1900* 24 (1984); and Kristen Poole, "*Dr. Faustus* and Reformation Theology," in *Early Modern English Drama: A Critical Companion*, ed. Garrett A. Sullivan, Patrick Cheney and Andrew Hadfield (Oxford: Oxford University Press, 2005). Robert Logan has developed the discussion by suggesting that Shakespeare's most significant artistic inheritance from Marlowe was "an inventiveness with various forms of dramaturgical ambiguities," adding that "both of these playwrights resolutely refused to resolve these ambiguities." See *Shakespeare's Marlowe: The Influence of Christopher Marlowe on Shakespeare's Artistry* (Aldershot: Ashgate, 2007), 221.

[18] See Annabel Patterson, *Censorship and Interpretation: The Conditions of Writing and Reading in Early Modern England* (Madison: University of Wisconsin Press, 1984); Joel Altman, *The Tudor Play of Mind: Rhetorical Inquiry and the Development of Elizabethan*

of thought to Marlowe's dramatic oeuvre, suggesting that he might be "the first English playwright to script dialogical dramas that inscribe the multiplicity and indecidibility of human experience, thereby anticipating, and perhaps even precipitating, the greater achievements of Jacobean tragedy."[19]

Each of the chapters in this book will engage in some of the further exploration of the ambiguity of the plays that Deats calls for, and as a whole my argument is sympathetic to the notion that Marlovian tragedy anticipates the indeterminacy of Jacobean drama. In his landmark study *Radical Tragedy*, Jonathan Dollimore characterizes that indeterminacy in the following terms:

> In Jacobean tragedy, the rejection of metaphysical harmony provokes the rejection of aesthetic harmony and the emergence of a new dialectic structure. Coherence comes to reside in the sharpness of definition given *to* metaphysical and social dislocation, not in an aesthetic, religious or didactic resolution *of* it. Thus the alternative to such resolution is not necessarily "irresolution" in the sense of intending, yet failing to dispose of contradictions. On the contrary, it may be that contradictory accounts of experience are forced into "misalignment," the tension which this generates being a way of getting us to confront the problematic and contradictory nature of society itself.[20]

Dollimore's eloquent account of the irresolution of Jacobean tragedy might apply equally well to Marlowe's dramatic work in a way that it wouldn't for Marlowe's contemporaries. This is not to say that Marlowe was the only playwright of his time whose plays resisted resolution or focused on dislocation; Shakespeare is of course famed for his complex characterization, and critics such as Simon Shepherd, Ruth Lunney and John Parker have argued that the earlier morality drama, from which Marlowe is usually credited with having made a decisive and trend-setting break, is itself invested with a greater degree of complexity and dramatic ambiguity than is generally assumed.[21] But, as I hope this book will demonstrate, Marlowe's drama insists on moral ambiguity and indeterminacy to an extent that is not seen again until Shakespeare's Jacobean tragedies. Rather than offering an "aesthetic, religious, or didactic resolution" of dislocation, which Dollimore implies is characteristic of earlier drama, Marlowe's work steadfastly

---

Drama (Berkeley: University of California Press, 1978); and Ernest B. Gilman, *The Curious Perspective: Literary and Pictorial Wit in the Seventeenth Century* (New Haven, CT: Yale University Press, 1978).

[19] Deats, "Marlowe's Interrogative Drama," 125.

[20] Jonathan Dollimore, *Radical Tragedy: Religion, Ideology and Power in the Drama of Shakespeare and his Contemporaries*, 3rd ed. (Basingstoke: Palgrave Macmillan, 2004), 39.

[21] See Simon Shepherd, *Marlowe and the Politics of Elizabethan Theatre* (London: Harvester Wheatsheaf, 1986); Ruth Lunney, *Marlowe and the Popular Tradition: Innovation in the English Drama Before 1595* (Manchester: Manchester University Press, 2002); and John Parker, *The Aesthetics of Antichrist: From Christian Drama to Christopher Marlowe* (London: Cornell University Press, 2007).

resists resolution. His distinctiveness in this respect can be seen by looking at the work of George Peele, a contemporary whose plays are in many ways similar to, or at least derivative of, Marlowe's.[22] Both *The Battle of Alcazar* and *David and Bethsabe* imitate Marlovian, and particularly Tamburlanean, rhetoric, often explicitly. Muly Mahamet, when scoffing at the prospect of facing the might of Amurath's army, invokes his men to "Convey Tamburlaine into our Afric here" (1. 2. 35),[23] and Peele does his best to convey the sonority of Marlowe's verse into his own work: Tamburlaine's "pampered jades of Asia" (Two. 4. 3. 1), for instance, become "shepherd's-dogs of Israel" (187)[24] in *David and Bethsabe* and "proud malicious dogs of Italy" (5. 1. 126) in *Alcazar*. Peele's drama, however, lacks entirely the tension which this book examines in Marlowe's work. While *Alcazar* does dramatize the results of a disunited state, its heroes and villains are portrayed unilaterally as such; in contrast to *Tamburlaine*, the ambitious upstart here gets his comeuppance, and the correct order of things is reassuringly and unquestioningly restored at the play's close, a comfort which Marlowe does not grant to his audience.

The irresolution of Marlowe's plays is bound up with the interest they exhibit in unity. This interest takes different shapes in different plays: in *Doctor Faustus* the focus of the protagonist is on the unification of knowledge, a pursuit informed by contemporary Hermetic philosophy which privileged unity as the most divine of states; in *Tamburlaine* we witness the attempt of the protagonist not only to reduce the complexity of the world to a map but also to impose unity upon the competing aspects of his own subjectivity. The other plays deal with unity on a broader level: *Dido, Queen of Carthage* engages with and critiques mytho-historical narratives that collapse disparate cultural heritages into a unified concept of common origin; *The Jew of Malta* interrogates the ideological uses of unifying state rhetoric; and *Edward II* and *The Massacre at Paris* dramatize the conflicts inherent in theories of kingship which at once invest a sovereign with absolute power and at the same time conceptualize a unity between the sovereign and his subjects. What is common to all of the unifying ideals explored in Marlowe's drama is that they each find the aforementioned ambiguity of the plays insurmountable. In the indeterminate play worlds Marlowe creates – worlds which are stubbornly resistant to resolution – unifying projects like those of Faustus and Tamburlaine unravel and rhetorics of unity such as those employed in *The Jew of Malta* are shown to be illusory.

---

[22] On the relationship between Marlowe's work and Peele's, see Annaliese Connolly, "Peele's David and Bethsabe: Reconsidering Biblical Drama of the Long 1590s," *Early Modern Literary Studies* Special Issue 16 (October 2007), <http://purl.oclc.org/emls/si-16/connpeel.htm> (accessed 26 July 2013); Peter Berek, "*Tamburlaine*'s Weak Sons: Imitation as Interpretation Before 1593," *Renaissance Drama* 13 (1982); and Richard Levin, "The Contemporary Perception of Marlowe's Tamburlaine," *Medieval and Renaissance Drama in England* 1 (1984).

[23] George Peele, *The Battle of Alcazar*, in *The Stukeley Plays*, ed. Charles Edelman (Manchester: Manchester University Press, 2005).

[24] George Peele, *David and Bethsabe*, in *Minor Elizabethan Drama (I): Pre-Shakespearean Tragedies* (London: J. M. Dent & Sons, 1929).

Of course, the consideration of unity, particularly on the level of the individual, is not new in early modern or even Marlowe studies. Influential cultural materialist studies by Jonathan Dollimore and Catherine Belsey, which theorize the early modern subject as a discursive entity that is fractured and discontinuous, reject the notion of the unified, transcendent individual conceived of by post-enlightenment liberal humanism.[25] For Dollimore, and also for new historicists like Stephen Greenblatt, the notion of the disunified subject was accompanied by the rejection of the idea, most famously propounded by E. M. W. Tillyard, that early modern drama abhorred chaos and tended towards a vindication of order and hierarchy; for them, the stage was a space for interrogation and subversion (although opinions on how effective a motor of political change early modern drama was differ between cultural materialist and new historicist critics).[26] These ideas have been influential in Marlowe studies (indeed, Greenblatt, Dollimore and Belsey all discuss Marlowe's plays in their landmark works, and Deats engages with their ideas in her study of the plays),[27] not least because Marlowe's transgressive persona (whether an historical actuality or the product of mythography) renders him particularly apt to be read as a playwright of dissolution. This study builds on these critical foundations: it reads the plays as always insisting on the potential for dissolution and as conceiving of identity as multivalent, discontinuous and even fractured. Where this study differentiates itself from previous readings is that it considers not just the ways in which Marlowe's plays negate unity, but also the way in which they focus on the pursuit or illusion of unity in the process of negating it.

Before closing this introductory chapter, I would add a couple more notes on the rationale of this volume. Firstly, I steer clear of incorporating Marlowe's biography into my reading of his plays. I do so in part because a number of substantial biographical studies of Marlowe have appeared in the last decade, each providing biographically infused critical readings of his works, but also because I find myself in agreement with Lukas Erne that biographical approaches to Marlowe's work often tend towards circularity in that they extrapolate Marlowe's character from his literary work and then base readings of the literary work upon that extrapolation.[28] Secondly, I have limited the scope of this volume to

---

[25] See Catherine Belsey, *The Subject of Tragedy: Identity and Difference in Renaissance Drama* (London: Methuen, 1985), and Dollimore, *Radical Tragedy*.

[26] See Stephen Greenblatt, *Renaissance Self-Fashioning: From More to Shakespeare* (Chicago: Chicago University Press, 2005), and E. M. W. Tillyard, *The Elizabethan World Picture* (London: Penguin, 1990).

[27] Sara Munson Deats, *Sex, Gender, and Desire in the Plays of Christopher Marlowe* (Newark: University of Delaware Press, 1997).

[28] See Lukas Erne, "Biography, Mythography, and Criticism: The Life and Works of Christopher Marlowe," *Modern Philology* 103, no. 1 (August 2005). For a similar breakdown of the problems of author-centric readings of Marlowe, one with which I concur, see Clare Harraway, *Re-Citing Marlowe: Approaches to the Drama* (Aldershot: Ashgate, 2000), 1–17. Una Ellis-Fermor provides an early example of the circular trend of interpreting Marlowe's life through his works and then vice-versa, when she states that

Marlowe's drama, omitting discussion of his poems and translations (although I will refer to these where appropriate). This is partly due to considerations of space, but also because it is in the drama that the subject which this book explores is at its most evident and most interesting; the tensions inherent in drama, a form which offers competing voices without a mediating narrative guide, provide the perfect conditions for the exploration of the idea of unity and the performance of its negation.

The first chapter of this volume will consider *Dido, Queen of Carthage* in relation to mytho-historical narratives of empire employed in the justification of fledgling imperial activity being carried out by Elizabeth's England. Marlowe's problematic depiction of epic male heroism and divine authority highlights the fictiveness of these narratives, which reductively collapse English history into the mythos of ancient Rome and Troy. The following chapter will be devoted to a discussion of both parts of *Tamburlaine the Great*, concentrating on the dual projects of unification that their eponymous hero embarks upon. As well as displaying an unswerving drive to conquer the world (known and unknown) in its entirety and "reduce it to a map" (4. 4. 80), Tamburlaine also struggles to maintain a unilateral projection of himself. Despite being amongst the more successful of Marlowe's protagonists, Tamburlaine's achievements, I will argue, are ironically undercut, pointing up the impossibility of mastering either the diversity of the world or the indeterminacy of the subject. *Doctor Faustus* will be the focus of my third chapter, which reads the play as presenting the inevitability of failure in any attempt to achieve unified knowledge. Faustus's adoption of magic associates him with contemporary modes of religio-philosophical thought that were esoteric in their most authentic form but also filtered widely into mainstream consciousness, and that stated as their ultimate goal the achievement of intellectual and spiritual unity. Through Faustus's decline from his more serious ambitions to the satisfaction of banal whims, and through the ambiguous generic structuring of the play – at once early modern and medieval – Marlowe presents another world in which unity is a forlorn dream rendered impossible by the deep-seatedness of ideological difference and the self-interest of individuals. The self-interest of

---

"The peculiar difficulties which beset Marlowe's biographers are inherent in the subject, for little is known of his life and some of his most important works are incomplete or survive only in corrupt texts; but the task of gathering together indications and of interpreting from them the nature of the mind and character of the man whom they reveal, promises a reward before which the difficulties are insignificant." *Christopher Marlowe* (London: Methuen, 1927), xi. A recent example of a work in which tenuous biographical claims have been applied to readings of the plays is Park Honan's *Christopher Marlowe: Poet and Spy* (Oxford: Oxford University Press, 2005), while Charles Nicholl's *The Reckoning: The Murder of Christopher Marlowe*, rev. ed. (London: Vintage, 2002), provides an entertaining yet speculative account of Marlowe's death that has been influential in Marlowe biography and criticism. More cautious and profitable approaches to biographically infused readings of Marlowe's work are to be found in David Riggs's *The World of Christopher Marlowe* (London: Faber and Faber, 2004) and Lisa Hopkins's *Christopher Marlowe: A Literary Life* (Basingstoke: Palgrave, 2000).

individuals, and its relationship to the common interest of the society at large, provides the focus of the fourth chapter of this book, which discusses both *The Jew of Malta* and *The Massacre at Paris*. Through the depiction of the marginal figure of the Jew, and through the dramatization of intense religious discord, Marlowe explores the tensions and relationships between the individual and the multitude, as played out in politics and religion. In these plays in which amorality is the norm rather than the exception, we are shown both the dishonesty and the efficacy of religion as a state tool for suppressing its citizens' self-interested actions. In these plays, I will suggest, Marlowe gives what people want to be real – unity under a religious banner – and, bubbling immediately below the surface, what *is* real – a society comprising a collection of individuals whose actions and allegiances are determined only by their desire for power or profit. The final chapter of this volume looks at *Edward II*. That this play deals with a state wracked by disunity is obvious, yet, more interestingly, Marlowe presents in it a world in which the prospect of resolution is philosophically inconceivable – the play is concerned with hierarchical world views that fundamentally contradict yet still depend upon one another. As in *The Jew of Malta*, this play coolly demonstrates the difference between unitary theories of authority and the actuality of factional *Realpolitik*. Overall, by reading the plays in terms of their focus on unity, and the relationship between that focus and the drama's marked indeterminacy, this book aims to build on existing criticism which posits Marlowe's work as interrogative and transgressive, and to provide a new lens through which to view the relationship between the work and the cultural discourses from which it emerged.

Chapter 1
Building a Statelier Troy:
Dido, Queen of Carthage

Dido, Queen of Carthage, like the later *The Jew of Malta*, is a play which makes use of its audience's preconceptions and expectations, complicating them to create an atmosphere of moral ambiguity in which its numerous concerns are developed. Marlowe takes a story with which the educated members of the courtly audience would have been familiar: the portion of Virgil's *Aeneid* (books One and Four) in which the hero, Aeneas, is temporarily distracted from his anointed task of re-establishing Troy in Italy by a love affair with a north-African queen. In Virgil's epic order is restored when Aeneas comes to his senses and sets sail for Italy, leaving Dido to commit suicide, an unfortunate but necessary instance of collateral damage in the hero's mission. Likewise, a generous portion of the audience would have been aware of the Galfridian tradition which held that the people of England were direct descendants from Aeneas through his great-grandson Brutus, who founded "Brutayne" after being banished from Italy for shooting his father in a hunting accident. There were plenty of reasons, then, for Elizabethan playgoers to expect an Aeneas with whom they could identify and whom they could admire. This chapter will explore Marlowe's exploitation and subversion of these expectations, and the ambiguity this engenders, in detail. Against this background of moral ambiguity, I will argue, *Dido* explores the conflict between personal desire and social duty, not simply in the case of Aeneas, but also for Dido and the Olympian gods, and the reaction of individuals when that conflict is irreconcilable. It is by way of this concentration on incompatibility and conflict that *Dido* interrogates the concepts of authority and of authorization. Marlowe's portrayal of the classical gods, in contrast to their representation in Virgil's *Aeneid*, diminishes their authority, and, by extension, the perceived necessity of Aeneas's journey. In doing so, it engages critically with a recurring discourse of authorization in which the legend of Dido and Aeneas is central. Just as Aeneas's task is to create a new empire authorized both by divine sanction and by its direct association with ancient Troy, so the story itself, in its many guises, has been used to authorize various imperial enterprises, from those of Augustan Rome to those of the England of Elizabeth. This chapter will discuss the play's interrogation of reductive tendencies, displayed both within the legend of Dido and in contemporary politics of empire, to seek authorization through association with and replication of history, both real and mythological. Furthermore, it will examine the application of this authorization to programmes of expansion which reproduce the familiar at the expense of diversity, with the overall aim of eliding the kind of incompatibilities that are dramatized in Marlowe's play.

Moral Ambiguity

In re-telling the story of Aeneas's sojourn at Carthage, Marlowe trades in a currency with which his audience, particularly if the play was performed for the educated elite at court,[1] would be very familiar. While there had been a medieval tradition, exemplified by Lydgate's *Troy Book*, of representing Aeneas as a villain complicit in King Priam's murder,[2] Marlowe's play appears to adhere more closely to the version of events as told in *The Aeneid*, in the process automatically imbuing Aeneas with a Virgilian gravitas.[3] The reading of Marlowe's Aeneas as a grand epic hero and masculine exemplar was prevalent in much twentieth-century criticism of the play. J. B. Steane, writing in the mid-twentieth century, suggests that the celestial imagery of the play's early Olympian scenes provides a "setting made for man: the magnificence which the world offers to the human being great enough to take it. Aeneas is such a man."[4] Steane's enthusiastic (and distinctly gendered) account of Marlowe's Aeneas implies the standard expectations of the hero of a Virgilian epic: a man great enough to bear the focus of a work of such great scope must be a great man indeed. For Irving Singer, an epic hero "must always be bigger than life, as a way of carrying the reader's eye or the listener's ear beyond the particularity of any single person, episode, or event."[5]

On the face of it, there is good reason to afford Marlowe's Aeneas the dignity of his Virgilian forebear. After all, in terms of plot, there are few differences between Marlowe's account and Virgil's; Aeneas arrives at Carthage, distraught at the sack of Troy, and is accommodated generously by Dido, with whom he shares a love affair, before being reminded of his higher purpose and setting sail for Italy. Meanwhile, Dido, unwilling to continue her life without him, commits suicide. Marlowe expands the involvement of Iarbas, inventing both his infatuation with

---

[1] On *Dido* as a court play, see Brian Gibbons, "'Unstable Proteus': *The Tragedy of Dido Queen of Carthage*," in *Christopher Marlowe*, ed. Brian Morris (London: Ernest Benn Limited, 1968). See also Martin Wiggins, "When Did Marlowe Write *Dido, Queen of Carthage*?" *Review of English Studies* 59, no. 241 (2008).

[2] In Lydgate's account Aeneas is instrumental in the decision to allow the horse into the city. Later that night Priam awakes during the slaughter of his subjects, aware that "there was treason / Falsely compassed unto his city / By Antenor and also by Enee [Aeneas], / Of whose malice he was no more in doubt," and a short while later is murdered "While Antenor and Enee stood beside." Cited in Vivien Thomas and William Tydeman, eds., *Christopher Marlowe: The Plays and Their Sources* (London: Routledge, 1994), 4–5, lines 6316–9, 6418.

[3] The extent of *Dido*'s debt to *The Aeneid* is disputed. J. B. Steane suggests that, although it has been claimed that up to a third of the play is directly translated or paraphrased from Virgil, "not more than one-seventh or one-eighth of the play follows Virgil with any closeness." See *Marlowe: A Critical Study* (Cambridge: Cambridge University Press, 1964), 51–2. Whatever proportion of the play is taken, directly or indirectly, from Virgil, the close relationship between it and the Augustan epic is undeniable.

[4] Steane, *Marlowe: A Critical Study*, 31.

[5] Irving Singer, "Erotic Transformations in the Legend of Dido and Aeneas," *Modern Language Notes* 90, no. 6 (1975): 767.

Dido and Anna's with him, creating for him an integral role in Aeneas's departure.[6] Marlowe also introduces the comic episode with Cupid and the octogenarian nurse, and amplifies the scale of the carnage at the play's climax, but Aeneas's actions are essentially the same here as they are in Virgil.

Notwithstanding this, the Aeneas we get is not the Aeneas we expect. Steane's account of the play's language and imagery as a setting made for a great man overlooks the fact that the play doesn't even bear his name. This honour, of course, goes to its principal female character. Instead of being a man capable of bearing the weight of a great epic or tragedy, Marlowe's Aeneas is weak-willed, indecisive, and a serial abandoner of women. It is not only in the title of the play that Dido enjoys precedence over Aeneas. Although she is the victim of an Olympian ruse at the hands of Juno and Venus, Dido takes action throughout the play, while Aeneas remains passive, even submissive. This tendency is glimpsed when he appeals to Dido to repair his fleet:

> Yet, Queen of Afric, are my ships unrigg'd,
> My sails all rent in sunder with the wind,
> My oars broken, and my tackling lost,
> Yea, all my navy split with rocks and shelves;
> Nor stern nor anchor have our maimed fleet;
> Our masts the furious winds struck overboard:
> Which piteous wants if Dido will supply,
> We will account her author of our lives.
> (3. 1. 104–11)[7]

This account, one of many delivered by Aeneas regarding hardships he has encountered, culminates in a submission – perhaps rhetorical, but nonetheless prophetic – of his autonomy to Dido, who immediately responds by demanding he stay at Carthage. Similarly, Aeneas's vacillations after embarking on a romantic relationship with Dido are indicative of a comically weak will. When he is first persuaded of his need to leave Carthage and seek out Italy, and shortly afterwards of the necessity of his staying, his decisions are presented as being made for, and not by, him. When apparently choosing to leave Dido without her knowledge, Aeneas provides the audience with his reasons for leaving:

> Carthage, my friendly host, adieu,
> Since destiny doth call me from the shore;
> Hermes this night descending in a dream
> Hath summon'd me to fruitful Italy;
> Jove wills it so, my mother wills it so;

---

[6] See Fred B. Tromly, *Playing With Desire: Christopher Marlowe and the Art of Tantalization* (Toronto: University of Toronto Press, 1998), 48.

[7] Christopher Marlowe, *Dido Queen of Carthage and The Massacre at Paris*, ed. H. J. Oliver (London: Methuen, 1968). All subsequent quotations from *Dido* are from this edition.

Let my Phoenissa grant, and I then go.
Grant she or no, Aeneas must away.
(4. 3. 1–7)

Aeneas appears to exhibit a moment of assertiveness here, but it is notable that everybody's will but his own is alluded to in these lines. In case the point was missed, his total surrender to Dido when she catches him leaving, combined with his childlike refusal to accept responsibility for it, firmly re-establishes what Brian Gibbons calls his "pathological" passiveness:[8]

> AENEAS: O princely Dido, give me leave to speak;
>   I went to take my farewell of Achates.
> DIDO: How haps Achates bid me not farewell?
> ACHATES: Because I fear'd Your Grace would keep me here.
> DIDO: To rid thee of that doubt, aboard again:
>   I charge thee put to sea, and stay not here.
> ACHATES: Then let Aeneas go aboard with us.
> DIDO: Get you aboard, Aeneas means to stay.
> AENEAS: The sea is rough, the winds blow to the shore.
> DIDO: O false Aeneas, now the sea is rough,
>   But when you were aboard 'twas calm enough!
>   Thou and Achates meant to sail away.
> AENEAS: Hath not the Carthage Queen mine only son?
>   Thinks Dido I will go and leave him here?
> DIDO: Aeneas, pardon me, for I forgot
>   That young Ascanius lay with me this whole night.
> (4. 4. 17–32)

The balance of power in this passage is firmly – comically even – in favour of Dido, whose remonstrations call to mind a stern schoolmistress administering discipline to errant pupils (a parallel which may be significant, given that the play was written for and acted by a boys' company. I will return to this later). Yet Aeneas appears to be guilty of negligence as well as passivity, apparently having forgotten to take his son with him when making his escape. This oversight represents not only a neglect of his familial duty, but also of the divine quest that he claims necessitates his departure; Ascanius is a very necessary link in the ancestral chain that will lead to Augustus (and further on to Queen Elizabeth), a point which Hermes makes very clear when he reminds Aeneas whose prophecy it is that needs to be fulfilled:

> Vain man, what monarchy expect'st thou here?
> Or with what thought sleep'st thou in Libya shore?
> If that all glory hath forsaken thee
> And thou despise the praise of such attempts,
> Yet think upon Ascanius' prophecy
> And young Iulus' more than thousand years.
> (5. 1. 34–9)

---

[8] Gibbons, "Unstable Proteus," 44–5.

Indeed, it is Aeneas's overlooked son, "bright Ascanius," who, according to Jupiter's declaration in the opening scene of the play, "Shall build his throne amidst those starry towers / That earth-born Atlas groaning underprops" (1. 1. 96–9). The son that Aeneas seems to have been either calculating or absent-minded enough to leave behind at Carthage is actually the focus of the prophecy to which he seems to attach such unlimited importance. It is because Dido believes this act of negligence is beyond his capabilities that she eventually acquiesces to his insistence that he hadn't intended to leave. The audience knows better, however.

As well as lacking the kind of decisiveness the audience might have expected from a Virgilian hero, Marlowe's Aeneas also proves to be a chivalric failure. We are given an early warning of Aeneas's propensity to utterly fail women in his account to Dido of the sack of Troy, which details his inability to save firstly his wife Creusa, secondly Cassandra and thirdly Polyxena from the myrmidon horde (2. 1. 265–88). The account of the sack of Troy ominously prefigures the events that will transpire throughout the rest of the play; his ineptitude at performing the most fundamental of chivalric duties – the rescue of beleaguered females – is only further confirmed by his abandonment of Dido.[9] On a lighter note, his failure to recognize Dido's erotic advances in the cave scene provides another instance of comedy at his expense:

> AENEAS: Why, what is it that Dido may desire
>   And not obtain, be it in human power?
> DIDO: The thing that I will die before I ask,
>   And yet desire to have before I die.
> AENEAS: It is not aught Aeneas may achieve?
> DIDO: Aeneas? No, although his eyes do pierce.
> AENEAS: What, hath Iarbas anger'd her in aught?
>   And will she be avenged on his life?
> DIDO: Not anger'd me, except in ang'ring thee.
> AENEAS: Who, then, of all so cruel may he be
>   That should detain thy eye in his defects?
> DIDO: The man that I do eye where'er I am,
>   Whose amorous face, like Paean, sparkles fire,
>   When as he butts his beams on Flora's bed.
>   Prometheus hath put on Cupid's shape,
>   And I must perish in his burning arms.
>   Aeneas, O Aeneas, quench these flames!
> AENEAS: What ails my queen? Is she fall'n sick of late?
> (3. 4. 6–23)

---

[9] Sara Munson Deats notes the difference between this account and that of the Virgilian source: "Marlowe radically abbreviates one episode in Virgil to render Aeneas almost indifferent to the loss of his wife Creusa, expands another to stress the Prince's pusillanimous desertion of the priestess Cassandra, and adds yet a third to narrate his failure to rescue Polyxena from the cruel Myrmidons." "Marlowe's Interrogative Drama," 111.

Aeneas's evasion of the meaning of Dido's blatant insinuations here seems every bit as pathological as the passiveness described by Brian Gibbons. Aeneas's romantic ineptitude is highlighted by the fact that, in keeping with his passive nature, he is wooed by Dido and not the reverse. This tended to trouble mid-twentieth-century critics: Steane recognizes in Dido's seizing of the initiative "a kind of perversion," and William Leigh Godshalk declares their love to be "as unnatural in its own way as that between Jupiter and Ganymede."[10] Neither critic seems to acknowledge the comic aspect of Dido's assumption of the traditionally masculine role in the relationship, however. The lavish protestations of love offered by Dido, the victim of Cupid's dart, to a clueless Aeneas make the cave scene reminiscent of Titania's wooing of Bottom whilst under the influence of a love potion in *A Midsummer Night's Dream*.[11] Whether the wooing of Aeneas by a woman represents comedy or unnatural perversion, the effect is brought about by his failure to fulfil the masculine protocol associated with the epic or tragic hero.[12] In fact, it is effectively Dido rather than Aeneas who takes up that role, a point observed by Singer: "If anyone is the hero in Marlowe's play, it is Dido herself. And I speak of her advisedly as a 'hero' rather than a 'heroine.' For the passivity of the Marlovian Aeneas progressively forces her into a more and more active role in their relationship."[13]

Dido's heroic status in the play is mirrored throughout by Aeneas's emasculation. Traditional gender roles are subverted before the cave scene, when, shortly after being struck by Cupid, Dido articulates her romantic designs on Aeneas in what is close to being a blazon, a poetic device usually employed to aesthetically anatomize the female visage:

O dull-conceited Dido, that till now
Didst never think Aeneas beautiful!
But now, for quittance of this oversight,
I'll make me bracelets of his golden hair;
His glistering eyes shall be my looking glass,

---

[10] Steane, *Marlowe: A Critical Study*, 34, and W. L. Godshalk, "Marlowe's *Dido, Queen of Carthage*," *English Literary History* 38, no. 1 (March, 1971): 8.

[11] Tromly also observes a resonance between the two plays' comic treatment of artificially induced infatuation, stating that "[in] both plays, the stimulus creates a response of instantaneous (and thus comic) dotage. And in both plays the scene raises serious questions about the irrationality of love." See *Playing With Desire*, 58. See also Annaliese Connolly, "*A Midsummer Night's Dream*: Shakespeare's Retrospective on Elizabeth I and the Iconography of Marriage," in *Goddesses and Queens: The Iconography of Elizabeth I*, ed. Annaliese Connolly and Lisa Hopkins (Basingstoke: Palgrave, 2008).

[12] This view is echoed by Harold Levin, who states that "Aeneas, a hero at Troy and again in Latium, cuts an unheroic figure at Carthage, where he is not so much the romantic lover as the capricious object of Dido's passion." *Christopher Marlowe: The Overreacher* (London: Faber and Faber, 1961), 34.

[13] Singer, "Erotic Transformations," 781.

His lips an altar, where I'll offer up
As many kisses as the sea hath sands.
(3. 1. 81–7)[14]

This effeminizing mode of address is not used exclusively by Dido. Aeneas and his fellow Trojans address one another with notable affection; Aeneas refers to "my Achates" (1. 1. 175), and, when the friends are re-united, their joyous greetings are decorated with decidedly unmanly epithets:

> AENEAS: O what destinies
>   Have brought my sweet companions in such plight?
>   O tell me, for I long to be resolv'd!
> ILIONEUS: Lovely Aeneas, these are Carthage walls.
> (2. 1. 59–62)

Upon first meeting Aeneas, Dido chastises him for lacking in masculine and noble self-assertiveness, charging him to "remember who thou art; speak like thyself" (2. 1. 100). By this point, we have already seen Aeneas articulate his woe through the use of the curiously feminine example of the tearful grief of a mother at the loss of her children:

> O my Achates, Theban Niobe,
> Who for her sons' death wept out life and breath,
> And, dry with grief, was turn'd into a stone,
> Had not such passions in her head as I.
> (2. 1. 3–6)

Marlowe's Aeneas, then, falls well short of the expectations that the contemporary audience would have associated with a Virgilian epic hero. Rather than proving himself to be worthy of bearing the weight of legend on his masculine shoulders, Aeneas avoids responsibility and vacillates throughout the play, usually appearing to have self-interest, rather than any heroic calling, primarily at heart.

Authority and Ambiguity

As is always the case in Marlowe, however, no single character bears the play's burden of culpability. Any of the faults attributed above to Aeneas, and arguably more, can also be attributed to the divine Jupiter himself, as well as his fellow Olympians. The play foregrounds the frivolity of the gods by opening with a homoerotic scene between Jupiter and his youthful cup-bearer, Ganymede:

> Come, gentle Ganymede, and play with me:
> I love thee well, say Juno what she will.
> (1. 1. 1–2)

---

[14] On dramatic uses of the blazon, see Deborah Uman and Sara Morrison, eds., *Staging the Blazon in Early Modern English Theater* (Farnham: Ashgate, 2013).

These opening lines, vaguely reminiscent of the inviting tone of "The Passionate Shepherd," instantly underscore the existence of divine conflict, as familiar human domestic concerns between husband, wife and lover are played out in an Olympian setting.[15] While the nature of the conflict is all too human, the magnitude of its potential consequences is certainly of a greater order, as we are reminded when Jupiter tells us what Juno has coming to her if she appears disapproving of his young lover:

> By Saturn's soul, and this earth threat'ning hair,
> That, shaken thrice, makes nature's buildings quake,
> I vow, if she but once frown on thee more,
> To hang her meteor-like 'twixt heaven and earth,
> And bind her hand and foot with golden cords,
> As once I did for harming Hercules!
> (1. 1. 10–15)

This passage suggests an Olympus that is a site of perennial and historic conflict. As well as the overt description of the unpleasant fate with which Juno is threatened, Jupiter reminds us that it is a punishment he has already bestowed upon her on a previous occasion on which she had displeased him. We are reminded of the ease with which he is capable of wreaking destruction on the earth, and all of this he swears by the soul of his father Saturn, whom he himself usurped in order to take the throne of Olympus. As dangerous as Jupiter's power to punish and destroy, however, is his apparent willingness to dismiss his divine responsibilities in favour of personal fulfilment. After vowing to punish those who challenge Ganymede's newfound position of prominence, Jupiter goes on to promise further devastation, this time simply according to Ganymede's whim: having already promised to have Vulcan dance for his entertainment, and to pluck him feathers from Juno's peacock and Venus's swans, he goes on to proclaim that

> Hermes no more shall show the world his wings,
> If that thy fancy in his feathers dwell,
> But, as this one, I'll tear them all from him,
> Do thou but say, 'their colour pleaseth me'.
> (1. 1. 38–41)

Jupiter shows not only a willingness to create conflict out of spite, but also to prevent his fellow gods from doing their divinely allotted duty in order to entertain his lover (in this case the very deity whose contribution will prove to be vital

---

[15] Patrick Cheney argues that, in this moment of self-quotation, Marlowe "uses a strategy of self-authorship to advance his theological critique, for the great deity of the Olympian pantheon voices the famous erotic invitation of Christopher Marlowe. The playwright does not simply reverse the traditional process advocated in Scripture, in which the individual imitates God or Christ; he reconfigures the central hierarchy of culture, divesting the deity of divine power." *Marlowe's Counterfeit Profession: Ovid, Spenser, Counter-Nationhood* (Toronto: University of Toronto Press, 1997), 110.

in ensuring the successful realization of Aeneas's destiny). These egotistically motivated destructive tendencies are not unique to Jupiter: all of the gods in the play appear capable of bearing long-standing grudges, and this is certainly the case with Juno and Venus, whose spiteful encounter and subsequent conspiracy to substitute a disguised Cupid for Ascanius effectively provide the catalyst for the tragic events of the play. What is noticeable is the likeness of these gods to human beings; they have greater powers and responsibilities, but they are subject to the same desires, vices and corruptions. In the words of Roma Gill, "Marlowe shows us the gods ... off duty."[16]

According to Steane, the pettiness of the play's deities is a symptom of the author's lack of artistic sensitivity, and tendency to resort to bombast:

> These gods are petty childish humans who have all the worlds to play with. They are not, I think, seen by the *author* as childish. He gives no hint of critical burlesque: he is probably offering them in a high spirited, deliberately "outrageous" manner, enjoying the freedom which their power and exuberant sports, desires and enmities gives to the imagination.[17]

In another extreme, Godshalk suggests that, by opening the play with a scene dealing with homosexual love (which is "by common judgment, completely without worth"), Marlowe simply seeks to distance the disapproving, and evidently male, audience from the occupants of the stage: "The homosexual love here evinced forces the playgoer, assuming that he is normally oriented toward the opposite sex, to stand aloof from the action, to evaluate critically the words of the old god and the young boy. The viewer can hardly sympathise with what he sees and hears."[18] Both of these arguments fail to do justice to Marlowe's subtlety as a dramatist. To dismiss the Olympian material as superficial exuberance is to ignore its consistency with the rest of the play's content; the conflict between personal desire and allotted responsibility that is seen in Jupiter, Juno and Venus will be played out in far greater detail in the shape of Dido and Aeneas's affair. Similarly, to suggest that Marlowe includes a scene of homoerotic play in order to excite a homophobic response from the audience is to fail to acknowledge the differences between twentieth- and sixteenth-century conceptions of sexuality, as well as the differences between both of these and the sexual attitudes of Augustan Rome.[19]

---

[16] Roma Gill, "Marlowe's Virgil: *Dido Queene of Carthage*," *Review of English Studies* 28, no. 110 (May 1977): 144.

[17] Steane, *Marlowe: A Critical Study*, 47.

[18] Godshalk, "Marlowe's *Dido, Queen of Carthage*," 3.

[19] Bruce R. Smith, for example, suggests that to "distinguish 'homosexual' men from 'heterosexual' men is ... a distinctively twentieth-century way of constructing sexuality ... Homo*sexual behaviour* may be a cross-cultural, transhistorical phenomenon; homo*sexuality* is specific to our own culture and to our own moment in history." *Homosexual Desire in Shakespeare's England: A Cultural Poetics* (Chicago: University of Chicago Press, 1991), 12. For further historicized accounts of early modern sexuality, see Gregory W. Bredbeck, *Sodomy and Interpretation: Marlowe to Milton* (Ithaca, NY: Cornell University Press, 1991),

Rather than provoking the audience's disapproval, or simply providing decoration, the passages involving the gods, especially by virtue of their placement in the early parts of the play, serve to deny the audience a stable moral framework on which to build their interpretation of the play. Beings of the highest order are here subject to the same whims as those of the lowest, and, rather than setting a divine example of harmony, show themselves to be liable to decadence and self-interest. Marlowe's depiction of the divine as no better or worse than the mortal is by no means a new concept (Matthew Proser, for example, asserts its debt to Ovid),[20] but is certainly incongruous in terms of the *Aeneid*, in which two things Virgil leaves us certain of are the seriousness of the task allotted to Aeneas, and the seriousness of those by whom it is allotted.[21]

By relieving the gods of their divine seriousness, Marlowe by extension diminishes the sense of pressing urgency surrounding Aeneas's mission. As Deats states, "The vagaries of Marlowe's quarrelling and conniving gods vitiate their authority, invalidating their heroic commands."[22] It is less easy when reading Marlowe's *Dido* to be convinced of the necessity of Aeneas's leaving than it is when reading Virgil's *Aeneid*. Indeed, it would have been even less easy to take seriously the dictates of the gods when seeing *Dido* than it is when reading it, given that the title page suggests that it was "Played by the Children of her Maiesties Chappell." As Mary E. Smith suggests, the fact that the play was performed by, and hence written for, a boys' company is more than a side issue: "Dido is a play written for boys and intended to be performed by them; unless this idea is borne firmly in the mind, nothing will fall properly into place, and once it is, many things will."[23] The capricious and self-absorbed nature of Marlowe's gods is brought into sharper focus by the fact that they would have originally been played by children – the juvenility of their behaviour is spelled out visually on stage. Similarly, the vacillations of Aeneas and the obsession of Dido take on a different character altogether when one considers the stature of the actors playing them. Marlowe presents us with a deflated version of heroic epic that is diminished in scale in every sense.[24] Smith has noted the undercutting effect of the play's

---

and Mario DiGangi, *The Homoerotics of Early Modern Drama* (Cambridge: Cambridge University Press, 1997). I discuss this subject in more detail in Chapter 5.

[20] Matthew Proser, "*Dido Queene of Carthage* and the Evolution of Marlowe's Dramatic Style," in *"A Poet and a Filthy Playmaker": New Essays on Christopher Marlowe*, ed. Kenneth Friedenreich, Roma Gill and Constance B. Kuriyama (New York: AMS, 1988), 85. Patrick Cheney identifies Marlowe as constructing his career in imitation of Ovid and in opposition to the Virgilian course taken by Edmund Spenser in *Marlowe's Counterfeit Profession*.

[21] See Douglas Cole, *Suffering and Evil in the Plays of Christopher Marlowe* (Princeton: Princeton University Press, 1962), 84.

[22] Deats, "Marlowe's Interrogative Drama," 111.

[23] Mary E. Smith, "Staging Marlowe's *Dido Queene of Carthage*," *Studies in English Literature, 1500–1900* 17, no. 2 (Spring 1977): 178.

[24] A 2003 production of *Dido* at the Globe Theatre emphasized this often overlooked aspect of the play by setting the action in a children's playground and dressing its divine

scenes of adult passion being performed by child actors, arguing that Marlowe "understood the disparity between actor and role and intended to make use of it."[25] Tromly argues along similar lines, stating that "Especially in the case of Marlowe's unprepossessing version of Aeneas ... we cannot be sure whether we are watching a child actor playing the part of a hero, or a hero acting like a child."[26] The result of this is often comical, but does not dictate that we cannot take the play seriously. Marlowe's play, and the performance of it by young boys, highlights the pettiness of human concerns, attributing them to gods as well as mortals. The audience is denied the moral certitude of a higher calling which ultimately dictates how things should and must be, and which lends authority to earthly pursuits. Instead, mortals and gods alike are cut adrift, looking out for themselves in an interminable network of conflict and conspiracy, and it is against this background that the audience must interpret the action.

Duties and Desires

The focus of the play is often characterized as a conflict between desire (gendered feminine) and duty (masculine), as experienced by Aeneas, who is torn between his dual positions as lover of Dido and servant of Jupiter and Troy. While this is undoubtedly a central concern, the play's dramatization of incompatibility and conflict is more complex than this. As discussed above, the play does begin with an apparently simple conflict between desire and duty; Jupiter's desire for Ganymede seems to be incompatible with his duties as king of the gods, as highlighted by his daughter Venus when she interrupts his lovemaking, reprimands him for his behaviour and demands that he return his attention to the plight of his grandson:

> GANYMEDE: I would have a jewel for mine ear,
>   And a fine brooch to put in my hat,
>   And then I'll hug with you an hundred times.
> JUPITER: And shalt have, Ganymede, if thou wilt be my love.
>   *Enter* VENUS
> VENUS: Ay, this is it! You can sit toying there,
>   And playing with the female wanton boy,
>   Whiles my Aeneas wanders on the seas,
>   And rests a prey to every billow's pride.
> (1. 1. 46–53)

Venus goes on to make clear that the wind that is battering Aeneas's fleet is the work of Juno and Hebe. It is impossible for Jupiter to fulfil his duties in a way

---

characters in oversized clothing. See review in *The Independent* (London), 25 June 2003, and Lisa Hopkins, *Christopher Marlowe: Renaissance Dramatist* (Edinburgh: Edinburgh University Press, 2008), 64–5.

[25] Smith, "Staging Marlowe's *Dido*," 190.
[26] Tromly, *Playing With Desire*, 54.

which will satisfy all of his fellow gods, or indeed in a way which will satisfy both his wife and his daughter – his duties as father and husband conflict with his duties as king. Of course, the main plot with which the play is concerned is characterized by similar incompatibilities. The conflict faced by Aeneas is well documented as being one between personal desire and duty, and usually interpreted as fatally weighted in the latter direction. Cole, for example, states that "Aeneas' suffering ... reveals his deepest concerns and ties, and makes it all the more inevitable that he should later be able to break the personal tie of love for Dido, in response to his higher duty."[27]

What is often overlooked is that Aeneas's bond to Dido is not simply one of desire. Indeed, Aeneas's behaviour speaks much less of desire than Dido's does, and, as discussed earlier with regard to the cave scene, his erotic sensibility is shown to be markedly dull in comparison to hers. Deats notes this disparity, stating that "In all of their scenes together, ... Dido's passion remains the galvanising force, with Aeneas' affection only a flickering reaction to her burning desire."[28] Instead, it might be argued that his bond to Dido is one of duty, in much the same way as his responsibility to Troy and to Jupiter – in this case the duty is that of a husband. Marlowe's play is much more suggestive of a conjugal bond between Dido and Aeneas than are his sources: Deats observes that neither Virgil nor Ovid includes an exchange of wedding jewels between the lovers in their versions of the tale.[29] Furthermore, Virgil has Aeneas justify his decision to leave Carthage by denying the validity of his union with Dido, claiming to have made her no promises: "I shall say only a little. It never was my intention to run away without your knowing, and do not pretend that it was. Nor have I ever offered you marriage or entered into that contract with you."[30] Marlowe suppresses this aspect of the source, having Aeneas instead leave without attempting to defend his position, and without suggesting any illegitimacy in their relationship. The Marlovian version of the epic narrative refuses to undermine the formality of the union, meaning that, rather than facing an emotionally difficult yet morally transparent choice between feminine self-gratifying desire and divine masculine duty, Aeneas is positioned between two duties – one as a Trojan and one as a husband – which cannot both be fulfilled. Aeneas's position as Dido's husband, Margo Hendricks contests, is both demonstrated by the scenes of gift-giving and necessitated by its political expediency: "Sichaeus's robe and his seat at Dido's side empower Aeneas in a way the status of Dido's guest could not. Both the chair and the robe symbolize the power of a husband, not a guest; and as such, they represent a powerful

---

[27] Cole, *Suffering and Evil*, 78.

[28] Sara Munson Deats, "The Subversion of Gender Hierarchies in *Dido, Queene of Carthage*," in *Marlowe, History and Sexuality: New Critical Essays on Christopher Marlowe*, ed. Paul Whitfield White (New York: AMS Press, 1998), 168.

[29] Ibid., 169.

[30] Virgil, *The Aeneid: A New Prose Translation*, trans. David West (London: Penguin, 1990), Book 4, 337–40.

incentive for Aeneas."[31] Marlowe, however, leaves us uncertain on this point: whether Aeneas's acceptance of Sichaeus's finery and wedding jewels constitutes wedlock is cast into some doubt by a similar exchange at the opening of the play in which Jupiter bestows Juno's wedding jewels upon Ganymede, an act which hardly seems to signify their official union, but rather, in Venus's words, a juvenile instance of "toying" and "playing" (1. 1. 50–51).

Another point often neglected by critics is the fact that the relationship represents a conflict of interests for Dido as well as for Aeneas, since she seems unable to perform her duty as the queen and protector of Carthage while also being the lover of Aeneas. When Anna suggests the possibility of a negative public response to Dido's decision to parade Aeneas through the streets as the new king of Carthage, her response is very much that of the tyrant:

> Those that dislike what Dido gives in charge
> Command my guard to slay for their offence.
> Shall vulgar peasants storm at what I do?
> The ground is mine that gives them sustenance,
> The air wherein they breathe, the water, fire,
> All that they have, their lands, their goods, their lives;
> And I, the goddess of all these, command
> Aeneas ride as Carthaginian king.
> (4. 4. 71–8)

This rhetorical performance of political power ironically accompanies the surrender of sovereign power in her own land to Aeneas; only two scenes later we see him drawing up plans to turn the "petty walls" of what was her city into a "statelier Troy" (5. 1. 2, 4). In the climactic scene of the play, Dido herself acknowledges the incompatibility of her love for Aeneas and her duty to her state, by saying to Anna, "Now bring him back and thou shalt be a queen, / And I will live a private life with him" (5. 1. 197–8). She is well aware of the need to abandon one concern before pursuing the other. As with Aeneas, however, it can be argued that the conflict of interests experienced by Dido is not reducible to a dichotomy of duty and desire, or, as Ian McAdam puts it, of conflicting desires to both rule and submit.[32] Emily Bartels, for example, suggests that a number of more complex motives dictate Dido's actions in the play, and that they are to a great extent political. She states that "in offering her body and her kingdom to Aeneas, Dido acts not transgressively as lover but appropriately as host; her actions evoke and comply with a code of hospitality that demands reciprocity – in her case, marriage."[33] For Bartels, "Phoenician" Dido, herself a colonial presence in Carthage, seeks to

---

[31] Margo Hendricks, "Managing the Barbarian: *The Tragedy of Dido, Queen of Carthage*," *Renaissance Drama* 23 (1992): 171.

[32] Ian McAdam, *The Irony of Identity: Self and Imagination in the Drama of Christopher Marlowe* (London: Associated University Presses, 1999), 63.

[33] Emily Bartels, *Spectacles of Strangeness: Imperialism, Alienation and Marlowe* (Philadelphia, PA: University of Philadelphia Press, 1993), 35.

solidify her political position through an ennobling union with a heroic figure of divine descent; lust is a secondary concern: "However much Dido may be touched by desire, here, as in the *Aeneid*, her offer of her hospitality, kingdom, and self and her attempts to instate Aeneas as her husband are political moves, constructed to authorize her power."[34] Bartels's highlighting of the *Aeneid* as well as Marlowe's play here is apt. In Virgil's account politics are taken very much into consideration in Dido's courtship of Aeneas, as demonstrated by Anna's advice to her sister:

> Have you forgotten what sort of people these are in whose land you have settled? On the one side you are beset by invincible Gaetulians, by Numidians, a race not partial to the bridle, and the inhospitable Syrtes; on the other, waterless desert and fierce raiders from Barca ... I for my part believe that it is with the blessing of the gods and the favour of Juno that the Trojan ships have held course here through the winds. Just think, O my sister, what a city and what a kingdom you will see rising here if you married such a man![35]

Political self-preservation, then, may be as much on Dido's agenda as desire for Aeneas or duty to Carthage.

The reading of Dido's actions as astute political manoeuvres is problematized, however, by the fact that we cannot ascertain to what degree she is actually their instigator. For large parts of the play, Dido acts and speaks under the influence of Cupid's dart, and, as such, the extent to which her desires are the result of her agency remains ambiguous. Cupid's external influence on Dido is evident shortly after he tricks her in the duality of her speech to Iarbas:

> DIDO: Why stay'st thou here? thou art no love of mine.
> IARBAS: Iarbas, die, seeing she abandons thee!
> DIDO: No, live, Iarbas; what hast thou deserv'd,
>   That I should say thou art no love of mine?
>   Something thou hast deserv'd – Away, I say,
>   Depart from Carthage, come not in my sight!
> IARBAS: Am I not King of rich Gaetulia?
> DIDO: Iarbas, pardon me, and stay a while.
> CUPID: Mother, look here.
> DIDO: What tell'st thou me of rich Gaetulia?
>   Am I not Queen of Libya? Then depart.
> (3. 1. 39–49)

Any suggestion that Dido is here toying with Iarbas of her own volition is potentially undermined by the comic scene which effectively mirrors this one. In it, Dido's nurse is struck by Cupid and experiences a similar divergence of wills:

> Blush, blush for shame, why shouldst thou think of love?
> A grave and not a lover fits thy age.

---

[34] Ibid., 45.
[35] Virgil, *The Aeneid*, Book 4, 38–49.

> A grave? Why? I may live a hundred years:
> Fourscore is but a girl's age; love is sweet.
> My veins are wither'd, and my sinews dry;
> Why do I think of love, now I should die?
> (4. 5. 29–34)

In Dido's case, this duality of voice does not last long; the persona which displays contempt for Iarbas and infatuation with Aeneas is soon dominant, suggesting, one might argue, that she is no longer in control of, or responsible for, her actions. Indeed, Aeneas himself seems to come to this conclusion when Hermes reveals to him the substitution of Cupid for Ascanius, to the extent that it may be seen to ease his conscience prior to leaving for Italy:

> This was my mother that beguil'd the Queen
> And made me take my brother for my son:
> No marvel, Dido, though thou be in love,
> That daily dandlest Cupid in thy arms!
> (5. 1. 42–5)

Again, however, this view cannot go unchallenged. The extent of Dido's agency in her actions subsequent to her initial encounter with Cupid is dependent on the audience's interpretation of the play's mode of representation; is Cupid, for example, to be viewed as an entity in his own right who exerts external influence over Dido, or is he, and the effect of his dart, an externalized representation of her own human emotions, essentially a dramatic emblem? The implications of this question are suggested by Deats:

> From an illusionist perspective, therefore, Dido lacks agency; she is reduced to a puppet, pathetic but not tragic. However, when viewed from an emblematic perspective, with Cupid and the supernatural personae generally functioning as allegorical correlatives for the human characters' psychological traits (Cupid = passion, Hermes = Ambition), both Aeneas and Dido can be seen as either multifaceted characters, demonstrating the complexity and ambiguity traditionally associated with tragic figures, as the fragmented, discontinuous subjects of the medieval drama, or as rhetorical constructs in the gender debate in which the playtext engages.[36]

The play leaves unanswered a number of questions that it raises about agency: are Dido and Aeneas compelled by forces external to them or are they in control of their own fates? Given that the play's gods are every bit as fractious and petty as its humans, can their will be said to carry any authority? If the will of the gods does not carry authority, are the play's humans obliged to carry it out? If the play's characters are in possession of their own wills, is that will motivated by desire or reason, assuming the two can be thus separated? Marlowe's undermining of

---

[36] Deats, "Gender Hierarchies," 171.

the authority that the *Aeneid* invests in the gods, together with the complicating of the dichotomy that it plays out between duty and desire, removes from the play a central source of authority, creating a moral indeterminacy that has been reflected in the critical response to it over the last sixty or so years. H. J. Oliver sees this as one of its weaknesses, contending that "These interpretations differ so much that they cannot all be in accord with Marlowe's intention; and it may even be in part the dramatist's fault that they exist."[37] On the contrary, it is precisely this multivalence that allows the play to function as an interrogation of authority and authorization; as Gibbons notes, it is important that we see ambiguity as an integral device and not a failing of the play.[38]

Creating Authority

The multiple dilemmas faced by the characters in *Dido, Queen of Carthage*, then, occur in a complex climate of moral indeterminacy. Instead of the conflict between righteous duty and selfish desire that we see in Virgil's *Aeneid*, Marlowe's *Dido* presents its protagonists in the grip of moral conundrums to which no solution is right: the human self-interest and Machiavellian policy demonstrated by Marlowe's Olympian gods mean that divine endorsement and moral authority are not the same thing. In this morally ambiguous environment, legitimizing associations with illustrious predecessors, mythological or otherwise, become priceless, as moral authority is sought to justify actions which further the personal interests of the perpetrator. In this context, I will argue, Marlowe's selection of the Dido and Aeneas myth as his source material is as significant as the play's content. In revising Virgil's account of the myth, Marlowe engages in and interrogates a discourse of legitimization that has run for over one-and-a-half millennia, and, in doing so, brings the focus of *Dido* away from classical Carthage and on to Elizabethan England.

Immediately apparent to the audience of *Dido* is the affinity of Aeneas with Troy. The first two acts of the play resonate with lamentation at the hero's separation from his homeland; the intensity of Aeneas's longing for his lost home and its representatives – "O Priamus, O Troy, O Hecuba!" (2. 1. 105) – seems to outweigh that of his professed love for Dido later in the play. The separation of Aeneas from Troy utterly disorientates him: he and his men, during their early exchanges, repeatedly express unfamiliarity with their surroundings and mistrust of their senses.[39] This disorientation is unsurprising, given the extent to which Troy is presented as being integral to his identity. When the disguised Venus asks

---

[37] H. J. Oliver, introduction to *Dido Queen of Carthage and The Massacre at Paris*, xxxix.

[38] Gibbons, "Unstable Proteus," 45.

[39] "Where am I now? These should be Carthage walls" (2. 1. 1); "saving air, / Is nothing here, and what is this but stone?" (2. 1. 13–14); "Achates, though mine eyes say this is stone, / Yet thinks my mind that this is Priamus" (2. 1. 24–5); "I hear Aeneas' voice

Aeneas who he is, he responds first with his civil allegiance, and second with his name: "Of Troy am I, Aeneas is my name" (1. 1. 216). When Dido repeats the request in the following act, Aeneas's more contemplative reply, again focused on Troy, is suggestive of an existential crisis:

> Sometime I was a Trojan, mighty Queen;
> But Troy is not; what shall I say I am?
> (2. 1. 75–6)

Divested of the authority of his association with an extant Troy, Aeneas lacks a narrative through which to construct his sense of self. Elsewhere, however, Aeneas seems to attempt to retain or recover a sense of authority and identity by repeatedly evoking Troy, as if it is a portable entity that exists wherever he is. The conception of a mobile Troy living in Aeneas is first promoted by his mother Venus in her complaints to Jupiter at the plight of the homeless men stranded on the ocean:

> Poor Troy must now be sack'd upon the sea,
> And Neptune's waves be envious men of war;
> Epeus' horse, to Aetna's hill transform'd,
> Prepared stands to wrack their wooden walls,
> And Aeolus, like Agamemnon, sounds
> The surges, his fierce soldiers, to the spoil.
> (1. 1. 64–9)

Venus's speech, designed to arouse sympathy in Jupiter for the repeated woes suffered by Aeneas and his men, also re-affirms her son's Trojan identity: it is not simply a group of soldiers that is at the mercy of the waves, but the mighty city of Troy itself, reliving perpetually its moment of great crisis. The same conceit is utilized by Aeneas himself, who, once the men have landed on unidentified shores, declares that "Priam's misfortune follows us by sea" (1. 1. 143). Again, Troy is evoked when Aeneas first encounters signs of civilization, in the shape of Carthage's walls:

> Methinks that town there should be Troy, yon Ida's hill,
> There Xanthus stream, because here's Priamus –
> And when I know it is not, then I die.
> (2. 1. 7–9)

Aeneas's rhetorical transplantations of Troy to his own location are representative of his inability to come to terms with the fact of the city's destruction, and as such are pathetic devices, yet they also have political undertones. In repeatedly evoking his homeland, Aeneas rehabilitates and legitimizes his identity: he is nowhere an outsider, nowhere destitute of status, if Troy, with its associated glory, follows

---

but see him not, / For none of these can be our General" (2. 1. 45–6); "You are Achates, or I deceiv'd" (2. 1. 49).

him everywhere. Indeed, the transportability of Troy is a politically necessary concept for Aeneas; his mission is not simply to build a new city in Italy, but quite specifically to build another Troy there. Similarly, any doubt that the play's conflicts raise over the success of this mission is not to do with *whether* a new Troy will be built, but *where* it will be built: Aeneas makes clear his intention to transform Carthage into a "statelier Troy" (5. 1. 2) after Dido has persuaded him to remain in Africa.

Crucially, however, the concept of a mobile Troy that is so essential to Aeneas is also useful to Dido. Aeneas is able to take complete ownership of the cultural gravitas of Troy as the physical city no longer exists to lay claim to it; as in Venus's account of their tribulations at sea, Aeneas and his colleagues are a mobile synecdoche for all of the cultural and historical import of a city that no longer exists, but which might exist again. This is a luxury that the fugitive Dido, whose homeland of Tyre continues to exist in her absence, is not afforded. A union with Aeneas has the potential to lend Dido some of the lustre and authority that comes from association with a city that has, judging by her eagerness to hear the story of the sack of Troy, already become legend. Indeed, the play accentuates her need for this association by suppressing her lineage; Hendricks has noted that, while the play lingers over Aeneas's patrilineal descent, Dido's Tyrian past is largely erased, instead foregrounding her status as an African queen. Hendricks argues that this has the effect of loading onto Dido contemporary "assumptions about the behaviour and dispositions of the peoples of Africa," yet it also renders her rootless, associated only with a land in which she is an alien.[40] Union with Aeneas, and thus with Troy, can potentially provide Dido with a self-fashioning narrative that the play otherwise denies her.

Dido cannot enjoy the benefits of association with Aeneas for long, however, because there is no way that Aeneas can stay in Carthage. This is not because Jupiter wills it so, nor is it because Aeneas is inevitably brought round to a pressing sense of duty to the memory of Troy. Aeneas has to leave Carthage for Italy because he is the focus of a myth written retrospectively with the purpose of associating Rome and its first emperor with ancient Troy – the very creation of the myth is an exercise in the legitimization of post-republican Rome. Through Virgil's epic, Augustan Rome appropriates the lustre of ancient Troy and also of Aeneas's Olympian lineage, which leads to the goddess Venus, and, by extension, to Jupiter (members, of course, of the Roman Pantheon, which, in another instance of legitimizing assimilation, correlates with that of the ancient Greeks). Marlowe's play points ironically to this fact at the point of Aeneas's departure, where the dialogue reverts to direct quotation of the *Aeneid*:

> DIDO: And woeful Dido, by these blubber'd cheeks,
> By this right hand, and by our spousal rites,
> Desires Aeneas to remain with her:
> *Si bene quid de te merui, fuit aut tibi quidquam*
> *Dulce meum, miserere domus labentis: & istam*

---

[40] Hendricks, "Managing the Barbarian," 174.

Oro, si quis adhuc precibus locus, exue mentem.
AENEAS: *Desine meque tuis incendere teque querelis,*
   Italiam non sponte sequor.
(5. 1. 133–40)

Critical explanations of this intrusion of Latin have tended to suggest that Marlowe was either too intimidated by Virgil's brilliance to attempt a translation of these pivotal lines, or at least that his admiration of them led him to decide on their inclusion in the play.[41] Rather, as Timothy Crowley has argued, their inclusion serves to highlight the story's origin at the very point at which Aeneas leaves to follow his destiny. Aeneas's final line of the passage quoted above – "*Italiam non sponte sequor*" [it is not of my own free will that I seek Italy] – delivered in Virgil's Latin, implies that the external force that necessitates his departure is coming not from Jupiter but from Virgil himself.[42]

The story of Dido and Aeneas, then, is embedded in a discourse of political legitimization achieved by telling stories, a discourse which Marlowe's version interrogates from within: *Dido, Queen of Carthage* both engages in and criticizes the history of authorization by myth of which it is the latest instalment. Indeed, Aeneas's welcome in Carthage is fully secured when he tells Dido the story of the sack of Troy, a story which, it is implied in Dido's request to hear it, has already been adapted to serve the purposes of a number of different tellers:

> May I entreat thee to discourse at large,
> And truly too, how Troy was overcome?
> For many tales go of that city's fall
> And scarcely do agree upon one point.
> Some say Antenor did betray the town,
> Others report 'twas Sinon's perjury;
> But in all this, that Troy is overcome,
> And Priam is dead; yet how, we hear no news.
> (2. 1. 106–13)

Aeneas's tale firmly establishes Dido's sympathy, and cements his foothold in Carthage. Dido displays her awareness of the persuasive power of narrative when, whilst attempting to convince Aeneas to abandon his mission to Italy, she proposes to decorate the sails of his ship with a selective version of his city's history,

---

[41] See H. J. Oliver, ed., *Dido, Queen of Carthage and The Massacre at Paris*, 81n. Una Ellis-Fermor states that "On two occasions he quotes directly from the original, as if half afraid, at such moments of crisis as the final parting or the dying speech of Dido, to trust translation." *Christopher Marlowe*, 19. Levin, rather less kindly, describes this burst of direct quotation as "an evasion" that "smells of the university." *The Overreacher*, 33.

[42] See Timothy Crowley, "Arms and the Boy: Marlowe's Aeneas and the Parody of Imitation in Marlowe's *Dido, Queen of Carthage*," *English Literary Renaissance* 38, no. 3 (2008). On the relationship between Marlowe's Aeneas and Virgil's see also Emma Buckley, "'Live, false Aeneas!': Marlowe's *Dido, Queen of Carthage* and the Limits of Translation," *Classical Receptions Journal* 3, no. 2 (2011).

detailing "The wars of Troy, but not Troy's overthrow" (3. 1. 113–24). Dido's, and Marlowe's, adaptations might be seen as simply engaging with Renaissance notions of artistic creativity; according to Troni Y. Grande:

> In the Renaissance, writerly invention is understood in its rhetorical sense as a new arrangement of what has been previously known, rather than (in the sense it later acquires in the Romantic era) as an original discovery of the yet unknown: hence all forms of writing to a Renaissance mind appear in the light of "translation," since even "original" compositions in the vernacular invariably refer back to a prior narrative source.[43]

Marlowe's *Dido*, it could thus be suggested, is a re-arrangement of a prior source like any other Renaissance composition. Yet Marlowe's play is notable in the extent to which it draws attention to the adaptation it is enacting, and in its awareness of the ends to which the myth has been adapted in the past: adaptation is a concern in a play which Marlowe has himself adapted from a story that Virgil has in turn adapted from Homer. In each case, the fact of the adaptation, as well as the content of the literature, carries authorizing significance.

As a creative act needs a precedent, so a political act needs authorization from a prior example or association, real or fictional. The settlement of the British Isles by Aeneas's great-grandson Brutus, an event attested to by medieval chroniclers such as Geoffrey of Monmouth, had been largely established as myth by the late sixteenth century, but not to the extent that it was no longer useful to state iconography.[44] Attributing the genesis of civilized England to the arrival of Brutus provided Elizabeth with a genealogy tracing back through classical Rome, Troy, Aeneas and the Olympian pantheon. This was a catalogue of potent ancestral associations too good for a state embarking on fledgling expansionist enterprises to dismiss. Indeed, as Hendricks observes, the explosion of international and intercultural contact around the Mediterranean and further afield in the sixteenth century, with its related opportunities, anxieties and confrontations, gave rise to the idea that national identity was in need of coherent definition.[45] It is in this period that John Dee begins to push for a "British Empire," a coinage typical of the mythologizing propaganda of the time in that it both looks forward to the nation being an imperial power in its own right and looks back to its time as Roman *Britannia*.[46] In emphasizing the concept of an imperial England and stressing its

---

[43] Troni Y. Grande, *Marlovian Tragedy: The Play of Dilation* (London: Associated University Presses, 1999), 80.

[44] Lisa Hopkins contends that the notion of Britain's Trojan descent "had been immortalized in the popular pseudo-history of Geoffrey of Monmouth, and though humanist historians like Polydore Vergil had subsequently declared it to be a myth, Brutus remained a potent icon of national pride." See "We Were the Trojans: British National Identities in 1633," *Renaissance Studies* 16, no. 1 (2002): 37.

[45] Hendricks, "Managing the Barbarian," 166.

[46] On Dee's encouragement of Elizabeth to embark on an imperial campaign, see Benjamin Woolley, *The Queen's Conjuror: The Life and Magic of Dr Dee* (London: Flamingo, 2002), 129–38.

historical and ancestral links with the Roman Empire, Dee participates in a long-standing tradition of English propaganda which extends back to the Middle Ages and particularly to Monmouth's *Historia Regum Britanii*. The mythical ancestry proposed by Monmouth is revivified in 1577 and 1586 by the first and second editions of Holinshed's *Chronicles*, the pseudo-historical treatise that was so influential a source for early modern dramatists. Alongside these chronicles stand works such as Richard Hakluyt's *The Principal Navigations, Voyages, Traffiques and Discoveries of the English Nation*, which supplemented assertions of imperial ancestry with an imagined history of intrepid exploration that predated those of rival European states. As Jack Beeching points out in his edition of *The Principal Navigations*, "Hakluyt does his best to prove that the English were travellers even before the Crusades; perhaps because any tradition is a comfort, even a fake one."[47]

Implicit in all of these discourses is an assertion that England can lay claim to foreign lands (in particular the New World) by virtue of the putative exploits of its erstwhile inhabitants: Dee's manuscript *Brytanici Imperii Limites*, written specifically for the Queen, detailed prior claims to western territories that originated in the voyages of King Arthur and the putative Atlantic crossing made by the Welsh prince Madoc in 1170.[48] At a time when England is ambitiously looking forward to an imagined era of empire, it is also reaching back in order to find authority for its vision. This was particularly important to the English, Hendricks claims, as inhabitants of a nation on the periphery of Europe with no obvious colonial history.[49] *Dido, Queen of Carthage*, then, details a story that is crucial in the mythical sequence of events that together form England's imperial heritage – Aeneas's departure to Italy is necessary not only for the formation of Rome, but for the formation of England.

Reduction/Repetition

This relationship between the beginnings of English expansionism and the use of history and myth as a legitimizing and authorizing device is, I argue, a focus of Marlowe's *Dido, Queen of Carthage*. Marlowe uses the Dido and Aeneas myth to comment upon imperial expansionism as a paradoxically reductive enterprise, and on the use of historical and mythological precedent in a process of national self-fashioning as a contributory factor in that reductiveness. Aeneas makes an ideal focus for any literary work which aims to comment upon the concept of empire, since in his transplantation of Troy to Italy he becomes the first colonizer of note in western cultural history (although it is worth remembering that Aeneas's establishment of a new Troy is not an act of expansion – he is relocating

---

[47] Richard Hakluyt, *Voyages and Discoveries: The Principal Navigations, Voyages, Traffiques and Discoveries of the English Nation*, ed. Jack Beeching (London: Penguin, 1972), 9.
[48] Woolley, *The Queen's Conjuror*, 133.
[49] Hendricks, "Managing the Barbarian," 179–80.

Troy rather than extending its territories). Furthermore, as has been mentioned earlier in this chapter, Dido's own position as a foreign occupier in Carthage entails further colonial implications which cannot be ignored in a reading of the play as a comment upon imperial expansion. The relationship between Dido and Aeneas, whilst presenting a dilemma between personal desires and public or divine duties, also constitutes, in Bartels's words, "a conflict of cultures and colonizing powers."[50]

Notable in the play's dealing with the idea of colonial expansion is the repetitive or reproductive quality it attributes to it. Throughout the play we are reminded that Aeneas's goal is not to expand Troy but to bring it back into existence. Jupiter informs us within the first hundred lines of the play what the successful completion of Aeneas's duty will bring about:

> Which once perform'd, poor Troy, so long suppress'd,
> From forth her ashes shall advance her head,
> And flourish once again that erst was dead.
> (1. 1. 93–5)

The motif of resurrection is revisited in other parts of the play. Ilioneus, when chastising Aeneas for neglecting higher duties in favour of Carthaginian indulgence, demands

> Why, let us build a city of our own
> And not stand lingering here for amorous looks.
> Will Dido raise old Priam forth his grave
> And build the town again the Greeks did burn?
> No, no, she cares not how we sink or swim,
> So she may have Aeneas in her arms.
> (4. 3. 37–42)

Shortly afterwards, we see Aeneas articulate the same idea, confidently stating (before being told by Hermes to move on again) that "Here will Aeneas build a statelier Troy / Than that which grim Atrides overthrew" (5. 1. 2–3), a desire that is foreshadowed upon his arrival at Carthage when he believes he can see a statue of Priam at the city walls. Geoffrey of Monmouth's *Historia* makes use of the same motif with direct reference to the birth of Britain: in a scene analogous to Hermes's appearance to Aeneas, Brute is advised by the goddess Diana to seek out an island "past the realms of Gaul," for

> There by thy sons again shall Troy be builded;
> There of thy blood shall Kings be born, hereafter
> Sovran in every land the wide world over.[51]

---

[50] Bartels, *Spectacles of Strangeness*, 29.

[51] Geoffrey of Monmouth, *History of the Kings of Britain*, trans. Sebastian Evans, rev. Charles W. Dunn (London: J. M. Dent & Sons, 1963), 18.

Whilst he is not engaged in a project of expansion, Aeneas's desire to found another Troy is reflected in the common practice of contemporary expansionist states naming new territories abroad after familiar towns and cities at home; in being synonymous with a part of the motherland, expansionist territories inherit the cultural and historical significations of the name bestowed upon them. Again, Geoffrey of Monmouth provides a parallel here. His *Historia* makes retrospective use of this system of mimetic naming in its attribution to early London of the title "Trinovantum," or New Troy.[52] As Hendricks has shown, Spain has similar links with Carthage: its city Cartagena is a legacy of a bygone Carthaginian imperial presence in the Iberian peninsula, and one of its new colonies in South America is given the same name. Hendricks argues that Aeneas's abandonment of Dido, as dramatized in Marlowe's play, asserts English superiority over Spain, since England is intrinsically linked with Troy and Spain with Carthage: "In light of the 1585 conquest and sacking of Cartagena, Marlowe's audience would have recognized immediately the allegorical parallels between that event and Dido, envisioning this third defeat of Carthage as a prophetic confirmation of England's racial and imperial heritage."[53] For Hendricks, Marlowe's *Dido* contributes to a discourse of legitimization that asserts England's heritage and destiny as being synonymous with imperial dominance. Deanne Williams, conversely, reads Marlowe's Dido as an analogue of Elizabeth, nonetheless still concluding that the play "celebrates a ruler known for her chastity and her empire."[54] While both of these positions are compelling, I am not entirely persuaded by the contention that the play acts as an earnest endorsement of Elizabethan imperial policy. Rather, Marlowe's version of the story makes use of England's propagandist self-association with Aeneas in order to interrogate imperial power and the means of its justification.

Marlowe's *Dido* suggests that imperial expansion is a paradoxically reductive enterprise. While expansion is experienced subjectively by the colonizing state as a broadening of horizons, it is experienced by all others as a reduction of diversity. As has been discussed, Aeneas, as his descendant Brute will later do, plans not to build a new city but to reproduce ancient Troy, at the expense of whatever alien land he chooses to do it in; at one point this looks as though it will be Carthage, but eventually, once he has been re-acquainted with his divine/Virgilian mission, it is Italy, where, as audience members familiar with Virgil's *Aeneid* will have known, his new Troy will absorb the various Latin peoples.

This process of homogenization would have been pertinent to the contemporary audience, which was living in a period in which maritime representatives of England were encountering and, in some cases, attempting to subdue difference in foreign climes. The immediacy and vitality of these encounters is evinced by

---

[52] Ibid., 27–8.
[53] Hendricks, "Managing the Barbarian," 179.
[54] Deanne Williams, "Dido, Queen of England," *English Literary History* 73, no. 1 (2006): 32. Cheney also considers Dido's relationship to Elizabeth, particularly as mythologized in Spenser's *The Faerie Queene*. See *Marlowe's Counterfeit Profession*, 99.

accounts such as that of Thomas Hariot, possibly an acquaintance of Marlowe's, in his *Brief and True Report of the New Found Land of Virginia*, and those collated by Richard Hakluyt in his *Principal Navigations*. Both of these texts, as well as providing journalistic accounts of encounters with difference, also offer advice on how it might be eradicated. Hariot suggests that it "may bee hoped if meanes of good government bee vsed, that they may in short time be brought to ciuilitie, and the imbracing of true religion,"[55] while Hakluyt's encouragement to the Queen implies a more aggressive programme of religious enlightenment:

> If upon a good and godly peace obtained, it shall please the Almighty to stir up Her Majesty's heart to continue with transporting one or two thousand people ... she shall by God's assistance, in short space, work many great and unlooked for effects, increase her dominions, enrich her coffers, and reduce many pagans to the faith of Christ.[56]

By necessity, Elizabeth's "increase" must be matched by a reduction elsewhere. Beyond even the explicit advocacy of eliminating the diversity of alien peoples, these accounts are bound by the limitations of only being able to describe the alien in terms of the familiar – they perform a linguistic act of homogenization. Hariot in particular describes several examples of Virginia's flora and fauna by comparing it to that of England, and even accompanies illustrations of the native inhabitants with images of ancient Pictish inhabitants of the British Isles, "to showe how that the Inhabitants of the great Bretannie haue bin in times past as sauuage as those of Virginia."[57] Christopher Hodgkins identifies the same Virgilian mytho-historical discourse at work in the rhetoric of English New World expansion under King James:

> Significantly, the Virgilian legend provided striking parallels, and thus a potent paradigm, for the fledgling Jamestown enterprise: in book 7 of the *Aeneid*, Virgil imagines Latium as a place of sylvan rusticity inhabited by a warrior race under a noble chieftain looking to give his daughter in dynastic marriage to a prophesied foreign prince with whom he will share equal rule ... Thus a Virgilian Virginia could recapitulate the master epic, promising another cycle of imperial regeneration, with Rolfe an Aeneas of sorts, chief Powhatan as a transatlantic Latinus, Pocahontas the new Lavinia, and Jamestown yet another Troy.[58]

Dido, Queen of Carthage, then, engages in a narrative that was central to the construction of a colonial national identity. But Marlowe's play does not advocate

---

[55] Thomas Hariot, *A briefe and true report of the new found land of Virginia* (London: 1590), STC (2nd ed.) / 12786, 25.

[56] Hakluyt, *Voyages and Discoveries*, 37.

[57] Hariot, *A briefe and true report*. This passage appears in the supplementary collection of illustrations, Sig. E.

[58] Christopher Hodgkins, *Reforming Empire: Protestant Colonialism and Conscience in British Literature* (London: University of Missouri Press, 2002), 124–6.

or provide propaganda for the expansion of a monolithic imperial state; it has too much sympathy for the alien victim and not enough for the Trojan – and by extension Anglo-Roman – colonizer. It accentuates too acutely the arbitrariness of power and the moral ambiguity of political and personal motivations for it to be considered an endorsement of the assertion of political power. As I will suggest elsewhere in this book, Marlowe's plays tend to problematize rather than endorse. Instead, in *Dido* as much as in his other plays, he presents the world as an indeterminate and ambiguous place which is resistant to reductive, unifying projects, be they the imperial pursuits of Aeneas or those of Elizabeth.

Chapter 2
Reduced to a Map:
Tamburlaine the Great, Parts One and Two

> I will confute those blind geographers
> That make a triple region in the world,
> Excluding regions which I mean to trace,
> And with this pen reduce them to a map.
> (One. 4. 4. 77–80)[1]

So says Tamburlaine to Zenocrate in response to her plea for mercy on behalf of the city of Damascus. This quotation is indicative of one of Tamburlaine's, and the plays', main concerns: the projection of a vast world onto a page is mirrored in the efforts of the protagonist both to subdue the known world and unify it under his yoke, thus establishing forever his unsurpassable might.

While Tamburlaine's attempts to make a single region of the world, and map it accordingly, are undoubtedly the focus of the plot, the plays are not simply concerned with physical space. As well as reducing the world to a map, Tamburlaine, I will argue, attempts to perform a similar act of reduction upon himself – to present through rhetoric and stagecraft his three-dimensional self as a two-dimensional image. The image is that of a relentless war machine, and is entirely monolithic; Tamburlaine's projection strives to suppress any suggestion of elements of his identity which diverge from it.

This chapter will argue that Marlowe's plays, however, prove to be more complex than Tamburlaine's performance: the variety inherent in a world that spans the miles of the Earth and not the inches of a page is too great for Tamburlaine to appropriate. Similarly, his attempted act of reduction upon himself meets insurmountable obstacles. Just as a map cannot represent its subject without the aid of simplification and distortion, Tamburlaine finds that complexity, both of the world and of himself, stands firmly in the way of the fashioning of a unified self. The plays are in fact riddled with ambiguity and confusion on a number of levels. The various conflicting religious ideologies present in the two plays are mirrored in an apparent theological confusion displayed by Tamburlaine himself, and the endorsement of Christianity that an audience might expect to see never in fact materializes. The plays repeatedly highlight the physical complexity of the body, and the idea of its being a composite of parts rather than a single whole; Tamburlaine's fatal distemper brings about the last of several deaths in the plays which are explained in detailed biological terms that emphasize the ever-present

---

[1] Christopher Marlowe, *Tamburlaine*, ed. J. S. Cunningham. All subsequent quotations from the plays are from this edition.

potential for bodily disharmony. The warlord's affection for Zenocrate provides another challenge to his project of implacable self-representation. The world of *Tamburlaine*, both for its audience and for its protagonist, is one that obstinately resists reduction. Tamburlaine finds himself and his surroundings to be too mutable to be entirely appropriated into a campaign of singular self-fashioning, and, similarly, the audience is faced with a moral labyrinth in which no reward seems to come of virtue. It is this tension between Tamburlaine's reductive goals and the complexity of the world he inhabits that will form the focus of this chapter.

Tamburlaine and Reduction

A feature of the *Tamburlaine* plays that is foregrounded throughout the two parts is Tamburlaine's conscious representation of himself, both to the audience and to his enemies. Paramount in this representation is his use of language. From as early as the prologue to Part One, which promises that "you shall hear the Scythian Tamburlaine / Threat'ning the world with high astounding terms" (One. Prologue. 4–5), clear indication is given that Tamburlaine's use of language is going to be central to the plays. This importance is further emphasized in the opening scene, in which Mycetes proves unable to verbalize his anger:

> Brother Cosroe, I find myself aggrieved
> Yet insufficient to express the same,
> For it requires a great and thund'ring speech:
> Good brother, tell the cause unto my lords;
> I know you have a better wit than I.
> (One. 1. 1. 1–5)

Mycetes's inability to engage in "great and thund'ring speech" prefigures his incapacity to fulfil the role of a king, just as his delegation of the responsibility of kingly oration to Cosroe anticipates the eventual loss of his crown to his more eloquent brother. Not all of Tamburlaine's adversaries share Mycetes's verbal impotence, however. Indeed, the increasing audacity of Tamburlaine's achievements is illustrated by the fact that, as the conqueror moves from one martial feat to the next, each new adversary seems always to be more rhetorically adept than the last. Mycetes's unwillingness to speak contrasts sharply with Bajazeth's prophecy of victory upon his introduction in Act 3, for instance:

> You know our army is invincible:
> As many circumcisèd Turks we have
> And warlike band of Christians renied
> As hath the ocean or the Terrene sea
> Small drops of water when the moon begins
> To join in one her semicircled horns.
> (One. 3. 1. 7–12)

The Turkish Emperor's boasts are followed by the raging words of the Soldan of Egypt, Tamburlaine's final opponent in Part One:

> A monster of five hundred thousand heads,
> Compact of rapine, piracy, and spoil,
> The scum of men, the hate and scourge of God,
> Raves in Egyptia, and annoyeth us.
> (One. 4. 3. 7–10)[2]

This progression in Tamburlaine is noted by J. B. Steane, who states that "by presenting [Mycetes] first, Marlowe defines the base of a pyramid of which Tamburlaine will be the apex," and by Harold Levin, who observes that the "drama is built up on rivalries like a tournament, where each new contender is more formidable than the last."[3] In a tournament in which the measure of each contender is their mastery of rhetoric, a quick and a venomous tongue equates to great martial power, and nobody in either play has a tongue as quick or as venomous as Tamburlaine's; as Mark Thornton Burnett notes, the protagonist "is drawn as a master of linguistic power."[4] Up until the latter part of the second play, Tamburlaine's boasts prove to be prophetic, and are delivered with a linguistic self-awareness that is illustrated when he commends Theridamas's use of the imperative mood, asserting that "Will and Shall best fitteth Tamburlaine" (One. 3. 3. 41).

Furthermore, other characters in the plays often pass comment on the persuasive significance of Tamburlaine's words and their inevitable vindication, a pertinent example arising from Tamburlaine's persuasion of Theridamas to join his ranks:

> THERIDAMAS: Not Hermes, prolocutor to the gods,
>   Could use persuasions more pathetical.
> TAMBURLAINE: Nor are Apollo's oracles more true
>   Than thou shalt find my vaunts substantial.
> (One. 1. 2. 209–12)

Not only are his words stirring, they are also "substantial," possessing a "working" utility (One. 2. 3. 25).

---

[2] While the second half of the final line of this quotation may seem absurdly bathetic to a modern ear, more severe inflections of the verb "annoy" would have been available to an early modern audience. The *OED* gives the following obsolete definition of "annoy" as a transitive verb: "2. To be hateful or distasteful to; to trouble, irk, bore, weary." The modern sense is considerably lighter in tone: "3. To affect (a person) in a way that disturbs his equanimity, hurts his susceptibilities, or causes slight irritation"; "annoy, v.," *OED Online*, June 2014, Oxford University Press, <http://www.oed.com/view/Entry/7938> (accessed 26 June 2014).

[3] J. B. Steane, *Marlowe: A Critical Study*, 89, and Levin, *The Overreacher*, 52.

[4] Mark Thornton Burnett, "*Tamburlaine the Great, Parts One* and *Two*," in *The Cambridge Companion to Christopher Marlowe*, ed. Patrick Cheney (Cambridge: Cambridge University Press, 2004), 128.

As important as language to Tamburlaine's projection of himself is his appearance. Both plays bustle with references to the potency of his looks, typified by the following speech by Techelles:

> As princely lions when they rouse themselves,
> Stretching their paws and threat'ning herds of beasts,
> So in his armour looketh Tamburlaine:
> Methinks I see kings kneeling at his feet,
> And he with frowning brows and fiery looks
> Spurning their crowns from off their captive heads.
> (One. 1. 2. 52–7)

Just as Tamburlaine's words are prophetic, so his appearance seems to convey grave portent. As with his talent for oration, Tamburlaine is all too aware of his ability to portray "ugly death" (One. 3. 2. 72) with his brows. The importance of this ability is foremost in his advice to his three sons in the early stages of the second play:

> For he shall wear the crown of Persia
> Whose head hath deepest scars, whose breast most wounds,
> Which, being wroth, sends lightning from his eyes,
> And in the furrows of his frowning brows
> Harbours revenge, war, death and cruelty.
> (Two. 1. 3. 74–8)

Tamburlaine's concern with appearance corresponds to a distinction that runs throughout the plays between being something and being perceived to be something. Tamburlaine, when delivering an invigorating speech to his newly acquired charges, says of his enemies that

> They shall be kept our forcèd followers
> Till with their eyes they view us emperors.
> (One. 1. 2. 66–7)

As Burnett states, "to be an emperor ... is not simply to act as one but to be seen as one."[5] Indeed, the impression that the audience gets of Tamburlaine's might comes almost entirely from his language and descriptions of his appearance by himself and the plays' other characters; while Marlowe clearly suppresses the putative lameness of the historical figure upon whom the plays are based, for all of the physical actions he undertakes on stage there is little in the plays that would prevent a director casting an immobile protagonist rather than the strapping hero of the dramas' tradition.[6]

---

[5] Ibid., 138.

[6] When discussing *Tamburlaine*, Levin suggests that the expanse of Marlowe's dramatic vision means that in his plays language assumes a performative quality; words are substituted for action that is of too large a scale for the stage: "Driven by an impetus towards

As John Gillies has noted, Tamburlaine's influence over his supporters and his enemies is essentially the same as that he wields over the audience: his power is expressed through the dramatic media of spectacle and language.[7] For the majority of both plays, the characters with whom Tamburlaine shares the stage are, like the members of the audience, passive spectators and auditors, becoming active speakers only to verbalize the profound effect that Tamburlaine's words and looks have had upon them. As listeners and watchers they both mirror and prompt the response of the audience, accentuating throughout a shared inferiority to the protagonist. Tamburlaine's own manipulation of dramatic and literary spectacle is of paramount importance to his self-construction. The punishments that he hands out to his vanquished foes are theatrical in persuasion: the caged Bajazeth, together with the kings who draw Tamburlaine's chariot, are reduced to spectacles in "vulgarised pageants."[8] Tamburlaine's brow, which other characters report to be capable of figuring and portraying (One. 2. 1. 21, 3. 2. 72), seems to perform a function akin to that of a literary text. Furthermore, his expressions of his own ambitions are often delivered in terms that involve some form of inscription. It is with a pen that Tamburlaine threatens to reduce the world to a map, and he evokes a similar idea when he warns Bajazeth that "Those wallèd garrisons will I subdue, / And write myself great lord of Africa" (One. 3. 3. 244–5). Just as Tamburlaine dares God out of heaven, he correspondingly attempts to usurp Marlowe's role by promising to write himself unilaterally as a conqueror; to allow other characteristics to infiltrate his self-representation would be to dilute his power. C. L. Barber states that "In *Tamburlaine* nothing can be envisaged except as it aggrandizes the hero's identity. Otherness is a challenge which must either be incorporated or destroyed."[9] Barber here refers to Marlowe's project in writing the *Tamburlaine* plays, yet the account he provides less accurately describes Marlowe's *modus operandi* than it does Tamburlaine's. As the geographer reduces the world to a map, and as the playwright reduces it to a stage, Tamburlaine attempts to reduce himself to a two-dimensional image, one that "figures" potent ferocity. His approach to achieving this goal is uncompromising and monolithic. As Una Ellis-Fermor states in her description of the first play, *Tamburlaine* is "a study of the irresistible power of a mind concentrating upon an end which it pursues with an unsleeping singleness of purpose."[10]

---

infinity and faced with the limitations of the stage, the basic convention of Marlovian drama is to take the word for the deed. Words are weapons; conflict perforce is invective, verbal rather than physical aggression; through musters and parleys, wars of nerves are fought out by exchanging boasts or parrying insults." *The Overreacher*, 62.

[7] John Gillies, "*Tamburlaine* and Renaissance Geography," in *Early Modern English Drama: A Critical Companion*, ed. Garrett A. Sullivan Jr., Patrick Cheney and Andrew Hadfield (Oxford: Oxford University Press, 2006), 45.

[8] Burnett, "*Tamburlaine the Great, Parts One* and *Two*," 138.

[9] C. L. Barber, "The Death of Zenocrate: 'Conceiving and subduing both' in Marlowe's *Tamburlaine*," *Literature and Psychology* 16 (1966): 18.

[10] Ellis-Fermor, *Christopher Marlowe*, 29.

Geography and Reduction

Among the most striking features of *Tamburlaine the Great* is its insistent evocation of the exotic through what must have been, to an early modern audience, alien-sounding place names. At the end of the first scene of the first play, by which time there have already been numerous references to Persia, Afric, Persepolis, the Western Isles, the Caspian Sea, Eastern India and Graecia, Ortygius crowns Cosroe while speaking the following lines:

> And in assurance of desired success
> We here do crown thee monarch of the East,
> Emperor of Asia and of Persia,
> Great lord of Media and Armenia,
> Duke of Assyria and Albania,
> Mesopotamia and of Parthia,
> East India and the late-discovered isles,
> Chief lord of all the wide vast Euxine Sea
> And of the ever-raging Caspian Lake.
> Long live Cosroë, mighty emperor!
> (One. 1. 1. 160–69)

References of this type persist throughout the first play and are equally prevalent in the second: Natolia, Argier, Tripoli, Azamor, Tunis, Tesella, Biledull, Guallatia, Gibraltar, Machda, Canarea, Cazates, Manicar, Cubar, Borno, Damasco and more are all mentioned in the space of one hundred lines in Act 1 Scene 3, for example.

The insistent naming of places serves a clear aesthetic purpose in the plays, lending them a peculiar exoticism and providing Marlowe with endless opportunity to experiment with the rhythms of his blank verse line. The significance of this feature goes beyond the aesthetic, however; rather than just places, it is the mapping of places that is of particular interest to both plays. When Cosroe says to Menaphon that "Men from the farthest equinoctial line / Have swarmed in troops into the Eastern India" (One. 1. 1. 119–20), he is not just talking about space, but about space as it appears on a map. Both plays contain important sequences that refer directly to, or include, maps: in Part One, Tamburlaine promises to reduce the world to a map, calling upon cartography to signify to Zenocrate his unerring martial ambition (One. 4. 4. 75–84), while in Part Two Tamburlaine, on his deathbed, orders his subordinates to

> Give me a map, then let me see how much
> Is left for me to conquer all the world,
> That these my boys may finish all my wants.
> (Two. 5. 3. 123–5)

In the following lines Tamburlaine summarizes his martial achievements, tracing his own progress on the map and indicating to his sons the direction in which they might further expand his empire after his death.

Nor is it just any map which Tamburlaine requests. As Seaton convincingly shows, the plays' expansive campaigns are painstakingly plotted by "Marlowe's finger"[11] on the pages of the *Theatrum Orbis Terrarum*, the unprecedented world atlas compiled by Abraham Ortelius. There is a cruel irony in Tamburlaine's interest in the cartography of the *Theatrum*; the drive behind Ortelius's grand vision, Paul Binding asserts, was the irenic promotion of international harmony:

> Religious tolerance – if any one subject dominated the lives of Ortelius and his circle, it was this, and the *Theatrum* is, among other things, an expression of its maker's ardent belief in its importance. How else could countries exist in the peaceful juxtaposition that we find on the printed page?[12]

The image of the entire world lying undisturbed on a page evokes, for Ortelius, a sense of community among the inhabitants of the physical object it depicts. For Tamburlaine, however, the reduction of the world into a conceivable unified whole makes it seem all the more conquerable. As Garrett Sullivan Jr. notes, Tamburlaine's campaign is predicated upon the elimination of variety, upon the creation of a homogenous world in his own image: "If Tamburlaine is to bring 'excluded regions' into his new geographical frame, he makes plain that their inclusion will go hand-in-hand with their extinction: they are to be conquered and renamed after Tamburlaine and Zenocrate."[13] The new geography of Ortelius and Mercator, with its systematic reduction of the variety of the world to a single image on a flat page, seems ideal for Marlowe's voracious protagonist. Stephen Greenblatt notes the aptness of the mathematically regular new cartography, devoid of the typological significance of its medieval forebear, as a device to aid Tamburlaine's project; both the systematic Ortelian map and the bare Elizabethan stage, he suggests, divest space of its value, transforming it "into an abstraction," which is then "fed to the appetitive machine."[14] In the words of Bernhard Klein, "the map turns into an imaginative correlative of [Tamburlaine's] monstrous military exploits, the fantasy of an empty canvas on which to paint his own private empire."[15] Greenblatt also rightly suggests that the life of the appetitive machine is always ultimately unfulfilled – after all, the final reference to a map

---

[11] Ethel Seaton, "Marlowe's Map," in *Marlowe: A Collection of Critical Essays*, ed. Clifford Leech (Englewood Cliffs, NJ: Prentice Hall, 1964), 42.

[12] Paul Binding, *Imagined Corners: Exploring the World's First Atlas* (London: Review, 2003), 15.

[13] Garrett A. Sullivan Jr., "Geography and Identity in Marlowe," in *The Cambridge Companion to Christopher Marlowe*, ed. Patrick Cheney (Cambridge: Cambridge University Press, 2004), 235. The same author elsewhere identifies this impulse in Tamburlaine with contemporary policies of standardization of measures in England. See "Space, Measurement and Stalking Tamburlaine," *Renaissance Drama* 28 (1997).

[14] Greenblatt, *Renaissance Self-Fashioning*, 195.

[15] Bernhard Klein, *Maps and the Writing of Space in Early Modern England* (Basingstoke: Palgrave Macmillan, 2001), 17.

in the play comes when Tamburlaine pores over one on his deathbed to see what remains unconquered.

That Tamburlaine's appetite cannot be fulfilled is not only due to a constitutional insatiability, however. Marlowe invests his fourteenth-century protagonist with an anachronistic ambition to reinvent the globe in its sixteenth-century image. In his final speech he directs the attention of his children to the map to indicate the piece of real estate, "westward from the midst of Cancer's line ... Wherein are rocks of pearl that shine as bright / As all the lamps that beautify the sky," that he most wishes he had been able to subdue (Two. 5. 3. 146, 156–7). The land he describes is, of course, America. And, of course, Tamburlaine *must* die with it unconquered, as the historical figure upon whom he is based expired some eighty-seven years before its discovery by inhabitants of the Mediterranean world. The internal confusion brought about by this modern figure existing in a pre-modern setting is apparent when, having previously sworn to confute the blind geographers who make a triple region of the world, he seems by Act 4 of the second play to have downgraded his ambition, promising now only the conquest of "all the triple world" (4. 3. 63).

Nor, I wish to show, is the process of reduction as manageable for Tamburlaine as he or Greenblatt suggest. Sullivan argues that the reduction of space into a homogenous and digestible form "is not the only available spatial model in the play," suggesting that the representation of Damascus, with its affiliations with Tamburlaine's wife Zenocrate and the appeals and subsequent slaughter of its virgins, is too complex for it to be reduced to a mere set of coordinates like so many of the plays' other locations.[16] I am in agreement with Sullivan here, but would extend the point by suggesting that the plays' fascination with the reductive process both of conquest and of new cartography is accompanied by, or perhaps contingent upon, a profound uneasiness about it. This unease is not dissimilar to that expressed in Alexander Barclay's 1509 translation of Sebastian Brant's *The Ship of Folys of the Worlde*, which, albeit from a pre-Ortelian perspective, nevertheless offers the following warning to would-be geographers:

> Ye people that labour the worlde to mesure
> Therby to knowe the regyons of the same
> Knowe first your self, that knowledge is most sure
> For certaynly it is rebuke and shame
> For man to labour, onely for a name
> To knowe the compass of all the worlde wyde
> Nat knowing hym selfe, nor howe he sholde hym gyde.[17]

Brant's admonition warns of the hubris inherent in presuming to understand the world in its entirety, particularly when the task of understanding oneself is such an all-encompassing one in its own right. Yet Tamburlaine attempts to enact the same

---

[16] Sullivan Jr., "Geography and Identity in Marlowe," 234.
[17] Cited in Klein, *Maps and the Writing of Space*, 21.

process of two-dimensional abstraction upon himself as a map does with three-dimensional physical space, wishing to present, or construct, himself unilaterally and unequivocally as a warrior king. When Tamburlaine promises to "write himself great lord of Africa" (One. 3. 3. 245), he presumably intends to use the same pen with which he will reduce the world to a map. Tamburlaine's geographical conception of the world, rather like his conception of himself, is a distorted simplification. Crystal Bartolovich, commenting on the plays' fascination with the exotic, articulates elegantly the impossibility of Tamburlaine's self-appointed task:

> these "foreign place names" are effects of a properly unrepresentable totality, not only because Tamburlaine's world does not yet (and never does fully) exist, nor because large parts of the globe are still terra incognita for Marlowe's audience in the late 1590s, nor even because the world of the putative speaker does not coincide with the moment in which it was presumably spoken, but rather because "the world" – being a set of increasingly vast and complex relations, always in flux – can nowhere appear in its totality; we only know it as an effect of these relations.[18]

Tamburlaine is able to think in absolutes because his view of the world and of himself is based on a reductive misconception which bypasses the variety and complexity inherent both in the world and in himself; it is the gap between this world view and the complexity of "reality" which guarantees his failure, and which I will discuss in the rest of this chapter.

Moral Ambiguity

Tamburlaine's reductive world view is set into stark relief not only by the complex realities of his own world, but also by our own ambivalent responses to him. Tamburlaine has traditionally been the subject of divergent critical approaches which place him either as an Elizabethan role model or as a deplorable tyrant, approaches in which judgements of Marlowe's own sympathies often figure. Is modern distaste at Tamburlaine's moments of extreme cruelty simply a response born of an anachronistic moral landscape, or is Marlowe's Scythian warlord likely to have excited a similar response from an Elizabethan audience?

Peter Berek has approached the question by examining numerous dramatic imitations of the *Tamburlaine* plays which seem calculated to capitalize on their success. These imitations, Berek suggests, "make clear that overreaching ambition and self-display deserve blame, not praise," and in doing so reflect audiences' reactions to Marlowe's plays. For Berek, whether Marlowe intended them to or not, Elizabethan audiences saw in Tamburlaine an impressive but reprehensible figure representing the folly of overreaching ambition.[19] In contrast, Richard Levin's

---

[18] Crystal Bartolovich, "Putting Tamburlaine on a (Cognitive) Map," *Renaissance Drama* 27 (1997): 50.
[19] Berek, "*Tamburlaine*'s Weak Sons," 59.

examination of contemporary responses to the plays concludes that their protagonist received an overwhelmingly sympathetic reaction.[20] Several critics have arrived at a similar conclusion to Levin by reading the *Tamburlaine* plays in conjunction with the swell of militaristic discourse that appeared in print in the 1580s and 1590s. This discourse both theorized and valorized military achievement and tended to betray an anxiety about the effeminacy of England's male youth.[21] T. M. Pearce argues that the plays capitalize on a contemporary undercurrent of opinion which held that modern youth lacked discipline and had become increasingly effeminized and given to leisure. Marlowe, Pearce asserts, would have been in full agreement with Sir Humphrey Gilbert, whose 1570 proposals for reform of the education system, had they been approved, "would have set up a military academy designed to provide England with young Tamburlaines."[22] As such, he delivered a pair of plays that not only provided a powerful moral example to England's youth, but also a counterblast to anti-theatrical polemicists like Stephen Gosson who argued that the theatre exerted an effeminizing influence on its audiences.[23] Paul H. Kocher argues that Tamburlaine's killing of his son, Calyphas, often cited as the most repulsive act committed in either play, is misunderstood by modern critics, who overlook contemporary military law when appraising it.[24] William J. Brown, in identifying Foxe's *Actes and Monuments* as a source for Part One, suggests that Tamburlaine's ruthless and ritual humiliation of the vanquished Bajazeth is enacted as divine retribution for his prior persecution of Christians, and would have been met with "complete sympathy and approval."[25]

More recent critical accounts of the *Tamburlaine* plays have tended to complicate this divergence between reading them as either valorizations of a masculine military ideal or a condemnation of unchecked ambition. Nina Taunton notes that Tamburlaine observes some of the dictates of the martial literature of the period but contravenes others, making him "a problematic figure of command."[26] Alan Shepard, meanwhile, complicates the practice of reading Tamburlaine in terms of a homogenously conceived notion of militarism by noting the variety of attitudes present in militaristic writing of the period.[27] Where some texts prescribe

---

[20] Richard Levin, "The Contemporary Perception of Marlowe's Tamburlaine."

[21] On militaristic writing in the late sixteenth century, and its relation to the literature of the period, see Nick de Somogyi, *Shakespeare's Theatre of War* (Aldershot: Ashgate, 1998); Nina Taunton, *1590s Drama and Militarism: Portrayals of War in Marlowe, Chapman and Shakespeare's "Henry V"* (Aldershot: Ashgate, 2001); and Alan Shepard, *Marlowe's Soldiers: Rhetorics of Masculinity in the Age of the Armada* (Aldershot: Ashgate, 2002).

[22] T. M. Pearce, "Tamburlaine's 'Discipline to His Three Sonnes': An Interpretation of *Tamburlaine Part II*," *Modern Language Quarterly* 15 (1954): 22.

[23] Ibid., 27.

[24] Paul H. Kocher, "Marlowe's Art of War," *Studies in Philology* 39 (1942): 223.

[25] William J. Brown, "Marlowe's Debasement of Bajazet: Foxe's *Actes and Monuments* and *Tamburlaine*, Part I," *Renaissance Quarterly* 24, no. 1 (1971): 41.

[26] Taunton, *1590s Drama and Militarism*, 58.

[27] Shepard, *Marlowe's Soldiers*, 43–6.

ferocity, others recommend clemency, meaning that a unilateral sense of the likely moral reaction to Tamburlaine's more extreme moments cannot necessarily be gleaned from military conduct books. This indeterminacy is reflected in Robert Logan's reading of the plays, in which he suggests that they "feed the desire of the English of the 1580s and 1590s for a heroic military commander" but that "in reflecting the harsh realities of war," they also "forcefully limn its extreme cost."[28] In its appreciation of the plays' ambiguity, Logan's reading complements interpretations by Daniel Vitkus and Sara Munson Deats which stress Tamburlaine's duality. In these readings, Tamburlaine is characterized by a moral ambiguity that simultaneously attracts and repels the audience. For Vitkus, "Tamburlaine is a paradoxical model of what to be or do, and what not to be or do," while Deats posits Part One in particular as a dual-aspect "Mars-Gorgon" portrait.[29]

I find these latter readings persuasive. The popularity of the first part of the play, implied in the prologue of the second, indicates that audiences must have responded to its protagonist, who dominates the stage so completely, with something other than just revulsion. Conversely, suggestions that the slaughter of innocent virgins or a father's murder of his son can be fully justified by contemporary military law overestimate the influence of bureaucracy over Christian morality and also ignore the reaction to the acts of the other characters on stage. These episodes, while displaying Tamburlaine's adherence to his word, also reveal a valuation of personal pride and individual honour over the lives of innocents that could hardly be more divergent from common Christian values, a fact that is not lost on Zenocrate, whose loyalties are tested when she looks upon the carnage of the vanquished Damascus:

> But most accursed, to see the sun-bright troop
> Of heavenly virgins and unspotted maids,
> Whose looks might make the angry god of arms
> To break his sword and mildly treat of love,
> On horsemen's lances to be hoisted up
> And guiltlessly endure a cruel death
> ...
> Ah Tamburlaine, wert thou the cause of this,
> That termest Zenocrate thy dearest love –
> Whose lives were dearer to Zenocrate
> Than her own life, or aught save thine own love?
> But see another bloody spectacle!
> (One. 5. 1. 325–40)

---

[28] Robert A. Logan, "Violence, Terrorism, and War in Marlowe's *Tamburlaine* Plays," in *War and Words: Horror and Heroism in the Literature of Warfare*, ed. Sara Munson Deats, Lagretta Tallent Lenker and Merry G. Perry (Lanham, MD: Lexington, 2004), 78.

[29] Daniel Vitkus, *Turning Turk: English Theater and the Multicultural Mediterranean, 1570–1630* (Basingstoke: Palgrave Macmillan, 2003), 65, and Sara Munson Deats, "Mars or Gorgon? *Tamburlaine* and *Henry V*," *Marlowe Studies: An Annual* 1 (2011): 101.

These words, spoken by the ostensibly guiltless Zenocrate, prompt a moral response from the audience, or indeed, as Matthew Greenfield has suggested, may even represent an onstage vocalization of the audience's opinion.[30]

An audience's experience of *Tamburlaine* is, I would argue, analogous to Tamburlaine's experience of his own world. In much the same way that Tamburlaine's attempts at reductive self-figuring meet with insurmountable complexities, an audience's sympathies and attempts at moral assessment are persistently complicated by the plays. In a series of bluffs, characters that exhibit the usual signifiers of virtue – adherence to Christianity, or enmity with Turks, for example – all prove to be problematic. An early modern audience would in all likelihood have been repulsed by those to whom they should be sympathetic, like the Christian King Sigismund, whose double-crossing appears all the more cowardly in the company of the unfailingly direct approach of Tamburlaine. They would be equally likely to have felt pity for those they might be expected to despise, like the Turkish Emperor Bajazeth, who is subjected to inhumane cruelty. And, through an appreciation of valour and the small matter of an extremely powerful common Islamic enemy, they would have been tempted to take the side of a conqueror whose actions are deplorable and whose Scythian ancestry allied him to a race considered "the epitome of savagery" in Elizabethan England.[31]

Religious Ambiguity

As highlighted earlier in this chapter, the geographical span of the *Tamburlaine* plays is comprehensive. A side effect of this imaginative scope is that the plays also exhibit a varied and sometimes confusing spectrum of religious systems of belief. Tamburlaine's own ambiguous theology is juxtaposed on stage with those of Turks and Catholic Christians, creating a spiritual melting pot that would be pertinent to English audiences who not only lived with Christian religious controversy on a regular basis, but were also aware of the Ottoman threat looming on the eastern horizon. While the Ottoman Empire proved useful to Protestant England by virtue of its persistent erosion of European Catholic territory, there is no doubt that Turks and Catholics were regarded with similar animosity. Far from providing a religious landscape ripe for unification, then, Marlowe depicts members of two religious denominations that are alien both to one another and to the members of the audience. To destabilize matters more, Tamburlaine's own theology has a markedly protean quality. While his frequent reference to Jove suggests ostensibly classical pagan beliefs, he also occasionally adopts elements of other faiths, and often displays a manifest confusion regarding the nature of divinity in general. According to Vitkus, "During the course of the two plays, Tamburlaine converts from his initial position as a pagan polytheist to an acceptance of Mahomet as

---

[30] Matthew Greenfield, "Christopher Marlowe's Wound Knowledge," *PMLA* 119, no. 2 (2004): 239.

[31] Hopkins, *Christopher Marlowe, Renaissance Dramatist*, 132.

'a god' – and then later he becomes an anti-Islamic scourge and destroyer who seeks to annihilate Islam as an established religious culture."[32] Indeed, the term "Jove" is itself laden with ambiguity in these plays, seeming as it does to refer variously to the Judaeo-Christian God and to classical Jupiter.[33] Nor is this pluralist approach to faith unique to Tamburlaine himself: after his defeat of the Christian Sigismond, Orcanes observes, "Now lie the Christians bathing in their bloods, / And Christ or Mahomet hath been my friend" (Two. 2. 3. 10–11). A short while later, Tamburlaine's Turkish enemy Callapine delivers the following order to his troops:

> Come, puissant viceroys, let us to the field –
> The Persians' sepulchre – and sacrifice
> Mountains of breathless men to Mahomet,
> Who now with Jove opens the firmament
> To see the slaughter of our enemies.
> (Two. 3. 5. 53–7)

The plays' Islamic characters seem willing to accept the divinity of Christ or Jove, providing, of course, it increases their chances of success in battle. The co-existence of Mahomet with pagan and Christian deities is evident in the thinking of Tamburlaine, who, when he speaks of "that Mahomet / Whom I have thought a god" (Two. 5. 1. 174–5), engages in a popular Christian misconception that Islamic faith worships the prophet Mohammed as divine. Indeed, the liberal distribution of godly status is exemplified when, at his wife's deathbed, Tamburlaine articulates the apotheosis of "divine Zenocrate" (Two. 2. 4. 1–37).

Present throughout the plays, then, is an ambiguous co-existence of various faiths, none of which is adhered to exclusively by its ostensible followers. Perhaps more ambiguous than the denomination of Tamburlaine's faith is his attitude towards the concept of divinity itself: from the beginning to the end of his campaign, Tamburlaine has trouble reconciling his earthly ambition with his spiritual duty. Nowhere is this more in evidence than in the following famous speech, which it is necessary to quote at length:

---

[32] Vitkus, *Turning Turk*, 51.

[33] Dena Goldberg argues that the use of "Jove" is a convenient route around the censor to a discussion of Christian theology, stating that "The use of *Jupiter* as a pseudonym for God goes back at least as far as *Everyman*; and there is nothing to distinguish these exotic deities from the Christian god, whether they are being called upon to defend the innocent or punish Tamburlaine's 'presumption.'" "Whose God's on First? Special Providence in the Plays of Christopher Marlowe," *English Literary History* 60, no. 3 (1993): 574. Goldberg overstates her case here; at points in the play Jove is clearly and elaborately depicted as the Olympian monarch, and as such is very much distinguishable from the Christian God, while Tamburlaine's self-fashioning as the scourge of God calls to mind a distinctly Old Testament theology. The indeterminacy of the referent "Jove" is maintained throughout the plays, and is entirely consistent with the spiritual vacillations of their characters.

> The thirst of reign and sweetness of a crown,
> That caused the eldest son of heavenly Ops
> To thrust his doting father from his chair
> And place himself in th'empyreal heaven,
> Moved me to manage arms against thy state.
> What better precedent than mighty Jove?
> …
> Our souls, whose faculties can comprehend
> The wondrous architecture of the world
> And measure every wand'ring planet's course,
> Still climbing after knowledge infinite
> And always moving as the restless spheres,
> Wills us to wear ourselves and never rest
> Until we reach the ripest fruit of all,
> That perfect bliss and sole felicity,
> The sweet fruition of an earthly crown.
> (One. 2. 7. 12–29)

This speech exhibits a characteristic confusion between the spiritual and the physical, the earthly and the divine. Jove's usurpation of the throne of heaven from Saturn, altogether an Olympian business, is here used as a precedent for earthly ambition, and the celebration of the human soul ends in an ironic pun when Tamburlaine evokes the "perfect bliss and sole felicity … of an earthly crown"; overall, therefore, the speech moves from an invocation of Jove to a rejection of all but earthly power. This apparent confusion of Tamburlaine's is not simply over a question of belief, but also of authority: Tamburlaine's attitude towards the power of Jove oscillates between reverent servitude and open hostility. Early in Part One, when recruiting Theridamas, Tamburlaine implies a contract of protection between himself and Jove:

> Draw forth thy sword, thou mighty man-at-arms,
> Intending but to raze my charmèd skin,
> And Jove himself will stretch his hand from heaven
> To ward the blow and shield me safe from harm.
> (One. 1. 2. 177–80)

By the final act of the first part, however, Tamburlaine's conception of this relationship seems to have altered altogether:

> The god of war resigns his room to me,
> Meaning to make me general of the world:
> Jove, viewing me in arms, looks pale and wan,
> Fearing my power should pull him from his throne;
> Where'er I come the Fatal Sisters sweat,
> And grisly Death, by running to and fro
> To do their ceaseless homage to my sword.
> (One. 5. 1. 451–7)

By the latter half of Part Two, raging obstinacy has given way to what could be interpreted either as servile obedience or doubt over Jove's existence:

> And till by vision or by speech I hear
> Immortal Jove say 'Cease, my Tamburlaine',
> I will persist a terror to the world.
> (Two. 4. 1. 199–201)[34]

This oscillation is characteristic of a protagonist that is racked with spiritual confusion. At various times he acknowledges the co-existence of deities from conflicting faiths, while at others he eschews the notion of divinity itself. This indecision undermines Tamburlaine's project of unilateral self-fashioning, since he doubts the very gods on whom he models himself. Furthermore, the decision to both act as an earthly scourge on Jove's behalf and to take Jove's divine rebellion as a precedent for his own actions leaves him in an irreconcilable position where, to succeed, he must simultaneously bow to Jove's authority and rebel against him. Several critics have noted the ironic ambivalence of Tamburlaine's relationship with the divine. J. S. Sullivan argues that "The self-styled scourge both invokes and repudiates divine authority, imitating God even in rebelling against Him,"[35] while Barber contends that "Marlowe explores remorselessly the ironies of seeking omnipotence by dependence, domination by surrender."[36] Furthermore, the very image of Tamburlaine as God's scourge is itself, according to Mark Hutchings, "beautifully ambiguous: scourge of God – God's servant to punish others – or – blasphemously – the scourge of God himself?"[37]

Tamburlaine and the plays' other characters may be forgiven for struggling to find singular conviction with regard to religious faith. The play-world in which they operate offers little assurance of the existence of any divine entity, benign or otherwise. Various religions are invoked by the myriad factions of the plays in order to promote equally depraved and irreligious martial campaigns, with victory seeming to come as a result of overwhelming power rather than as vindication

---

[34] Harold Levin notes the transformations in Tamburlaine's relationship with Jove, although he attributes to it a more teleological progression than I do: "Jove, whom [Tamburlaine] had been naming as his exemplar and patron, now seems to be his rival and enemy. Whereas he has justified his subversions by recalling how the Olympians overthrew Saturn, now he would seem to be on the side of the Titans." *The Overreacher*, 69.

[35] Sullivan, introduction to *Tamburlaine*, 73.

[36] Barber, "The Death of Zenocrate," 16.

[37] Mark Hutchings, "Marlowe's Scourge of God," *Notes and Queries* 51, no. 3 (2004): 246. Roy W. Battenhouse's examination of the play in terms of the "Scourge of God" as a contemporary theological concept does not suggest any ambiguity in the term, but argues that the concept itself serves as a vehicle for addressing apparently irreconcilable moral questions about warfare and sin: "The 'Scourge of God' concept, let us note, helps define a philosophical attitude toward war – the paradoxical outlook by which war is both justified (by sin) and condemned (by God)." "Tamburlaine, the 'Scourge of God,'" *PMLA* 56, no. 2 (1941): 340.

of a righteous cause. That said, we are equally unable to dismiss the idea of a prevailing divine force in *Tamburlaine*: could a Scythian shepherd have possibly been able to win the support of royal armies and subjugate huge portions of the known world without divine aid? And, despite Vitkus's assertion that "Nowhere does the play suggest that his death is the result of divine retribution,"[38] can we really dismiss the proximity of the onset of Tamburlaine's terminal illness with his burning of the Qu'ran and invitation of Mahomet to wreak "vengeance on the head of Tamburlaine" (Two. 5. 1. 194) as mere coincidence? Not according to Greenblatt: "The slaughter of thousands, the murder of his own son, the torture of his royal captives are all without apparent consequence; then Tamburlaine falls ill, and when? When he burns the Koran! The one action which Elizabethan churchmen themselves might have applauded seems to bring down divine vengeance."[39] The timing of Tamburlaine's illness in relation to his challenge to Mahomet is a typically Marlovian device; it is distant enough to be thought unrelated to the blasphemy, but also close enough to be considered a direct result of it.[40] This is the kind of environment in which the plays' spiritual concerns are played out; the unclear relationship between the heavenly and the earthly means that it is impossible to know whether a victory or defeat has been divinely inspired, and if so by which deity, and at the same time an entirely materialist faith in earthly power represents a risk that is not worth taking. It is this context which causes an oscillation within Tamburlaine between submissive faith in Jove's divine authority and total belief in his earthly power, and thus prevents him from creating a spiritually unified self-projection.

---

[38] Vitkus, *Turning Turk*, 63.

[39] Greenblatt, *Renaissance Self-Fashioning*, 202.

[40] A number of critics have argued in opposite directions on this issue. An example of the case for Tamburlaine's illness as the result of a divine intervention is provided by Steane, who argues that "if any placing can be assumed to be pointed and deliberate, this can. Within thirty lines of daring Mahomet to 'Come downe ... and work a myracle' he is struck by the fever which is to kill him." *Marlowe: A Critical Study*, 115, n. 1. Bartels, by contrast, argues that "Although Tamburlaine becomes distempered after explicitly challenging Mahomet's authority and burning the Koran, neither the play nor any of its characters make a definitive link between the two." *Spectacles of Strangeness*, 80. Closer to my own perception of the matter is Dena Goldberg's assertion that "it is due to this connection [between Christ and Mahomet in the play] that the Christian auditor (or critic) wants to see the hand of Mahomet in Tamburlaine's illness. It feels like blasphemy to deny it. And yet what does it mean to a Christian to conclude that Tamburlaine's death is due to the providential intervention of Mahomet?" "Whose God's On First?," 584. David Farr's production of an amalgamation of the two plays at the Barbican Theatre, London, caused controversy by omitting any suggestion that it is in fact the Qu'ran that Tamburlaine burns. Farr countered suggestions that this represented a pandering to Islamic sensibilities by stating that he wanted, and indeed that a censor-wary Marlowe may have wanted, the scene to represent an attack on *all* religion. See Hopkins, *Christopher Marlowe, Renaissance Dramatist*, 75–80.

Physiology

The religious uncertainty that besets Tamburlaine's mission is further compounded by internal physiological conflict, of which we are reminded at key moments of the plays. On the eve of Tamburlaine's death, his physician offers a remarkably complex diagnosis of the warlord's distemper, arrived at via an inspection of his urine:

> Your veins are full of accidental heat
> Whereby the moisture of your blood is dried:
> The humidum and calor, which some hold
> Is not a parcel of the elements
> But of a substance more divine and pure,
> Is almost clean extinguishèd and spent,
> Which, being the cause of life, imports your death
> …
> Your artiers, which alongst the veins convey
> The lively spirits which the heart engenders,
> Are parched and void of spirit, that the soul,
> Wanting those organons by which it moves,
> Cannot endure, by argument of art.
> (Two. 5. 3. 84–97)

The description offers an image of the internal self as a network of elements, interrelated but ultimately separate; it is of a single body made up of distinct parts, rather like a map. Indeed, Bernhard Klein has astutely observed that cartography and physiology were conceptually linked in the early modern period, particularly by virtue of "the ancient idea of the body as microcosm."[41] This much is plainly in evidence in the introduction to John Speed's 1611 atlas of Britain and Ireland, which avers that

> The State of euery Kingdome well managed by prudent government, seems to me to represent a Humane Body, guided by the soueraignty of the Reasonable Soule: the Country and Land it self representing the one, the Action and state affairs the other … And here, first wee will (by example of the best Anatomists) propose to view the *whole Body*, and *Monarchie* intire (as far as conueniently wee could comprise it) and after will dissect and lay open the particular Members, Veines and Ioints, (I meane the Shires, Riuers, Cities, and Townes).[42]

Educated members of the Elizabethan audience would have been familiar with the symbolic relation of the body to larger social institutions – the idea of the body politic, the state represented as a human body with each echelon of government and class of society assigned a body part resonant with their role in the state, was a commonplace – but in these plays the usual focus is inverted: rather than using

---

[41] Klein, *Maps and the Writing of Space*, 24.
[42] Cited in ibid., 40.

the familiar image of the body to illustrate the harmony of a well-run society, here the complexity and volatility of the body are insisted upon.[43] Rather than operating as a signifier of unity, the body is meticulously dissected throughout the plays, repeatedly being evoked as an uneasy coalition of disparate parts. As the plays undermine the ostensibly unifying potential of a map, so they place an unusual focus on the human body as complex biological construct.

Tamburlaine's "writing" of himself proves as difficult as the reduction of the world, because people are shown to be, like places, intricately complex entities. When Olympia's husband announces to her the severity of his battle wound, he does so in a manner which emphasizes the concept of the body as a whole made of parts, and demonstrates an extraordinary anatomical self-awareness:

> A deadly bullet gliding through my side
> Lies heavy on my heart; I cannot live.
> I feel my liver pierced, and all my veins
> That there begin and nourish every part
> Mangled and torn, and all my entrails bathed
> In blood that straineth from their orifex.
> Farewell sweet wife! Sweet son, farewell! I die.
> (Two. 3. 4. 4–10)

In the first play, after suffering defeat in battle at the hands of Tamburlaine, a wounded Cosroe stumbles on stage, complaining of the treachery used against him, but also of the injury done to him:

> An uncouth pain torments my grievèd soul,
> And death arrests the organ of my voice,
> Who, entering at the breach thy sword hath made,
> Sacks every vein and artier of my heart.
> (One. 2. 7. 7–10)

Here again the body is figured as a complex site, consisting of veins, arteries, organs, a heart and a soul. Cosroe also engages in that signifying practice that relates the body to a larger geographical entity – his wound becomes the breach in the wall of a town or fort succumbing to the siege of death.

Matthew Greenfield summarizes well the effect these passages have in promoting a consideration of the self as biological conglomeration:

---

[43] Other passages which foreground the physiological aspect of pain or death include Cosroe's continuation of his dying speech, in which he laments: "My bloodless body waxeth chill and cold, / And with my blood my life slides through my wound. / My soul begins to take her flight to hell, / And summons all my senses to depart: / The heat and moisture, which did feed each other, / For want of nourishment to feed them both / Is dry and cold …" (One. 2. 7. 42–8), and Bajazeth's account of his own starvation: "My empty stomach, full of idle heat, / Draws bloody humours from my feeble parts, / Preserving life by hasting cruel death. / My veins are pale, my sinews hard and dry, / My joints benumbed; unless I eat, I die" (One. 4. 4. 96–100).

Marlowe's scenes of self-dissection seem designed to have a similar effect, to make his audiences aware of the strangeness of their own experience of embodiment. It would be difficult to hear Marlowe's characters anatomize themselves and not think about one's internal architecture, with its convoluted spaces and its incessant and secret sucking, filtering, mixing, and transubstantiating.[44]

This focus is emphasized by Tamburlaine's response to Cosroe – the speech, quoted above, in which he cites Jove as his precedent. It contains the following much-quoted lines:

> Nature, that framed us of four elements
> Warring within our breasts for regiment,
> Doth teach us all to have aspiring minds.
> (One. 2. 7. 18–20)

The body, then, is not only a complex of interrelated entities, but also a site of conflict. Nature may teach us all to have aspiring minds, but it also allows our health, and our own individual nature, to depend upon an internal struggle over which we have no control. Marlowe allows us the idea that Tamburlaine's ethical judgements, his oscillating religious convictions and his barbarous and tyrannical actions are subject to a grim biological determinism.

The instability of human physiology is further accentuated in the plays' treatment of the protagonist's sons. Upon his deathbed, Tamburlaine addresses his two remaining heirs with a speech which asserts their inheritance of his being, both spiritual and physical:

> But sons, this subject, not of force enough
> To hold the fiery spirit it contains,
> Must part, imparting his impressions
> By equal portions into both your breasts:
> My flesh, divided in your precious shapes,
> Shall still retain my spirit though I die,
> And live in all your seeds immortally.
> (Two. 5. 3. 168–74)

Amyrus and Celebinus are imprints – "impressions" – of Tamburlaine, and, as his offspring, are made of his very flesh. This assertion of Tamburlaine's seems to hold water: the two sons are proud and warlike, apparently overflowing with the same ambition that drives their father. Frank Ardolino has noted Tamburlaine's determination "to protect and perpetuate his dominion by forcing his children into becoming copies of himself," and in some respects he would seem to have achieved success in this.[45]

---

[44] Greenfield, "Christopher Marlowe's Wound Knowledge," 237.

[45] Frank Ardolino, "The 'Wrath of Frowning Jove': Fathers and Sons in Marlowe's Plays," *Journal of Evolutionary Psychology* 2 (1981): 91. On the notion of the son as replica of the father, see Lynda E. Boose, "The Getting of a Lawful Race," in *Women, "Race," &*

Crucially, however, Amyrus and Celebinus are the remaining two survivors of what was a trio, Calyphas's absence from the scene owing to his having been murdered by his father as punishment for his refusal to take up arms. Whether his refusal to fight emanates from cowardice or from a coherently pacifist perspective, Calyphas's passivity presents a significant challenge to Tamburlaine's conviction that his sons represent impressions of himself. Ultimately, this is a challenge that he can only meet by denying Calyphas's parentage.[46] Towards the beginning of Part Two, he addresses Calyphas as "Bastardly boy, sprung from some coward's loins, / And not the issue of great Tamburlaine" (Two. 1. 3. 69–70), and later, shortly before performing his execution, asks "But where's this coward, villain, not my son, / But traitor to my name and majesty?" (Two. 4. 1. 89–90). Calyphas represents a significant problem for Tamburlaine's project of unilateral self-fashioning. He has set upon a mission to portray a self-image of uncompromising ferocity, yet his sons – supposedly extensions of himself – collectively display characteristics ranging from bellicosity to what he perceives as effeminate cowardliness. Tamburlaine's execution of Calyphas, then, ostensibly a martial punishment for cowardice, can also be seen as an attempt to suppress an element in his own character that is reflected in his son, a point which is taken up by Eugene Waith, who states that Tamburlaine enacts the murder as "almost a ritual killing – the extirpation of an unworthy part of himself."[47] When, in offering up to Jove the soul of Calyphas immediately prior to the murder, he finally acknowledges him as his son, this personal element to the process becomes more apparent:

> Here, Jove, receive his fainting soul again,
> A form not meet to give that substance essence
> Whose matter is the flesh of Tamburlaine,
> Wherein an incorporeal spirit moves,
> Made of the mould whereof thyself consists,
> Which makes me valiant, proud, ambitious,
> Ready to levy power against thy throne,
> That I might move the turning spheres of heaven:

Writing in the Early Modern Period, ed. Margo Hendricks and Patricia Parker (London: Routledge, 1994).

[46] Twentieth-century critics tended to dismiss Calyphas as a vacuous exemplar of cowardice, and as such perceived his punishment to be justified (see, for example, Kocher, "Marlowe's Art of War"). It has become increasingly common, however, to read Calyphas as a more complex and subversive figure. As early as 1970, M. M. Mahood contends that "Calyphas has the most character of [Tamburlaine's] three sons," while some years later Deats reads Tamburlaine's "cowardly yet daring" son as another of Marlowe's dual-aspect characters. Alan Shepard, as mentioned earlier in the chapter, has shown that the punishment carried out against Calyphas would not necessarily have been recognized as justified or fair. See, respectively, M. M. Mahood, *Poetry and Humanism* (New York: Norton, 1970), 63; Deats, *Sex, Gender, and Desire*, 155; Shepard, *Marlowe's Soldiers*, 44–5.

[47] Eugene M. Waith, "Tamburlaine," in *Marlowe: A Collection of Critical Essays*, ed. Clifford Leech (Englewood Cliffs, NJ: Prentice Hall, 1964), 84.

> For earth and all this airy region
> Cannot contain the state of Tamburlaine.
>   [*Stabs* CALYPHAS]
> (Two. 4. 1. 111–20)

Here Tamburlaine explicitly states Calyphas's unworthiness to occupy his great flesh, but the speech also accentuates his oneness with his son. The speech makes a seamless shift of focus from father to son, hinging on the phrase "the flesh of Tamburlaine"; the phrase, semantically and, in this speech, syntactically, applies both to the son and the father, emphasizing their essential sameness. In order to reassert his unflinching ferocity of character, Tamburlaine must excise that part of himself which reveals other characteristics, in this case one of his sons. In doing so he performs an act of reduction, and is also able to revivify his project of self-fashioning by the sheer brutality of the act. However, what the episode also shows is that this project is essentially self-destructive.

Love

A further challenge is presented to Tamburlaine's project in the shape of his relationship with Zenocrate: how can one consume oneself so comprehensively in a calling such as representing God's earthly scourge, and be a lover also? Amyras, when chastising Zenocrate regarding the object of her romantic attention, provides a simple answer: one cannot.

> How can you fancy one that looks so fierce,
> Only disposed to martial stratagems?
> Who when he shall embrace you in his arms
> Will tell how many thousand men he slew;
> And when you look for amorous discourse
> Will rattle forth his facts of war and blood,
> Too harsh a subject for your dainty ears.
> (One. 3. 2. 40–46)

Amyras's mischievous reproach, reminiscent of Prince Hal's teasing of Hotspur in *1 Henry IV*, is a measure of the success that Tamburlaine has achieved in convincing the majority of the plays' other characters of his monolithic persuasion – it is impossible for them to imagine him possessing the capacity for affection. Zenocrate's response, however, suggests that Tamburlaine's personality also incorporates a softer sensibility: he is an irrepressible warlord with "talk much sweeter than the Muses' song" (One. 3. 2. 50). Several critics have agreed, to an extent, with Zenocrate, in that his love for her is of perhaps equal importance to his territorial ambitions. Spence argues that Tamburlaine's "ardent and transforming love" for Zenocrate "has a force almost equal to his great historic passion for military power."[48] Fanta asserts that "Tamburlaine's claim to nobility goes deeper

---

[48] Leslie Spence, "Tamburlaine and Marlowe," *PMLA* 42, no. 3 (1927): 618.

than his military conquests," and reads Zenocrate as "an embodiment and object of expression of the milder strains of his character."[49]

There is plenty of evidence in the text to support these viewpoints. Nowhere does Tamburlaine seem to be more possessed of a tender heart than in the scene of Zenocrate's death, in which he articulates earth's loss and heaven's gain in her passing:

> Apollo, Cynthia, and the ceaseless lamps
> That gently looked upon this loathsome earth,
> Shine downwards now no more, but deck the heavens
> To entertain divine Zenocrate.
> The crystal springs whose taste illuminates
> Refinèd eyes with an eternal sight,
> Like trièd silver runs through Paradise
> To entertain divine Zenocrate.
> (Two. 2. 4. 18–25)

The pattern of this excerpt continues throughout Tamburlaine's speech, which is remarkable by virtue of its lack of reference to its speaker. In this speech, Barber notes, "there is, for once, deep reverence and a loss of self in contemplation of the harmony of the universe. Instead of appropriating the cosmos to aggrandize his identity, Tamburlaine envisages for a moment atonement with God through Zenocrate."[50] Key in this assessment of the speech, however, are the terms "for once" and "for a moment." Real as Tamburlaine's love for Zenocrate may be – and here, at the point of her death, it seems to be real – Tamburlaine elsewhere seeks to either suppress it or to subsume it into his more familiar martial discourse. If Tamburlaine can be said to be "letting himself go" in Zenocrate's death scene, then the other place in which he does so is in Part One, when, after articulating her hold over him, he muses on the essence of beauty:

> What is beauty, saith my sufferings, then?
> If all the pens that ever poets held
> Had fed the feeling of their masters' thoughts
> And every sweetness that inspired their hearts,
> Their minds and muses on admirèd themes;
> If all the heavenly quintessence they still
> From their immortal flowers of poesy,
> Wherein as in a mirror we perceive
> The highest reaches of a human wit –
> If these had made one poem's period
> And all combined in beauty's worthiness,
> Yet should there hover in their restless heads
> One thought, one grace, one wonder at the least,
> Which into words no virtue can digest.
> (One. 5. 1. 160–73)

---

[49] Fanta, *Marlowe's "Agonists,"* 14.
[50] Barber, "The Death of Zenocrate," 21.

Not only does Tamburlaine's sensitive musing here undercut his self-hewn image as warrior-orator, it also leads him to a very difficult conclusion: that beauty is something irreducible. It is this concept, of there being something in the world that cannot be mastered, that prompts the self-reproach of the following lines:

> But how unseemly is it for my sex,
> My discipline of arms and chivalry,
> My nature, and the terror of my name,
> To harbour thoughts effeminate and faint!
> (One. 5. 1. 174–7)

Tamburlaine's solution to this problem seems to be to unify romantic love and martial zeal. Only a couple of lines after reprimanding his own effeminacy, he is ready with the justifying assertion that "every warrior that is rapt with love / Of fame, of valour, and of victory, / Must needs have beauty beat on his conceits" (One. 5. 1. 180–82). This synthesis is played out in the protagonist's language later in the same scene, when the discussion of beauty is reflected in discourse on the carnage of war:

> And such are objects fit for Tamburlaine,
> Wherein as in a mirror may be seen
> His honour, that consists in shedding blood
> When men presume to manage arms with him.
> (One. 5. 1. 476–9)

The image of the mirror, echoing as it does his earlier discourse on beauty, suggests that war and beauty serve the same purpose to Tamburlaine: to intensify his self-projection. Despite this, he seems much more comfortable with the image in the mirror held up by the blood-stained and vanquished enemy than he does with that presented by the flowers of poesy. As such, with the exception of the two passages discussed above, when Tamburlaine discusses love he tends to articulate feeling using a fabric of military tropes: Zenocrate lays siege to his heart, is compared to the possession of the Persian crown, and is wooed with the promise of martial prizes (One. 1. 2. 82–104 and 5. 1. 135–56). Even Zenocrate, in response to Amyras's words of caution, defends the capacity of "mighty Tamburlaine" (One. 3. 2. 55) to be a lover by comparing his softer words with muses' songs of mythical conflicts.

In order to avoid the undermining of his warlike identity, then, Tamburlaine attempts to classify love as another branch of the constant warfare in which he is absorbed. Yet, as has been seen, there are two occasions on which this tenuous unification breaks down, and Tamburlaine seems to speak inspired by love in its own right. Tellingly, both of these scenes are also the only occasions in the plays, save for his death, in which Tamburlaine experiences genuine powerlessness; in the earlier scene he realizes the futility of attempting to master the abstract concept of beauty, while in the latter he demonstrates his frustration at his inability to prevent Zenocrate's death by giving the following futile order to Techelles:

>   Techelles, draw thy sword,
> And wound the earth, that it may cleave in twain,
> And we descend into th'infernal vaults
> To hale the Fatal Sisters by the hair
> And throw them in the triple moat of hell
> For taking hence my fair Zenocrate.
> (Two. 2. 4. 96–101)

Both of these moments of apparent powerlessness provoke immediate compensatory responses from Tamburlaine; in one case a simple and swift self-rebuke, in the other the destruction of a town and annihilation of its inhabitants. This wild retaliation in many ways prefigures the killing of Calyphas. Like his later filicide, it is an act of erasure which is performed in order to purge Tamburlaine of elements of his own character that fall beyond his sphere of control, and both acts of purgation are of such a ferocious nature as to give new vitality to his self-constructed image.[51]

Tamburlaine's attempt at fashioning a unified self-image, while convincing to the majority of the plays' other characters, is ultimately rendered unattainable by his own religious, physical, familial and emotional inconsistencies. He finds that, like beauty, the human personality is irreducible. There seems to be an unwitting acknowledgement of this shortly after Zenocrate's death, when Tamburlaine trains his remaining sons in the art of warfare. Up until this point, he has breezed through successive epic conquests without receiving as much as a scratch, and the ease of his victories has been suggested by the lack of any description of how they happen – they just, inevitably, do. This is, of course, part of the mystique of the image that Tamburlaine has built; the ease of his victories is reason enough to question whether he is in fact human, or, as he sometimes suggests, a vengeful instrument of God's ire. By the time his sons receive their martial training, however, the picture is beginning to disintegrate, and, rather than being left to imagine the force behind the great victories, we are presented with a detailed exposition of the "rudiments of war" (Two. 3. 2. 53–92). Furthermore, when scolding Calyphas for his cowardice, Tamburlaine cuts his arm as a demonstration of military virtue; after sweeping all before him completely untouched, he finally receives his first wound at his own hands, and, in a perverse reflection of the risen Jesus's encounter with St. Thomas, encourages his sons to search his wounds. Vitkus reads this scene as an aggrandizing moment, positing Tamburlaine's wound as "that of a god-like figure who cannot be harmed by human beings and can only be wounded when he

---

[51] This act of purgation is noted by Roger Sales, who highlights Tamburlaine's callous obliteration of Zenocrate's feminine and pacific influences after her death: "Tamburlaine wants to replace Zenocrate's influence over their children with his own. She asks him not to damage her after-life by responding rashly to her impending death. He burns a city to the ground and hangs up her picture outside his tent so that his soldiers will fight harder. He then kills the son who takes after his mother." *Christopher Marlowe* (Basingstoke: Macmillan, 1991), 82.

wills it to happen."[52] But the wound has an immediately demystifying effect: rather than looking like a god, Tamburlaine himself tellingly announces "Now look I like a soldier" (Two. 3. 2. 117). Christ's wounds prove that he is the risen saviour, but Tamburlaine's emphasize his mortality, something which up to this point an audience may have doubted. In the very act of demonstrating his invincibility he simultaneously reveals his vulnerability. In a sense this episode captures in microcosm the tension within Tamburlaine that this chapter has discussed. Here, as elsewhere in the plays, his projection of himself as an omnipotent being proves impossible to maintain. While the warlord's achievements are prodigious, the plays conclude with an insistence upon his failure to achieve his overarching aim of reducing the world to a map. Similarly, his equivalent project of reductive self-projection proves untenable. The unitary identity of warrior-god that Tamburlaine attempts to construct cannot withstand the multiplicity of competing forces – moral, religious, physiological, erotic – which it attempts to contain.

---

[52] Vitkus, *Turning Turk*, 68.

Chapter 3
"Resolve me of all ambiguities": *Doctor Faustus*

Doctor Faustus, Marlowe's most famous work, is a play that has attracted intense critical attention over a span of centuries. Among the many reasons for its continued prominence is its problematic nature. The play exists in two texts, both of which are markedly different from one another, and neither of which is considered to be entirely authoritative. For decades editors and textual scholars have disagreed over which text is a superior representation of Marlowe's play, and more recently over how one can even begin to tackle such a complex textual problem as this without stepping outside the remit of the modern editor. On a textual level, *Faustus* has resisted unification: a century of attempts to reduce it to a single text has culminated in the current consensus, cumbersome in practice but preferable in theory, that the play must continue to exist in two separate versions.[1] It is not only as an artefact that *Doctor Faustus* has been subject to such controversy, however. The play itself is shot through with ambiguity. The audience is shown the story of a morally barren scholar who rejects divinity in favour of the seductive power of Lucifer, yet at the same time seems to be invited to identify, and even sympathize, with him. The play appears to be variously a medieval morality play and a Renaissance tragedy, and also infiltrates a patently Christian theme with abundant images of classical mythology. It is this pervading ambiguity that has spawned the notably diverse range of critical responses to the play, leading *Faustus* to be seen as being amongst the most orthodox of moralistic Christian plays, and also as a subversive tract which glorifies the power of the human spirit.

In contrast to its ambiguity, however, I will argue that the play's protagonist is irrevocably driven towards unified and unequivocal knowledge. This desire is shared by a number of the leading lights of Marlowe's time, none more so than the Hermetic magus John Dee, upon whom the character of Faustus is sometimes said to be based.[2] Hermeticism, a system of philosophy popular amongst many of Marlowe's peers, posited the prime objective of man as a unified understanding of

---

[1] In this chapter I will, unless stated otherwise, quote from the 1604 text. I make this choice on the grounds that it seems to me the more coherent of the two versions, but in saying so I do not attempt to assert the originality or authority of the A text. For a discussion of the existence of the play in two texts, and the impact of this fact upon approaches to editing it, see my "Modern Problems of Editing: The Two Texts of Marlowe's *Doctor Faustus*," *Literature Compass* 2 (2005).

[2] See, for example, Frances Yates, *The Occult Philosophy in the Elizabethan Age* (London: Routledge & Kegan Paul, 1979), 115–25.

the universe, and made unification a vibrant concept amongst the intelligentsia of Elizabethan England. Just as the texts of *Doctor Faustus* have resisted unification, however, I will argue that the tragedy of Faustus lies in his absolute failure to achieve that unification of knowledge which he so desires, and that the play highlights the incompatibility of contemporary philosophical drives for unification with the inherent multiplicity of mankind.

Ambiguity

Perhaps the most fundamental ambiguity of *Doctor Faustus* is in the nature of its protagonist. Is Faustus a bad man, or simply foolish? If he is indeed bad or foolish, can he rightly be said to be a tragic hero? Is the audience meant to witness the demise of a man who has been overcome by the admirable Renaissance urge for human endeavour, or rather the fearful and just punishment of a faithless heretic? Critical discussion of the play over the last century has produced support for both sides of the argument. One does not have to delve deeply to find an orthodox Christian moral in *Doctor Faustus*. It is a play in which the protagonist, overflowing with boastful arrogance, sells his soul to Lucifer in return for twenty-four years of earthly indulgence, and ultimately pays the inevitable price of eternal damnation. As early as the prologue, we are given ample reason to anticipate a vehement propounding of Christian values:

> Excelling all whose sweet delight disputes
> In heavenly matters of theology;
> Till, swoll'n with cunning of a self-conceit,
> His waxen wings did mount above his reach,
> And melting heavens conspired his overthrow.
> For, falling to a devilish exercise,
> And glutted more with learning's golden gifts,
> He surfeits upon cursèd necromancy.
> (Prologue. 18–25)[3]

Faustus's descent from the study of "heavenly matters of theology" to the gluttonous partaking of "a devilish exercise" seems calculated to excite the disapproval of a Christian audience. Indeed, Arieh Sachs asserts the Christian outlook of the play, arguing that any interpretation which considers Faustus as a figure to be admired by the audience simply overlooks the religio-historical context in which the play was produced:

> To suggest that because Faustus does not seem to commit an infraction of what
> the modern liberal and utilitarian mind sees as morality he is an admirable

---

[3] Christopher Marlowe, *Doctor Faustus: A- and B-Texts (1604, 1616)*, ed. David Bevington and Eric Rasmussen. All subsequent quotations from the play are from the A-Text in this edition.

character and does not deserve his punishment is to put the play in a context entirely alien to it.[4]

Sachs's interpretation of the play as an exploration of religious despair and predestination is persuasive, and identifies many of the key moments of the play with these ardently Protestant themes. Leo Kirschbaum similarly states that "whatever Marlowe was himself, there is no more obvious Christian document in all Elizabethan drama than *Doctor Faustus*," while Robert Ornstein dismisses the notion of Faustus as the admirable humanist, arguing that "we are always aware that Faustus the aspiring Titan is also the self-deluded fool of Lucifer."[5]

Faustus's folly is often the main justification for orthodox readings of the play. The audience, the argument goes, cannot possibly have identified with a character who is simultaneously immensely proud of his intellect and sufficiently ignorant to pursue such a hopeless endeavour as a pact with Lucifer. Joseph T. McCullen contends that Faustus's downfall comes about as a result of his "culpable ignorance,"[6] and that the Elizabethan conception of wisdom, which emphasized the importance of self-knowledge and the application of ideas to practical causes, would leave little scope for the consideration of Faustus as anything other than a fool. As Mike Pincombe states, "For all Faustus's learning, he is still a *dilettante* when it comes to wisdom."[7] This argument is not without ammunition. Faustus knowingly signs away his soul, despite Mephistopheles's words of experience, warning him to "leave these frivolous demands, / Which strike a terror to my fainting soul!" (1. 3. 83–4). As if this was not enough, he then takes his academic scepticism to an absurd degree, challenging Mephistopheles, himself visible proof of the existence of hell, with the taunt: "Come, I think hell's a fable" (2. 1. 130). Indeed, despite the reputation he appears to wield in the academic world, the play gives cause to question Faustus's scholarly rigour. The syllogism that he constructs in the first soliloquy provides an example:

> Jerome's Bible, Faustus, view it well.
> [*He reads.*] *Stipendium peccati mors est.* Ha!
> *Stipendium*, etc.
> The reward of sin is death. That's hard.
> [*He reads.*] *Si peccasse negamus, fallimur*
> *Et nulla est in nobis veritas.*
> If we say that we have no sin,

---

[4] Arieh Sachs, "The Religious Despair of Doctor Faustus," *Journal of English and Germanic Philology* 63 (1964): 633.

[5] See Leo Kirschbaum, "Marlowe's *Faustus*: A Reconsideration," *The Review of English Studies* 19 (1943): 229, and Robert Ornstein, "The Comic Synthesis in *Doctor Faustus*," *English Literary History* 22, no. 3 (1955): 17.

[6] Joseph T. McCullen, "Doctor Faustus and Renaissance Learning," *Modern Language Review* 51 (1956): 9.

[7] Mike Pincombe, *Elizabethan Humanism: Literature and Learning in the later Sixteenth Century* (London: Longman, 2001), 169.

>   We deceive ourselves, and there's no truth in us.
>   Why then belike we must sin,
>   And so consequently die.
>   (1. 1. 38–47)

From the evidence that Faustus provides, his assertion is logically sound, but, through either ineptitude or wilful negligence, the biblical quotations upon which it is built are taken entirely out of their context, a fact observed by David Bevington:

> The first should read "For the wages of sin is death, but the gift of God is eternal life through Jesus Christ our Lord" (Romans 6.23); the second, "If we say we have no sin, we deceive ourselves, and truth is not in us. If we acknowledge our sins, he is faithful and just to forgive us our sins and to cleanse us from all unrighteousness" (I John 1.8). An Elizabethan audience, used to hearing disputations on Biblical texts, would presumably have been quicker than we to detect Faustus's fallacies.[8]

Faustus's erroneous syllogism, from an orthodox viewpoint, could be seen as representative of his greater plight: it is a lack of understanding of Christian faith and the forgiveness of God that leads him to reject it.

The stupidity of Faustus is further established by the profligate uses to which he puts his powers once he has indeed rejected divinity. In stark contrast to the lofty promises he makes to himself to "wall all Germany with brass" and "chase the Prince of Parma from our land" (1. 1. 90, 95), Faustus fritters away his four and twenty years in idle horseplay. Throughout the third and fourth acts he does little more than play practical jokes at the expense of the Pope and a lowly horse-courser, humiliate an injurious knight and perform magic tricks for the emperor, the Duke of Vanholt and his wife.[9] Gone are the designs on infinite knowledge that appeared to be his motive for signing the bond. Indeed, such is the gulf between the evocative statements of intent articulated in the first two acts and the trivial eventuality that ensues in the third and fourth that the play is often accused of poor structure and thematic inconsistency, and the less "serious" material attributed to the pen of an unnamed collaborator. One can equally argue, however, that the middle section of the play simply illustrates the transience and ultimate irrelevance of earthly power, and highlights the degree to which Faustus has been duped. As Greg justifiably asks, "Who but a fool, such a clever fool as Faustus, would dream that any power but evil could be won by a bargain with evil, or that truth could be wrung from the father of lies?"[10]

---

[8] David Bevington, "Marlowe and God," *Explorations in Renaissance Culture* 17 (1991): 4.

[9] The B text gives Faustus a task of some import by having him manufacture the escape of Bruno, the Imperial candidate for the papacy (3, 1–2). This more weighty endeavour is offset in this text, however, by the considerably greater attention paid to whimsical clownery that he engages in through Acts 3 and 4.

[10] W. W. Greg, "The Damnation of Faustus," in *Marlowe: A Collection of Critical Essays*, ed. Clifford Leech (Englewood Cliffs, NJ: Prentice Hall, 1964), 96.

In response to the argument for *Doctor Faustus* as a document of Christian morality, however, one can ask just how bad Faustus actually is, as besides a slap on the pate for the Pope, a joke at the expense of the knight and the sale of some questionable merchandise to the horse-courser, he does nothing to harm anybody other than himself. A critic such as Sachs might dismiss such a statement as born of a modern liberal judgement of an Elizabethan play, but some of Faustus's deeds are more likely to have brought the house down than to have excited censure. A Protestant audience would be more than willing to forgive Faustus for his jesting at the expense of the Pope, often himself figured as the antichrist, and his promise to "chase the Prince of Parma from our land" (1. 1. 95) is likely to have been met with unabashed admiration if the play was indeed performed in, or shortly after, the Armada year of 1588.[11]

Moreover, Faustus's folly need not exclude him from an audience's sympathies. As Maxwell points out, Faustus's error is a repeat of that made by Adam, the father of all humanity. Faustus and Adam both transgress after being overcome by curiosity, that most human of instincts. Indeed, the ubiquity of curiosity is reflected upon by Marlowe at other points in the play. In the scene which is often described merely as Faustus "hoodwinking" or "gulling" the horse-courser, we are provided with a comic mirror of the sins of Faustus and of Adam. Upon agreeing to sell the "horse," Faustus offers the horse-courser some advice:

> FAUSTUS: But I must tell you one thing before you have him: ride him not into the water, at any hand.
> HORSE-COURSER: Why, sir, will he not drink of all waters?
> FAUSTUS: O, yes, he will drink of all waters, but ride him not into the water. Ride him over hedge, or ditch, or where thou wilt, but not into the water.
> (4. 1. 123–9)

Within seven lines, the horse-courser returns in a state of fury, and reflects on what has happened since he left:

> But yet, like an ass as I was, I would not be ruled by him, for he bade me I should ride him into no water. Now I, thinking my horse had had some rare quality that he would not have had me known of, I, like a venturous youth, rid him into the deep pond at the town's end. I was no sooner in the middle of the pond but my horse vanished away and I sat upon a bottle of hay, never so near drowning in my life.
> (4. 1. 148–55)

The horse-courser has been given sound and unequivocal advice. Just like Adam and Faustus, he ignores it – or rather actively seeks to act contrary to it – on

---

[11] The date of *Doctor Faustus* has been a controversial issue throughout the play's critical history, with scholars favouring either a date of 1588/9 or 1592/3. For a significant case for the earlier date, see R. J. Fehrenbach, "A Pre-1592 English Faust Book and the Date of *Doctor Faustus*," *Library: The Transactions of the Bibliographical Society* 2, no. 4 (2001).

the assumption that some great knowledge is to be discovered. At worst, then, Faustus's sin is a heinous one to which we can all relate, while at best the sceptical curiosity displayed by him and the horse-courser, particularly in a Renaissance context of growing efforts in the fields of science, cartography and empire, is something to be understood and applauded.

Genre

These moral questions raise a further tricky question: if we cannot identify with or admire its protagonist, can *The Tragical History of Doctor Faustus* be considered "tragical" at all? In his *Poetics*, Aristotle is concise in identifying the ingredients of tragedy. He states that "Tragedy is an imitation of an action that is admirable, complete and possesses magnitude; in language made pleasurable ... performed by actors, not through narration; effecting through pity and fear the purification of such emotions."[12] The chief goal of tragedy is the therapeutic cleansing of residual feelings of pity and fear, achieved through a substantial but short-lived excitement of those emotions. This effect is not simply achieved by staging a spectacle of catastrophic misfortune, but is dependent upon careful and sensitive characterization and plotting:

> So it is clear first of all that decent men should not be seen undergoing a change from good fortune to bad fortune – this does not evoke pity or fear, but disgust. Nor should depraved people be seen undergoing a change from bad fortune to good fortune – this is the least tragic of all: it has none of the right effects, since it is neither agreeable, nor does it evoke pity or fear. Nor again should a very wicked person fall from good fortune to bad fortune – that kind of structure would be agreeable, but would not excite pity or fear, since the one has to do with someone who is suffering undeservedly, the other with someone who is like ourselves (I mean, pity has to do with the undeserving sufferer, fear with the person like us); so what happens will evoke neither pity nor fear.[13]

Nearly two thousand years later – in Marlowe's lifetime – echoes of Aristotle's definition of the genre can be heard in Philip Sidney's *An Apology For Poetry*:

> So that the right use of Comedy will (I think) by nobody be blamed, and much less of the high and excellent Tragedy, that openeth the greatest wounds, and showeth forth the ulcers that are covered with tissue; that maketh kings fear to be tyrants, and tyrants manifest their tyrannical humours; that, with stirring the affects of admiration and commiseration, teacheth the uncertainty of this world, and upon how weak foundations gilden roofs are builded.[14]

---

[12] Aristotle, *Poetics*, trans. Michael Heath (London: Penguin, 1996), 10.
[13] Ibid., 20–21.
[14] Philip Sidney, *An Apology for Poetry*, ed. Geoffrey Shepherd (London: Thomas Nelson and Sons, 1965), 117–8.

Sidney here invests tragedy with a more didactic and utilitarian purpose than does Aristotle, but the means that bring about the end – the stirring of admiration and commiseration – are synonymous with those in the Aristotelian definition.

If Faustus is neither a great man nor worthy of our sympathy, but rather a wicked man experiencing a fall from good fortune to bad fortune, then the play fulfils neither Aristotle's nor Sidney's criteria for tragedy. Indeed, the Christian subject matter of the play renders its classification as tragedy problematic. A characteristic traditionally displayed by tragic heroes, to give an example, is Hubris: excessive pride in the face of the gods. This, in the classical world of myriad jealous and interfering deities whose interests often conflict with one another, can be seen as an admirable, if ill-advised, quality. Pride in a Christian context, however, is the root of original sin, and to display it in the face of God is to commit outrageous blasphemy. The contradictions inherent in the idea of a Christian tragedy are indicative of a greater cultural tension between the established religious order, centred upon faith, and the newly flourishing humanism, largely defined by its revisiting of classical art and philosophy, centred upon knowledge.

J. C. Maxwell is aware of the implications inherent in these questions when he says "Faustus is Everyman, and his sin is a re-enactment of the sin of Adam – pride."[15] Maxwell's comparison of Faustus to Everyman, the quintessential figure of the medieval morality tradition, offers a potential solution to the problem of the play's genre, and suggests some telling parallels between the two plays. At the beginning of *Everyman*, the arrival of Death at once seals the inevitability of Everyman's fate, and sets in motion his journey towards spiritual emancipation. Faustus's contractual bond with Lucifer, also conducted early in the piece, provides a similar sense of inevitability, and, in an inversion of the plight of Everyman, sends him into a spiralling moral decline which terminates in damnation. There is, moreover, a consistent presence of traditional morality features in *Doctor Faustus*: psychomachia is provided through the interjections of the good and bad angels, and the counterbalancing forces of good and evil are represented on one side by the scholars and the Old Man, and on the other by Mephistopheles, Valdes and Cornelius. The pageant of the Seven Deadly Sins employs the traditional morality tool of casting abstract concepts as physical entities, while the episodic nature of the "middle" of the play, together with the alternating scenes that burlesque its main action, is very much in the style of the morality.[16]

To say that *Doctor Faustus* is a morality play, however, is to oversimplify the issue. It is worth remembering that Doctor Faustus could have been anyone, but was in fact someone: the play is based on the historical Johan Faustus, as he is represented in the *Faustbook* that was Marlowe's source. Furthermore, the morality features in the play are amply offset by its tragic elements. While the case against Faustus as a suitable tragic figure has been argued above, the play's prologue – that same source which is often employed as evidence of the

---

[15] J. C. Maxwell, "The Sin of Faustus," *The Wind and the Rain* 4 (1947): 50.

[16] See Nicholas Brooke, "The Moral Tragedy of *Doctor Faustus*," *The Cambridge Journal* 5 (1952): 665.

play's Christian orthodoxy – states that Faustus excels "all whose sweet delight disputes / In heavenly matters of theology" (Prologue. 18–19) – in his field he is indeed a great man, and clearly admired by his students. In his arrogant pride we have hamartia, in his final rejection of divinity and embrace of worldly pleasure in the form of the succubus Helen we have peripeteia,[17] and in the agonized final soliloquy there is a clear example of anagnorisis. Even the classical unities, which at first glance seem to have been ignored in the construction of the play, can be applied, in a sense: Faustus's diabolical contract covers a period of twenty-four years, conveniently matching the number of hours in one day; the scenes involving Robin, Rafe and Wagner comprise satirical comment on the main action rather than coherent subplots; and, although Faustus travels throughout Europe, all of the action could be said to occur in one "place" if we accept Mephistopheles's assertion that

> Hell hath no limits, nor is circumscribed
> In one self place, for where we are is hell,
> And where hell is must we ever be.
> (2. 1. 124–6)

What we have, it seems, is a play that can be shown to satisfy to a large degree the generic criteria of both the morality and the tragedy forms. It is often the interpretation of Faustus's character that leads to a preference for one form or another; as Bevington states, "it is the bifurcation of Faustus' own personality between base physical desires and Promethean aspiration that arouses dispute concerning the message of the play."[18] It is disapproval of Faustus's "base physical desires" that leads some critics to interpret him as an example in the morality tradition, and admiration of his "Promethean aspiration" that leads others to interpret him as a tragic figure. In whichever direction a critic leans, the generic apparatus can be found in the play to support their interpretation. The effect is described eloquently by Kristen Poole, who states that "the result of this generic intermingling is a world that is morally ambiguous, as both the old and the new, the angels and Faustus, seem alternately – or simultaneously – to be the subject of valorization and critique."[19]

---

[17] See Greg, Maxwell. Locating a specific moment of peripeteia in the play is somewhat hazardous. If one agrees with Greg and Maxwell that Faustus's irrevocable damnation is finally confirmed at the kiss with Helen, then there is little difficulty. However, if one agrees with Sachs, whose argument is that the play exhibits Calvinist tendencies, and that Faustus, as a despairing reprobate, is damned from the start, then peripeteia disappears from the play.

[18] David Bevington, *From Mankind to Marlowe* (Cambridge, MA: Harvard University Press, 1962), 254–5.

[19] Poole, "*Dr. Faustus* and Reformation Theology," 103. John Mebane, while asserting the play's status as a tragedy, makes a similar point: "*Dr. Faustus* is neither a morality play nor an unambivalent celebration of radical humanism; it is a tragedy which dramatizes a conflict between two irreconcilable systems of value, each of which, we may feel, has

The generic ambiguity of *Doctor Faustus* is reflected by the uncomfortable co-existence of the Christian theme and the abundant classical imagery that the play exhibits. In this case also, the distribution of classical and Christian imagery throughout the play is far from arbitrary. The connection between pagan mythology and aesthetic and artistic beauty, for instance, is highly significant: Faustus twice conjures Helen of Troy, "the face that launched a thousand ships" (5. 1. 91), and, when plagued with doubt over his contract, asks himself

> Have I not made blind Homer sing to me
> Of Alexander's love and Oenone's death?
> And hath not he that built the walls of Thebes
> With ravishing sound of his melodious harp
> Made music with my Mephistopheles?
> (2. 3. 26–30)

Just as classical imagery is here associated with sumptuous beauty, so it is elsewhere connected specifically to human ambition and potential. In the very first scene the Bad Angel assures Faustus that he can be "on earth as Jove is in the sky, / Lord and commander of these elements" (1. 1. 78–9), while, in the epilogue, the chorus laments the (tragic?) waste of human potential, saying

> Cut is the branch that might have grown full straight,
> And burnèd is Apollo's laurel bough
> That sometime grew within this learnèd man.
> (Epilogue. 1–3)

Tom McAlindon states that

> The prominence of mythological imagery in itself is hardly surprising in a Renaissance drama, especially one by Marlowe. But, as has been stated, this is mythology with a difference, mythology which invites moral and theological criticism. Aesthetically realized (how else could Faustus be bewitched?), its beauty contributes immensely to tragic irony.[20]

McAlindon argues that classical imagery in *Faustus* generally equates to magic, and falls strictly into line with the satanic campaign for Faustus's soul; the mythical comforts that Faustus receives, such as the kiss of Helen and the Harp-song of Amphion, are diabolical illusions, and the qualities that are described in classical terms – human potential, ambition, desire – are those that eventually get him damned. Again, however, a pertinent counter-argument would be to say that the very fact that these qualities, so markedly apparent in Faustus, are

---

at least partial validity and a genuine claim to our allegiance." *Renaissance Magic & the Return of the Golden Age: The Occult Tradition in Marlowe, Jonson, and Shakespeare* (Lincoln: University of Nebraska Press, 1989), 118.

[20] Tom McAlindon, "Classical Mythology and Christian Tradition in *Doctor Faustus*," *PMLA* 81, no. 3 (1996): 218.

described in classical terms – in the play's tragic register rather than its morality register – is confirmation that he is indeed a genuinely tragic figure. One thing that *is* certain is that this ambiguity is not incidental. The fact that critics cannot agree over whether this play represents the just punishment of a heinous man or the tragic fate of a great aspirer is symptomatic of the construction of the play, which implies that the aspiring intellectual nature of the Renaissance, drawing its inspiration from the recovery of classical culture, is entirely incompatible with orthodox Christian morality.

Unification

Towards the end of the first scene of *Doctor Faustus*, we see the protagonist excitedly soliloquize on the various rewards that he imagines will befall him once he has solemnized his pact with Lucifer. The majority of these fantasies are concerned with material wealth and martial power: he will have his spirits "fly to India for gold, / Ransack the ocean for orient pearl" (1. 1. 82–3), and invent "stranger engines for the brunt of war / Than was the fiery keel at Antwerp's bridge" (1. 1. 97–8). What is particularly noticeable in this passage is the far-reaching nature of Faustus's ambitions: he will "search *all* corners of the new-found world" (1. 1. 86), learn "the secrets of *all* foreign kings" (1. 1. 89), and ultimately "reign sole king of *all* our provinces" (1. 1. 96; my italics). This urge for a unified understanding of and dominance over the world is reflected later in Act 1, when, after having notified Mephistopheles of his intent to sell his soul, Faustus imagines himself unifying his provinces physically as well as politically:

> By him I'll be great emperor of the world
> And make a bridge through the moving air
> To pass the ocean with a band of men;
> I'll join the hills that bind the Afric shore
> And make that land continent to Spain,
> And both contributory to my crown.
> (1. 3. 106–11)

Perhaps the most significant of Faustus's unifying ideas, however, is the first that springs to his mind when he begins to muse on the power he is to wield:

> How am I glutted with conceit of this!
> Shall I make spirits fetch me what I please,
> Resolve me of all ambiguities …?
> (1. 1. 80–82)

Much has been made of the disparity between Faustus's exclamations of intent and his eventual achievements as a servant of Lucifer. As mentioned above, he does not engage in any of the forecast empire-building, does not extend his travels any further than the boundaries of Europe, makes little further reference to the amassing of wealth, and, rather than learning all of their secrets, seems content to serve as a court performer for foreign kings. The one item on Faustus's diabolical agenda that the audience does see him pursue, however, is the resolution of all ambiguity. His eagerness to be granted all-encompassing knowledge is exemplified by the swiftness with which he progresses from delivering the bond to requesting forbidden wisdom of Mephistopheles:

> MEPHISTOPHELES: Speak, Faustus. Do you deliver this as your deed?
> FAUSTUS [*Giving the deed.*]: Ay. Take it, and the devil give thee good on't.
> MEPHISTOPHELES: Now, Faustus, ask what thou wilt.
> FAUSTUS: First will I question with thee about hell.
>   Tell me, where is the place that men call hell?
> (2. 1. 114–20)

Shortly afterwards, when Mephistopheles presents Faustus with a book that facilitates the manipulation of the weather and the raising of armies, he seems decidedly more keen on asking for books "wherein I might behold *all* spells and incantations," "where I might see *all* characters and planets of the heavens, that I might know their motions and dispositions" and "wherein I might see *all* plants, herbs, and trees that grow upon the earth" (2. 1. 169–79; my italics). The pursuit of complete knowledge – the clearing up of ambiguities – seems of all the ambitions stated by Faustus to be the one given priority.

As well as being evident in his requests of Mephistopheles, Faustus's pursuit of unified knowledge is also consistent with the disillusionment that initially leads him to consider the study of magic. In his opening soliloquy, Faustus translates Ramus's definitive statement "*Bene disserere est finis logices*" into an interrogative form, asking "Is to dispute well logic's chiefest end?" (1. 1. 7–8). Logic, or "dialectic," was the prominent discipline in the Renaissance university arts course, with Marlowe's own Cambridge B.A. no exception. A good student of dialectic would be expected to have a sufficient mastery of language and logical thought to construct a convincing argument in support of any premise, however ludicrous it may seem, and similarly to dismantle an opponent's argument, however sound its reasoning may appear. What is *true* is not of concern, nor is it even ascertainable, as David Riggs writes: "The dialecticians' all-out investment in probability testified to their belief that certainty is either trivial or unattainable: for 'there is nothing which may not be disputed, and debated on all sides with great virtuosity. In all these matters, therefore, probabilities are examined, since necessities cannot be.'"[21] To dispute well, then, *is* logic's chiefest end, a dissatisfactory state of affairs for a man who wishes to be resolved of all ambiguities. Similarly frustrating for Faustus is that his knowledge in each of the various university disciplines is of no use outside of the confines of that discipline. Faustus may "level at the end of every art" (1. 1. 4), but this will only give him an understanding of discrete fields of knowledge, and not of the world itself. There is an echo of this frustration later in the same speech, when Faustus says

---

[21] Riggs, *The World of Christopher Marlowe*, 82. Riggs here quotes Lisa Jardine's translation of a passage in Lorenzo Valla's *Dialecticae disputationes*.

> Emperors and kings
> Are but obeyed in their several provinces,
> Nor can they raise the wind or rend the clouds;
> But his dominion that exceeds in this
> Stretcheth as far as doth the mind of man.
> (1. 1. 59–63)

While this passage relates to dominion rather than knowledge, the implications are the same: to rule in several provinces, or to have a mastery of distinct academic disciplines, is to fall short of the human potential that can be unleashed by magic, a potential which Faustus tellingly describes in terms of "the mind of man." Through magic, Faustus believes he can transcend the fragmentariness of human thought.

Of course, Faustus finds himself to be utterly misguided in his belief. Instead of being able to glean absolute knowledge from his conjuring, he soon discovers that there are questions that Mephistopheles cannot, or will not, answer. When Faustus asks about the nature of the movement of the heavens, he is less than happy with the response:

> FAUSTUS: But tell me, have they all one motion, both *situ et tempore*?
> MEPHISTOPHELES: All jointly move from east to west in four-and-twenty hours upon the poles of the world, but differ in their motion upon the poles of the zodiac.
> FAUSTUS: Tush, these slender trifles Wagner can decide.
> Hath Mephistopheles no greater skill?
> (2. 3. 44–50)

Upon delving further into the issue, Faustus has more cause to be disappointed:

> FAUSTUS: Well, resolve me in this question: why have we not conjunctions, oppositions, aspects, eclipses all at one time, but in some years we have more, in some less?
> MEPHISTOPHELES: *Per inaequalem motum respectu totius.*
> FAUSTUS: Well, I am answered. Tell me who made the world.
> MEPHISTOPHELES: I will not.
> (2. 3. 62–7)

Faustus's initial question raises a common contemporary interrogation of the Ptolemaic geocentric model: if the cosmos is structured in regular concentric circles, why do celestial phenomena occur with such irregularity? Mephistopheles's answer, which translates as "because of unequal movement with respect to the whole," is less than convincing; the vagueness of the explanation smacks of the kind of fudge that Faustus would expect to hear in the ambiguous academic disputes he wishes to escape from, a point highlighted by Mephistopheles's articulation of it in Latin. Faustus's response – "Well, I am answered" – strikes an ironic note. His disillusionment is only compounded when he is flatly refused an answer to the most fundamental of philosophical questions: who made the world? Perhaps we should not be surprised that it is after this disappointment that Faustus's ambitions seem to diminish to the extent that they are satiated by the fulfilment of trivial pleasures.

The failure of Faustus's main ambition is not entirely owing to Mephistopheles's inability or unwillingness to co-operate, however. As has been discussed, a prominent factor in Faustus's discontent with the academic world is the irresolvable nature of dialectic – he turns to magic because he believes it can resolve him of these ambiguities. Notwithstanding his symbolic rejection of logic and the other university disciplines in the opening soliloquy, though, Faustus continues to bear the hallmark of a trained dialectician throughout. Immediately after signing the bond, his response to Mephistopheles's first-hand account of hell is noteworthy:

> FAUSTUS: Come, I think hell's a fable.
> MEPHISTOPHELES: Ay, think so still, till experience change thy mind.
> FAUSTUS: Why, think'st thou then that Faustus shall be damned?
> MEPHISTOPHELES: Ay, of necessity, for here's the scroll
>   Wherein thou hast given thy soul to Lucifer.
> FAUSTUS: Ay, and body too. But what of that?
>   Think'st thou that Faustus is so fond
>   To imagine that after this life there is any pain?
>   Tush, these are trifles and mere old wives' tales.
> MEPHISTOPHELES: But, Faustus, I am an instance to the contrary,
>   For I am damned and am now in hell.
> FAUSTUS: How? Now in hell? Nay, an this be hell, I'll willingly be damned
>   here. What? Walking, disputing, etc.?
> (2. 1. 130–43)

Faustus's audacious challenging of Mephistopheles's understanding of hell may seem to be absurdly pig-headed, but it is a product of his academic conditioning. Despite having bemoaned the incapacity of logic to accommodate a unified understanding of the world, he finds himself slipping into an indulgence of an old university pastime of disputation precisely when Mephistopheles is offering him knowledge that is inaccessible to the rest of humankind; the practice of dialectic is so deeply ingrained in him that he casually comments that hell might not be so bad, provided he can spend his time there "walking, disputing, etc."[22] One might wonder whether, if he were granted access to universal knowledge, Faustus could find it within himself to accept it without questioning, without masking it once more in ambiguity.

"Magic"

It is worth considering why somebody who wishes to achieve a complete and unified understanding of the world might want to turn to magic in an attempt

---

[22] The prominence of dialectic in academia during Marlowe's university years is noted by Riggs, who states that "An aptitude for dialectic was the main criterion for admission to the colleges; a mastery of dialectic was the chief priority in appointments to college faculty. During Marlowe's time at Cambridge, the one university-wide intellectual controversy was about the right way of doing dialectic." *The World of Christopher Marlowe*, 79.

to achieve it. Furthermore, one might reasonably enquire as to what "magic" actually means in a Renaissance context. The association of Doctor Faustus with controversial practitioners of "magic" is invited explicitly by the play. Upon agreeing to learn the secrets of conjuring from Valdes and Cornelius, he is advised by his new patrons to

> haste thee to some solitary grove,
> And bear wise Bacon's and Albanus' works,
> The Hebrew Psalter, and New Testament;
> And whatsoever else is requisite.
> (1. 1. 155–8)

The Bacon referred to here is Roger Bacon, the thirteenth-century English philosopher with an interest in astrology and mathematics, whose notoriety as a conjurer was revitalized, possibly around the time *Doctor Faustus* was first being performed, by Robert Greene's *Friar Bacon and Friar Bungay*. Albanus probably refers to the Italian philosopher Pietro d'Albano, whose posthumous reputation was similarly infamous to Bacon's.[23] The inclusion of the Hebrew Psalter and the New Testament in this occult reading list is suggestive of a Christian Cabalist element to the conjuring of Faustus. Only a few lines earlier he has overtly aligned himself with a recent Cabalist and Hermetic philosopher by boasting that he will be "as cunning as Agrippa was" (1. 1. 119), and later, during his conjuration, he will draw attention to the Cabalist elements of his magic by announcing that "Within this circle is Jehovah's name, / Forward and backward anagrammatised" (1. 3. 8–9).

Besides these internal references, Faustus has often been equated with John Dee, most forcibly by Frances Yates, who argues that "audiences would inevitably have recognized Faustus as an unfavourable reference to Dee."[24] Yates further suggests that, as she sees occult philosophy as the central system of thought behind the Renaissance movement, and as Dee is its chief exponent in Elizabethan England, "we are in fact witnessing in this play a reaction against the Renaissance."[25] To whatever extent one accepts this reading, and, as I hope will become clear, I think it underestimates the complexity and ambiguity of the play, there is merit in the association of Faustus with the Elizabethan magus. Dee was certainly the most notorious practitioner of anything close to Faustus's magic in England, and, like Faustus (and like Giordano Bruno, another Hermetic magus who has attracted comparison with Marlowe's protagonist)[26] he took his magic on a momentous European tour and briefly enjoyed the patronage of the Holy Roman Emperor.[27] The "Lines, circles, signs, letters, and characters" that Faustus

---

[23] On the identity of "Albano," see Bevington and Rasmussen, *Doctor Faustus*, A-Text, 1. 1. 156, note.

[24] Yates, *The Occult Philosophy*, 120.

[25] Ibid., 119.

[26] See, for example, Hilary Gatti, "Bruno and Marlowe: *Doctor Faustus*," in *Christopher Marlowe*, ed. Richard Wilson (London: Longman, 1999).

[27] See Yates, *The Occult Philosophy*, 87–9, and Woolley, *The Queen's Conjuror*, 243–71.

"most desires" (1. 1. 53–4), as well as being "illustrated in some profusion" among the pages of the 1567 edition of Agrippa's *De Occulta Philosophia*,[28] can also be found liberally distributed throughout the 1570 English edition of Euclid's *Elements*, to which Dee appended his *Mathematical Preface* (a document in which he advises the reader to "Looke in the 27. and 28. Chapters, of the second booke, *De occulta Philosophia*").[29] Most obviously, the conjuring of Mephistopheles could be seen as a parody of the angel summoning for which Dee (like Agrippa before him) was so infamous.[30]

What is more important, or certainly more relevant to the current argument, than Faustus's specific association with John Dee, is his association with the Hermetic philosophy underpinning the magic that Dee practised and believed in. The discovery of the writings of the supposed Egyptian prophet Hermes Trismegistus by agents of the Medici family caused a furore in late fifteenth-century Italy. As Peter French states, "Their impact might be compared with a modern discovery of Dead Sea scrolls that revealed revolutionary information about Christianity, but even this is not a valid comparison because religion is not the all-embracing concern today that it was during the Renaissance."[31] The *Corpus Hermeticum*,[32] which was supposed to predate the work of Plato and Pythagoras and possibly even that of Moses,[33] espoused a philosophy which incorporated a monotheistic religious doctrine bearing a striking resemblance to that of Judaeo-Christianity, and incorporating an alternative creation myth.[34] The close relationship between some of its ideas and those of biblical texts, which it supposedly antedated, was considered astonishing at the time, but was deemed less remarkable in 1614 by the work of the philologist Isaac Casaubon, whose analysis of the texts showed

---

[28] See Gareth Roberts, "Marlowe and the Metaphysics of Magicians," in *Constructing Christopher Marlowe*, ed. J. A. Downie and J. T. Parnell (Cambridge: Cambridge University Press, 2000), 57–8.

[29] Euclid, *The Elements of Geometrie* (London: 1570), STC (2nd ed.) / 10560, Sig. C4.

[30] For a biography of Dee which focuses primarily on his ongoing attempts at angelic communication, see Woolley, *The Queen's Conjuror*.

[31] Peter French, *John Dee: The World of an Elizabethan Magus* (London: Routledge & Kegan Paul, 1972), 68.

[32] The text is sometimes referred to as the *Pimander*, after its first book. I shall refer to it here as the *Corpus Hermeticum*, or *Corpus*.

[33] The author of the preface to an early edition of the first English translation of the *Corpus Hermeticum*, named only as I. F., contends, despite there being strong evidence to the contrary by this point, that "This Book may justly challenge the first place for antiquity, from all the Books in the World, being written some hundreds of yeers before *Moses* his time, as I shall endeavour to make good." Hermes Trismegistus, *Hermes Mercurius Trismegistus his Divine pymander in seventeen books* (London: 1657), Wing / H1566, Sig. A3. I shall quote from this edition throughout the chapter. The *Corpus* was not available in English during Marlowe's lifetime, but Latin translations of it circulated widely.

[34] For a useful summary of the ideas expressed in the Hermetic texts, see Peter French, *John Dee*, 62–88. This chapter will go on to discuss some of these ideas in greater detail.

them to in fact date from early Christian times.[35] Such was the excitement at the point of their discovery, however, that Marsilio Ficino was ordered to postpone his ongoing translation of the works of Plato in order to prepare them for western consumption. Indeed, the fact that Ficino was absorbed in these two projects at the same time may have been significant, as he incorporated Hermetic ideas into his neoplatonic philosophy, which was to prove influential across Europe and throughout the Renaissance. The *Corpus* is a series of dialogues, predominantly between Hermes Trismegistus and "Mind," or Pimander – an articulation of the intellect of God – and between Hermes and his son Tat, and altogether represents a kind of religious philosophy which instructs man on how to regain his lost divinity and achieve oneness with God. Hermeticism became central to the thought of occult philosophers such as Giovanni Pico Della Mirandola, Francesco Giorgi and Heinrich Cornelius Agrippa. In the work of these philosophers, Hermeticism mingled with Christian doctrine, neoplatonism, and a Christianized version of the mystical Hebrew practice of Cabala, which applied divine numerological significance to letters of the Hebrew alphabet, facilitating the search for esoteric wisdom embedded in the Torah (Christian Cabalists used it to find evidence in the Old Testament of the divinity of Christ).[36] Despite their apparently esoteric and eccentric nature, Hermetic and Cabalist ideas were initially well received across Renaissance Europe. In fact, as demonstrated by the sixteen editions of Ficino's translation of *Pimander* in existence by the time the A-Text of *Faustus* had appeared, Hermeticism was rather popular; Frances Yates goes so far as to contend that occult thought formed the central driving force behind the Renaissance itself.[37] Whether one accepts this or not, Occultism was certainly taken very seriously by powerful Europeans; significant figures whose thinking it influenced included Phillipe Du Plessis Mornay and King Philip II of Spain, whose library contained over two hundred Hermetic texts.[38] Although he was never quite fully invited into the fold, John Dee's advice was often sought by the English court on matters of importance, and among the significant tasks entrusted to him was the selection of an astrologically favourable date for the coronation of Queen Elizabeth. Magic was also prominent in intellectual Elizabethan society. Dee himself was a member of the circle surrounding Henry Percy, "the wizard earl," which boasted a number of the great minds of the day, including the mathematician Thomas Hariot and, French claims, John Donne, Walter Ralegh and Christopher Marlowe.[39] Whether or not one accepts the assertion of a direct association between Marlowe and Dee (there is little more evidence for it than Marlowe's own alleged association

---

[35] See Anthony Grafton, "Protestant versus Prophet: Isaac Casaubon on Hermes Trismegistus," *Journal of the Warburg and Courtauld Institutes* 46 (1983).

[36] For concise accounts of the careers and legacies of these and other key figures in the development of Renaissance occult philosophy, see Yates, *The Occult Philosophy*, 9–59, and Mebane, *Renaissance Magic*, 22–72.

[37] See Yates, *The Occult Philosophy*.

[38] French, *John Dee*, 69.

[39] Ibid., 171.

with Hariot), it is evident that Hermetic ideas carried significant cultural capital in the time *Doctor Faustus* was written.

One of the key features of the Hermetic philosophy is its perception of the nature and potential of man, and its contrast with Judaeo-Christian beliefs on this matter. Peter French states that "though there are striking similarities between the *Pimander* [Hermetic text containing the creation myth] and Genesis, there is one fundamental difference: in the Hermetic treatise, man once was, and through his intellect can become again, like God. His original divine powers remain within him to be regenerated and used."[40] Man is created by a God who, it is stressed, is the only god (although, characteristically of this obscure text, a small number of passages seem to refer to more than one), and lives in a fallen state, a divine soul mired in a corrupt material body. Eventually, as in Christian tradition, man can achieve salvation, but the means by which this can happen are crucially different, indeed apparently opposed: rather than through faith, man regains his divine state through knowledge. Knowledge is valorized in the *Corpus* to the extent that ignorance becomes synonymous with the Christian idea of sin. Book Eight, entitled "That the greatest Evil in Man, is, The not knowing God," makes this clear:

> WHither [sic] are you carried, O men, drunkenwith [sic] drinking up the strong wine of ignorance? which seeing you cannot bear: why do you not vomit it up again?
> 2. Stand, and be sober, and look up again with the eyes of your heart; and if you cannot all do so, yet do as many as you can.
> 3. For the malice of Ignorance surroundeth all the Earth, and corrupteth the Soul, shut up in the Body, not suffering it to arrive at the Havens of Salvation.[41]

Crucial to this concept of understanding God as being the key to divine ascension is the notion of unity. God created the world through his intellect, and as such the world is a kind of articulation of his mind – the key to understanding the mind of God is understanding the world that it created. As human beings have been blessed above all other animals, they have the potential to understand God and share his intellect – the *Corpus* states that "*an earthly man, is a mortall God; and that the heavenly God, is an immortall man*"[42] – but to do so they must understand *everything*, as everything is the mind of God, and vice versa:

> 116. Or art thou ignorant, that as the parts of the World, are Heaven, and Earth, and Water, and Air; after the same manner the Members of God, are Life and Immortality, and Eternity and Spirit, and Necessity, and Providence, and Nature, and Soul, and Minde, and the Continuance or perseverance of all these which is called Good.
> 117. And there is not any thing of all that hath been, and all that is, where God is not.[43]

---

[40] Ibid., 74.
[41] Hermes Trismegistus, *Divine pymander*, 115.
[42] Ibid., 71.
[43] Ibid., 180.

This idea is reiterated succinctly later in the *Corpus*:

> 125. After this manner therefore contemplate God to have all the whole world to himself, as it were all thoughts, or intellections.
> 126. If therefore thou wilt not equal thy self to God, thou canst not understand God.
> 127. For the like are intelligible by the like.[44]

It is in this spirit that occult philosophers such as Pico della Mirandola and Agrippa attempted to develop philosophies which assimilated Hermetic, Hebrew and classical wisdom and sought to achieve a union between this fusion of thought and Christian theology. Of Francesco Giorgi, for example, Yates remarks:

> The word One, or Monas, falls constantly from Giorgi's pen, usually accompanied by a cluster of names of the authorities from whom he drives [sic] this concept. As Vasoli puts it, Giorgi wishes to be the carrier of a wisdom capable of including Hermes Trismegistus, Orpheus, Francis of Assisi, Plato and the Cabalists, Plotinus and Augustine, in the common understanding of the *arcana mundi*, and of the spiritual destiny of man in the return to the inaccessible One.[45]

It is this same spirit in which Dee creates his *monad* or "London Seal of Hermes," the symbol that adorned the frontispiece of his *Monas Hieroglyphica* and which apparently constitutes "a unified construction of significant astro-chemical symbols that embodied the underlying unity, or *monas*, of the universe,"[46] and, I suggest, in which Doctor Faustus announces his dissatisfaction with disparate academic disciplines and turns to magic in order to achieve an all-encompassing understanding of the world. Perhaps the most apt reflection of the Hermetic spirit of universal learning is in the following passage, referred to briefly earlier in the chapter, in which, having just been presented with a book of incantations, Faustus asks Mephistopheles to provide him with a variety of further learned texts:

> FAUSTUS: Thanks, Mephistopheles. Yet fain would I have a book wherein I might behold all spells and incantations, that I might raise up spirits when I please.
> MEPHISTOPHELES: Here they are in this book.   *There turn to them.*
> FAUSTUS: Now would I have a book where I might see all characters and planets of the heavens, that I might know their motions and dispositions.
> MEPHISTOPHELES: Here they are too.   *Turn to them.*

---

[44] Ibid., 155.
[45] Yates, *The Occult Philosophy*, 33.
[46] French, *John Dee*, 78. I. F., in his preface to the *Corpus Hermeticum*, attributes a similarly universal profundity to Hermes Trismegistus's work itself, stating, without forgetting to include a judicious caveat, that "he attained to, and transmitted to Posterity (although in an Ænigmaticall, and obscure style) the Knowledge of the Quintessence of the whole Universe." Hermes Trismegistus, *Divine pymander*, Sig. A4v.

FAUSTUS: Nay, let me have one book more – and then I have done –
   wherein I might see all plants, herbs, and trees that grow upon the earth.
MEPHISTOPHELES: Here they be.   *Turn to them.*
FAUSTUS: O, thou art deceived.
MEPHISTOPHELES: Tut, I warrant thee.
(2. 1. 169–82)

At every stage, Faustus's request for a book on a particular discipline is met with the revelation, the stage directions would seem to suggest, that the information required is in the book that Mephistopheles has already presented him with. Like the *Corpus Hermeticum*, or John Dee's *Monas Hieroglyphica*, this would seem to be a book containing the entire knowledge of the universe, providing one knows how to read it. This kind of learning, the *Corpus* makes clear, is essential to anyone who would achieve ascension:

> 128. Increase thyself unto an immeasurable greatnesse, leaping beyond every Body, and transcending all Time; become Eternity, and thou shall understand God: If thou believe in thyself, that nothing is impossible, but accountest thyself immortall, and that thou canst understand all things, every Art every Science, and the manner and custom of every living thing.[47]

This passage is redolent with the ambitions of Faustus in its insistence that one must assert one's own ability to understand every art, every science and the workings of all nature, and its overall tone calls to mind the arrogance for which he tends to be condemned by critics. The advice given here by Pimander provides a context for Faustus's boastfulness: he believes in himself, and his actions suggest that he may well account himself immortal. Indeed, the *Corpus* does not stop at recommending the maintenance of a healthy sense of self-esteem. We are in fact told that a lack of self-belief is evil:

> 131. But if thou shut up thy Soul in the Body, and abuse it, and say, I understand nothing, I can do nothing, I am afraid of the Sea, I cannot climb up into Heaven, I know not who I am, I cannot tell what I shall be; what hast thou to do with God? for thou canst understand none of those Fair and Good things; be a lover of the Body, and Evil.
> 132. For it is the greatest evil, not to know God.[48]

Faustus's arrogance, then, might be seen in a Hermetic context as a sign of piety rather than a hubristic flaw, a dogged determination to avoid the evil of submission to ignorance rather than a pig-headed obstinacy. Yet, of course, it must be remembered that Faustus clearly fails in his project, and is damned at the play's close. If we continue to read the play in the context of Hermeticism, why does this happen? While Faustus adopts the appropriate posture for the Hermetic magus in appearing to have total belief in his capacity to understand everything, the extent

---

[47] Hermes Trismegistus, *Divine pymander*, 155.
[48] Ibid., 156.

to which he respects or even understands the philosophical rationale for seeking this knowledge is questionable. A striking example of this negligence is to be found when Faustus muses on what uses his new powers will be put to:

> I'll have them fly to India for gold,
> Ransack the ocean for orient pearl,
> And search all corners of the new-found world
> For pleasant fruits and princely delicates.
> (1. 1. 84–7)

Book Ten of the *Corpus* contains a passage that is highly reminiscent of this:

> 120. And judge of this by thy self, command thy Soul to go into *India*, and sooner then thou canst bid it, it will be there.
> 121. Bid it likewise passe over the *Ocean*, and suddenly it will be there; Not as passing from place to place, but suddenly it will be there.
> 122. Command it to flie into Heaven, and it will need no Wings, neither shall any thing hinder it; not the fire of the Sun, not the *Aether*, nor the turning of the Spheres, not the bodies of any of the other Stars, but cutting through all, it will flie up to the last, and furthest Body.[49]

The passage in the *Corpus*, which uses its sense of scale and exoticism to illustrate the limitlessness of the potential of the liberated soul, is grossly degraded in Faustus's musings. In place of the soul are diabolical spirits, and rather than representing the process of coming to know God, India and the ocean serve to supply Faustus's material desires. As is evident from passages already quoted from the *Corpus*, the goal of the magus is essentially spiritual: the liberation of the divine soul from the trappings of the mortal body, achieved through contemplation. Faustus's search for knowledge, by contrast, is punctuated by the indulgence of banal pleasures of the flesh.

    The *Corpus Hermeticum*'s privileging of the soul over the body is similar to that of Christian tradition, and as such Faustus's fleshly indulgences are as sinful, or evil, to use the term from the *Corpus*, in a Hermetic context as they are in a Christian one. In this sense the crucial passage in Act 5 in which Faustus chooses the indulgence of the flesh, as represented by Helen of Troy, over the pious protestations of the Old Man constitutes as much a rejection of knowledge as it does a rejection of faith, since the *Corpus* explicitly equates the indulgence of the body with ignorance. Clearly, then, despite the Hermetic emphasis on knowledge as opposed to faith, there are a number of parallels between Hermeticism and Christianity, and a number of ways in which Faustus offends the tenets of both. It is worth examining the extent to which the focus of Hermeticism on knowledge represents a departure from Christian ethics. What, for example, is meant by "knowledge" in the *Corpus Hermeticum*? The following passage implies a formulation that places it firmly alongside belief:

---

[49] Ibid., 153–4.

50. When I say the things that are, I mean God; for the things that are, God hath; and neither is there any thing without him, nor he without any thing.
51. These things, O *Asclepius*, will appear to be true, if thou understand them; but if thou understand them not, incredible.
52. For to understand is to beleeve; but not to beleeve, is not to understand.[50]

Knowledge, or understanding, appears here not to be something acquired by learning, but the instantaneous product of an act of faith – before one can understand one must believe. In this context, lack of understanding begins to look a lot like religious despair, the sin to which the downfall of Faustus has often been attributed by critics.[51] When, in the final soliloquy, Faustus desperately cries "O, I'll leap up to my God! Who pulls me down?" (5. 2. 77), he reveals himself not only to be despairing of God's mercy but also to be the "lover of the body, and Evil," who "cannot climb up into Heaven" that Pimander describes in the passage quoted earlier. Faustus proves to be incapable of mastering the art of the magus. Rather than coming to know God, he must ask Mephistopheles who made the world, a question which, to add insult to injury, the servant of Lucifer is not able to answer. Furthermore, he never attains the unity of understanding which the *Corpus* prescribes as necessary, a unity which requires the synthesis of binary oppositions:

129. Become higher than all heighth, lower than all depths, comprehend in thy self, the qualities of all the Creatures, of the Fire, the Water, the Dry, and Moyst; and conceive likewise, that thou canst at once be every where in the Sea, in the Earth.
130. Thou shalt at once understand thyself, not yet begotten in the Womb, young, old, to be dead, the things after death, and all these together; as also, times, places, deeds, qualities, quantities, or else thou canst not yet understand God.[52]

Instead of allowing Faustus to merge such polarities, the play continually reminds us of their continued oppositional existence. Faustus states that "All things that move between the quiet poles / Shall be at my command" (1. 1. 58–9); he believes he can control everything in the world, but he cannot change its dichotomous structure. When nightfall brings about the ideal time for Faustus's conjuration, he utters the following words:

Now that the gloomy shadow of the earth,
Longing to view Orion's drizzling look,
Leaps from th'Antarctic world unto the sky
And dims the welkin with her pitchy breath,
Faustus, begin thine incantations.
(1. 3. 1–5)

---

[50] Ibid., 204.
[51] See, for example, Sachs, "The Religious Despair of Doctor Faustus."
[52] Hermes Trismegistus, *Divine pymander*, 155–6.

This evocative description of the arrival of darkness, as well as marking the occasion for the conjuration, again highlights the dual nature of the world: night has not simply descended, but has leapt from the Antarctic. When it is dark here, it is light elsewhere. The motif of bifurcation is sustained throughout the play. In direct contrast to his will for unification, Faustus's mental turmoil is represented by the regular visitations of angels representing good and evil, a dichotomy sustained in other relationships throughout the play: Faustus's loyal students oppose the forbidden learning of Valdes and Cornelius, and the pious Old Man, who offers Faustus the true path, constitutes the counterpoise to the temptation of the succubus Helen of Troy. Similarly, Faustus's plight culminates in an agonizing final soliloquy which plays out his anguished dilemma between up and down. As Jonathan Dollimore has noted, the play suggests a protagonist who himself possesses a fissured identity; throughout the play he refers to and addresses himself in the third person, and we see visual images of this fracture when he allows himself to be dismembered by the horse-courser in the interests of a confidence trick (4. 1. 169–85), and again when, in the B-Text, he is torn apart by devils at the point of his damnation (5. 3). For Dollimore, the "agonised irresolution" that Faustus experiences has its root in his fragmented subjectivity.[53]

In many ways Faustus is, to generalize somewhat, the victim of living on the fault line between a medieval scholastic world which promotes faith and piety, and a Renaissance humanist world which demands individualist endeavour and the pursuit of secular knowledge. With this in mind, a reading of the play in the context of Hermetic philosophy provides an interesting perspective, as Hermeticism attempts to reconcile the pursuit of knowledge with faith. Like the unity that Faustus tries to achieve in Marlowe's play, that unity foregrounded in Hermeticism, between religion and the pursuit of knowledge, and more widely the unity Renaissance occult philosophers attempted to establish between versions of Hermeticism, Cabala and Christian faith, is an uneasy one. Indeed, the internal tension evident in the work of Agrippa illustrates this well enough: his *De Occulta Philosophia*, the "indispensable handbook of Renaissance 'Magia' and 'Cabala,'"[54] shared a place in his oeuvre with *De Vanitate Scientiarum*, a work which displayed a great deal of scepticism and which claimed that all wisdom was vanity save for that of the Scriptures.[55] The apparent contradiction between these two works is mirrored by Faustus's oscillation from bombast to repentance. No intermediary position, it seems, is possible for him; he routinely changes allegiance from magic to Christ and back again. It also reflects, as Gareth Roberts astutely observes, the divergence of critical responses to the play: "The question of the interrelationship of these two Agrippan works, and the difficulty of finding a consistent reading of Agrippa, when these two important works seem to gesture in opposite directions, is illuminatingly analogous to the balance of two antithetical

---

[53] Dollimore, *Radical Tragedy*, 113.
[54] Yates, *The Occult Philosophy*, 37.
[55] French, *John Dee*, 41–4.

critical views of Marlowe's *Faustus*."[56] The ambiguous world of Marlowe's play is analogous to the atmosphere of religious and political disharmony in which late sixteenth-century Elizabethans, and Europeans in general, lived. It is perhaps no surprise that occult philosophy, which places such value on unity, should have become popular during the age of the Reformation and the Renaissance, a period of profound ideological seismic shift in Europe; perhaps a form of wisdom that united aspects of thought from sources as widely diverse as classical wisdom, magic, Hebrew Cabala and Christianity could potentially provide a solution to the religio-political schism of the time. The world which Marlowe creates, however, is a more cynical one than that. Here fracture is too profound, ideologies too incompatible, for any encompassing system of thought to reconcile them. Despite the popularity of Hermetic thought amongst the intelligentsia, those who openly based their beliefs upon it were still publicly viewed with mistrust. John Dee, for example, while utilized for his expertise, was generally kept at arm's length by the Queen and her privy council, doubtless a wise public relations policy, as Renaissance magi were generally the subject of relentless rumour.[57] Furthermore, while Hermeticism, by virtue of its emphasis on the potential of man, is concurrent with the ethos of Renaissance humanism, it also shares many of the difficulties of the revival of pagan wisdom in a Christian age; the Hermetic texts may display a remarkable correlation with Christian thought, but they also contain a number of fundamental differences. Thus, irenicists (campaigners for a unified church) who saw a Christianized version of Hermeticism as a solution to religious strife as it "contained doctrines common to both Protestants and Catholics, and therefore offered a unifying bond,"[58] not only faced the reality that in the aftermath of the Armada religious hostilities showed no sign of cessation, but also the fact that the idea of a truly Christian Hermeticism was one which faced insurmountable theological and philosophical obstacles. In a contemporary context of ideological fracture, not only in evidence through conflict between a Protestant England and European Catholic enemies, but also through the confused identity of a nation that had changed its religion three times in a century, a sceptical mind might find any suggestion of the possibility of unification, whether political, ideological or spiritual, ridiculous. *Faustus* may not represent, as Yates suggests, "the reaction against the Renaissance,"[59] but it does display a sceptical awareness of the incompatibility of different ideologies that co-existed in this period, an awareness reflected in the play's ambiguous structure: it can be a medieval morality, or it can be a Renaissance tragedy, but it cannot be both at the same time.

---

[56] Gareth Roberts, "Necromantic Books: Christopher Marlowe, Doctor Faustus and Agrippa of Nettesheim," in *Christopher Marlowe and English Renaissance Culture*, ed. Daryll Grantley and Peter Roberts (Aldershot: Scolar Press, 1996), 158.

[57] On the ambivalent reputation of John Dee as scholar on the one hand and dangerous conjurer on the other, for example, see Yates, *The Occult Philosophy*, 75–93.

[58] Roberts, "Necromantic Books," 156.

[59] Yates, *The Occult Philosophy*, 119.

Chapter 4
Individual and Multitude:
The Jew of Malta and *The Massacre at Paris*

When the governor of Malta, Ferneze, seizes the wealth of the rich Jew, Barabas, and justifies it as an act calculated to "save the ruin of a multitude" (1. 2. 98)[1] he evokes a concept – that of a unified people and a common good – that *The Jew of Malta* interrogates in a number of ways. The word "multitude" is ambiguous in the extent to which it denotes a collective group or a large number of individuals; the *OED*'s definitions include both "the populace; the public" and "the character, quality, or condition of being many; numerousness."[2] The play, I aim to show, exhibits a similar duality. It repeatedly evokes the possibility of community; despite the apparent social and political isolation of its central figure, it undermines assumptions about cultural and moral difference. It presents Christianity, Judaism and Islam as ostensibly clear distinguishing categories, but ultimately insists upon the common ground between the three faiths to the extent that the distinctions between them begin to appear arbitrary. Ultimately, however, it evokes the idea of a unified multitude only to undermine it, depicting a Malta whose inhabitants are united only by their unstinting individualism, and portraying categories such as nationality or religion as fantasies evoked either to conceal rampant self-interest or to create an illusory impression of unity. Crucially, the play does all of these things at a time when English pamphlets and sermons were betraying increasing levels of anxiety at a perceived atmosphere of discord in English society and were issuing pleas for the populace to become united once more. From the midst of this anxiety and idealist rhetoric, Marlowe offers in both *The Jew of Malta* and *The Massacre at Paris* brutally Machiavellian depictions of society as a constantly evolving struggle for power between self-seeking individuals that is barely kept below boiling point by arbitrary unifying concepts such as religion or nationhood – unifying concepts that are put in place and maintained by individuals whose interests they serve.

The Jew of Malta

In approaching *The Jew of Malta*'s treatment of unity and the relationship between the individual and the multitude, this chapter will touch upon some issues which

---

[1] Christopher Marlowe, *Doctor Faustus and Other Plays*, ed. David Bevington and Eric Rasmussen (Oxford: Oxford University Press, 1998). All subsequent quotations from the play are from this edition.
[2] "multitude, n.," *OED Online*, June 2014, Oxford University Press, <http://www.oed.com/view/Entry/123635> (accessed 26 June 2014).

have attracted considerable critical attention. Much recent criticism on the play has focused on the liminal position of Barabas as an early modern Jew: Richard Wilson and Daniel Vitkus have astutely read the play in terms of the intermediary position often assumed by prominent European Jews in trade and diplomacy in the Mediterranean, while Andrew Hiscock and Julia Reinhard Lupton have paid attention to the opportunities, as well as the limitations, that Barabas's position as a resident outsider present him.[3] A common feature of all of these readings is a sense of Barabas occupying a paradoxical state of simultaneous belonging and not belonging. This notion is important to this reading, but will be considered more broadly in terms of the play's interrogation of the possibility of belonging to any unified people or creed. In discussing the measures taken by characters in the play in order to establish unity, the chapter will discuss its well-established association with Machiavellian *realpolitik*. Of the numerous studies on this topic, three stand out. Irving Ribner argues that Marlowe had direct access to Machiavelli's work and that he "uses Machiavelli's political precepts ... because they are his precepts as well."[4] N. W. Bawcutt suggests that, while we cannot be sure whether or not Marlowe had read Machiavelli, his work subtly demonstrates sympathy with the "orthodox position" that the unbridled application of "Machiavellian" ideas, as popularly understood, would exert a corrosive influence on society.[5] Catherine Minshull builds upon an observation made by Bawcutt in order to argue that the play's prologue, which associates Barabas with Machiavelli, is a red herring, and that it is in fact Ferneze and his established regime on Malta that exhibit most clearly an alignment with Machiavellian thinking.[6] My intention here is not to establish the extent of Marlowe's acquaintance with or endorsement of Machiavelli's writing, but rather to highlight that the play's interest in Machiavellianism is symptomatic of a broader interest in the notion of the multitude as a unified collective, a notion to which both *The Discourses* (1531) and *The Prince* (1532) devote much discussion.

Moral Ambiguity

The play's prologue serves to both establish the association with Machiavelli and to mark out Barabas as an outsider – as distinct from the multitude.

---

[3]   Richard Wilson, "Another Country: Marlowe and the Go-Between," in *Renaissance Go-Betweens*, ed. Andreas Höfele and Werner von Koppenfels (Berlin: Walter de Gruyter, 2005), 177–99; Vitkus, *Turning Turk*, 163–98; Andrew Hiscock, *The Uses of This World: Thinking Space in Shakespeare, Marlowe, Cary and Jonson* (Cardiff: University of Wales Press, 2004), 52–82; Julia Reinhard Lupton, "The Jew of Malta," in *The Cambridge Companion to Christopher Marlowe*, ed. Patrick Cheney (Cambridge: Cambridge University Press, 2004), 144–57; Julia Reinhard Lupton, *Citizen-Saints: Shakespeare and Political Theology* (Chicago: University of Chicago Press, 2005), 49–72.

[4]   Irving Ribner, "Marlowe and Machiavelli," *Comparative Literature* 6, no. 4 (1954): 353.

[5]   N. W. Bawcutt, "Machiavelli and Marlowe's *The Jew of Malta*," *Renaissance Drama* 3 (1970): 48.

[6]   Catherine Minshull, "Marlowe's 'Sound Machevill,'" *Renaissance Drama* 13 (1982).

Machevil announces that "I count religion but a childish toy / And hold there is no sin but ignorance" (Prologue. 14–15), encapsulating the amoral policy of *The Prince* which so alarmed and influenced early modern Europe. From the mouth of this villainous archetype we hear the purpose of the forthcoming drama:

> I come not, I,
> To read a lecture here in Britainy,
> But to present the tragedy of a Jew,
> Who smiles to see how full his bags are crammed,
> Which money was not got without my means.
> (Prologue. 28–32)

Marlowe's ostensible alignment of Barabas with Machiavelli is patently suggestive, given the popular English identification of the Florentine theorist with "foreign, Catholic duplicity."[7] The play's protagonist, despite being Jewish, will enter the stage associated with the popish policy of Machiavelli, by devotion to which one may "attain / To Peter's chair" (Prologue. 11–12).[8] Yet his Jewishness alone is likely to have been sufficient to excite negative preconceptions in a contemporary audience. Stereotypical Elizabethan conceptions of Jews were complex and deep-seated, often focusing on a covetous preoccupation with material wealth, sometimes upon a tendency to commit acts of unspeakable barbarity, and generally highlighting their role as obstructers of the advancement of the Christian faith. In the words of Wilbur Sanders, Elizabethans had "a semantic complex of infidelity, treachery, inhumanity and rapacity informing the very use of the word 'Jew.'"[9] Barabas's Jewishness carries with it a poisonous set of associations which would have marked him as distinct from the characters with whom he shares the stage and would have distanced him from the viewing audience before uttering a word. As Stephen Greenblatt puts it, Barabas takes the stage "already trailing clouds of ignominy, already a 'marked case.'"[10] It might readily be argued that these expectations are entirely borne out by the action of the play – Barabas indeed

---

[7] Niccolò Machiavelli, *The Prince*, ed. Lucille Margaret Kekewich (Ware, Herts: Wordsworth Classics, 1997), xxii. On the Elizabethan popular conception of Machiavelli, Cole states that "Rapacity, avarice, ruthlessness, craft and deceit, treachery, diabolism – all these were summed up in the name of Machiavelli and in the 'policy' that became his notorious trademark," *Suffering and Evil*, 137; and Tromly argues that "The dominant attitude was to depict Machiavellianism as a lethal Continental disease which must be kept out of the innocent, enclosed world of England at all costs," *Playing With Desire*, 104.

[8] On early modern English identification of Jews with Catholic recusants, see Arata Ide, "*The Jew of Malta* and the Diabolic Power of Theatrics," *Studies in English Literature 1500–1900* 46, no. 2 (2006): 261–2.

[9] Wilbur Sanders, *The Dramatist and the Received Idea: Studies in the Plays of Marlowe and Shakespeare* (Cambridge: Cambridge University Press, 1968), 41. See also Vitkus, *Turning Turk*, 165, and Levin, *The Overreacher*, 84.

[10] Stephen Greenblatt, "Marlowe, Marx, and Anti-Semitism," in *Christopher Marlowe*, ed. Richard Wilson (London: Longman, 1999), 144.

turns out to be one of the most morally despicable characters in the history of English literature. Throughout the last three acts of the play he commits murder indiscriminately, and derives great pleasure from the process, even when plotting the poisoning of his own daughter, along with her entire convent.[11] Although unquestionably wronged, his responses to mischief done to him are absurdly disproportionate, and thus fly in the face of any contemporary moral code of revenge which might potentially serve to justify them. As Harold Levin puts it, "Barabas the Jew is a man with a grievance, but his retaliation outruns the provocation."[12] In keeping with the prologue, his Machiavellian pursuit of self-interest obviates any loyalty of any kind to anyone, and no self-promoting deceit is considered too shameful. This much is articulated by Barabas himself when he says to his daughter, "Be ruled by me, for in extremity / We ought to make bar of no policy" (1. 2. 273–4), and his advice to Ithamore is no less emphatic:

> First, be thou void of these affections:
> Compassion, love, vain hope, and heartless fear.
> Be moved at nothing; see thou pity none,
> But to thyself smile when the Christians moan.
> (2. 3. 170–73)

Through to the end of the play, Barabas does nothing to disassociate himself from Machiavellian thought; once he has assumed control of Malta he offers himself advice that is steeped in Florentine *realpolitik*:

> since by wrong thou got'st authority,
> Maintain it bravely by firm policy,
> At least unprofitably lose it not.
> (5. 2. 35–7)

This recalls the advice given in *The Prince* to heads of state who have achieved sovereignty by means of crimes. Machiavelli states that all evils necessary to consolidate one's newfound power should be conducted at once, rather than piecemeal, in which case they will be more keenly felt by the populace. As Barabas

---

[11] Barabas's precipitous descent into bloodlust in the final three acts of the play has led some commentators to suggest dual authorship. I do not see the change in tone as sufficient to warrant this suggestion. James R. Siemon notes that "It has been argued – largely on the basis of perceived disunity of style or tone – that the quarto reflects an extensive revision, probably by Thomas Heywood; but studies of vocabulary, spelling, metre and dramaturgy have generally supported the now widely held opinion that the quarto derives from some version of a Marlovian original." Introduction to *The Jew of Malta*, by Christopher Marlowe (London: A & C Black, 1994), xxxviii.

[12] Levin, *The Overreacher*, 79. For similar observations see David Bevington, "*The Jew of Malta*," in *Marlowe: A Collection of Critical Essays*, ed. Clifford Leech (Englewood Cliffs, NJ: Prentice Hall, 1964), 151, and James R. Siemon's introduction to *The Jew of Malta*, xxv.

intends to do, both of Machiavelli's examples in this chapter, Agathocles, King of Syracuse, and Oliverotto da Fermo, achieved their respective positions of power by inviting dignitaries to an assembly or banquet, and then slaughtering them.[13]

Despite establishing a network of unsavoury associations for Barabas, however, the prologue does end, not unlike those of *Tamburlaine* and *Doctor Faustus*, with an appeal to level-headed and objective judgement:

> I crave but this: grace him as he deserves,
> And let him not be entertained the worse
> Because he favours me.
> (Prologue. 33–5)

Such an approach to the play may find cause to withhold condemnation of Barabas. Crucial to our impression of him is his marked self-awareness. The most coherent enunciations of contemporary anti-Semitic stereotypes in the play are delivered not by its Christian characters, but by Barabas himself, as can be seen when he draws on the tradition of Jewish covetousness during an elaborate confession to the Friars Barnardine and Jacomo:

> I have been zealous in the Jewish faith,
> Hard-hearted to the poor, a covetous wretch,
> That would for lucre's sake have sold my soul.
> A hundred for a hundred I have ta'en,
> And now for store of wealth may I compare
> With all the Jews in Malta. But what is wealth?
> I am a Jew, and therefore am I lost.
> (4. 1. 54–60)

Crucially, Barabas is not speaking sincerely here, but rather deceiving the friars into thinking he is preparing for a conversion to Christianity. By delivering an account of a soul corrupted by avarice, the Jew tells the friars exactly what they want, and expect, to hear. The friars are fooled, but the audience is in on the joke. This exchange is echoed in Barabas's verbal tussle with Ithamore at the slave markets. Here each of the two combatants consciously appropriates the characteristics stereotypically applied to his religious denomination in a humorous attempt to prove himself the more execrable villain. Barabas's contribution is again comically absurd in its adherence to anti-Semitic prejudices, painting a self-portrait that luxuriates in poisoning and usury:

> As for myself, I walk abroad a-nights
> And kill sick people groaning under walls;
> Sometimes I go about and poison wells
> …
> Then after that I was an usurer,

---

[13] Machiavelli, *The Prince*, 32–6.

And with extorting, cozening, forfeiting,
And tricks belonging unto brokery,
I filled the gaols with bankrupts in a year,
And with young orphans planted hospitals,
And every moon made some or other mad,
And now and then one hang himself for grief,
Pinning upon his breast a long great scroll
How I with interest tormented him.
(2. 3. 175–99)

Greenblatt suggests that Barabas's identity "is to a great extent the product of the Christian conception of a Jew's identity."[14] But Barabas is not, as the prologue suggests he will be, simply a personification of anti-Semitic stereotypes. Rather, his histrionic performance of those stereotypes serves to highlight their fictive status, and positions him externally to them. He is fully aware of, and in dialogue with, the social forces that place him on the periphery of society. As Vitkus puts it, "the stereotype of the Jewish moneylender and poisoner is a role that Barabas irreverently appropriates but then exceeds."[15] In a sense, Barabas asserts his independence by distancing himself from reductive notions of Jewishness. Yet in another sense, since Jewishness was so readily associated with isolation and liminality, Barabas's separation from it facilitates a degree of unity with the audience that would otherwise be unavailable to him.

The irreverence described by Vitkus is important in this respect; underlying the reprehensible deeds which he commits is a charismatic disregard for any kind of moral code. He despatches his enemies with such elaborate verve and humour that the depravity of the situation is mitigated.[16] J. B. Steane has noted the significance of humour in establishing a rapport between Barabas and the audience, stating that "Laughter will bypass that countering reason and carry our inner allegiances into places where we have no sober intention of their going."[17] Furthermore, as Ruth Lunney has recently shown, his unusually frequent asides directly invite

---

[14] Greenblatt, "Marlowe, Marx, and Anti-Semitism," 148.

[15] Daniel Vitkus, "Turks and Jews in *The Jew of Malta*," in *Early Modern English Drama: A Critical Companion*, ed. Garrett A. Sullivan Jr., Patrick Cheney and Andrew Hadfield (Oxford: Oxford University Press, 2006), 61.

[16] The most famous commentary on the humour of the play is that of T. S. Eliot, who counters the common suggestion that the final three acts of the play represent a trivial departure from the serious matter of the first two: "If one takes *The Jew of Malta* not as a tragedy, or as a 'tragedy of blood', but as a farce, the concluding act becomes intelligible; and if we attend with a careful ear to the versification, we find that Marlowe develops a tone to suit his farce, and even perhaps that this tone is his most powerful and mature tone. I say farce, but with the enfeebled humour of our times the word is a misnomer; it is the farce of the old English humour, the terribly serious, even savage comic humour, the humour which spent its last breath in the decadent genius of Dickens." *Elizabethan Dramatists* (London: Faber and Faber, 1963), 63–4.

[17] Steane, *Marlowe: A Critical Study*, 172.

the audience to share in the elaboration of his plots.[18] According to Roger Sales, "The spectators share the secrets of Barabas's stagecraft and are therefore perhaps implicated in the original crime and its cover-up,"[19] while Greenblatt states that "Abigail, Don Mathias, and the nuns are killed off with remarkable ease and, in effect, with the complicity of the laughing audience."[20] That complicity serves to implicate the audience in Barabas's actions to the degree that to condemn him is also, to an extent, to condemn oneself. In achieving this effect, the play capitalizes on the potential for theatre to enact a form of unification on which Protestant polemic was not so keen. In a passage that strikingly anticipates Barabas's counting house soliloquy, the anti-theatrical writer Stephen Gosson reminds his readers that "the Carpenter rayseth not his frame without tooles, nor the Deuill his woork without instrumentes: were not the Players the meane, to make these assemblyes, such multitudes wold hardly be drawn in so narrow roome."[21] The theatre creates a multitude of its own, and in this case it is a multitude of which Barabas is at the centre.

Beyond his own actions and associations, our impression of Barabas is equally influenced by our response to the characters with whom he shares the stage. The play's Islamic characters are hardly a moral alternative to Barabas; Ithamore shows himself to be equally crooked, if less ingenious, while the more distant presence of Calymath and Callapine, who effectively hold the island of Malta to ransom, is suggestive of an Islamic empire that is at best opportunistic and at worst corrupt. Prejudice comes into play here also: as odious as the Elizabethan conception of the Jew may be, that of the Turk, subject of the Ottoman Empire that at the time was spreading its territories into western Europe, is certainly no better. More challenging for the contemporary audience, however, is the presentation of the play's Christians. The historical Knights of St John of Jerusalem, entrusted with the safekeeping of Malta after having lost Rhodes to the Ottoman Empire, were notoriously licentious. When Jean de La Cassière, the Order of Malta's leader, instigated a clampdown on immoral practices such as prostitution in the 1580s, his measures proved sufficiently unpopular to see him usurped and imprisoned by his followers.[22] Worse than this, however, they were Catholic, and ran the island with the blessing of the Spanish Emperor Charles V. Equally problematic is the company the knights keep in the play. They receive help in instigating a campaign

---

[18] Ruth Lunney, "Speaking to the Audience: Direct Address in the Plays of Marlowe and His Contemporaries," in *Christopher Marlowe the Craftsman: Lives, Stage, and Page*, ed. Sarah K. Scott and M. L. Stapleton (Farnham: Ashgate, 2010).

[19] Sales, *Christopher Marlowe*, 106. Levin states a similar case: "We, who overhear his asides and soliloquies, are his trustworthy confidants. We are therefore in collusion with Barabas. We revel in his malice, we share his guilt." *The Overreacher*, 94.

[20] Greenblatt, "Marlowe, Marx and Anti-Semitism," 145.

[21] Stephen Gosson, *The Schoole of Abuse* (London: 1579), STC (2nd ed.) / 12097, Sig. C3v–C4.

[22] See D. L. Farley-Hills, "Was Marlowe's 'Malta' Malta?" *Journal of the Faculty of Arts, Royal University of Malta* 3, no. 1 (1965).

against the Ottoman Empire from a Spanish sea captain, a dubious association in immediately post-Armada England. Marlowe's use of names accentuates this link: Ferneze, the island's governor, has a name uncomfortably resembling that of the Duke of Parma, Alessandro Farnese, who was the commander of the invasion force that the Armada had intended to deliver from Flanders to England's shores, and who had since been a thorn in the side of the Protestant Low Countries. The play's knights are clearly presented as Christians, but their enmity with Protestant England is foregrounded. Indeed, as Emily Bartels has shown, by inventing a situation in which no successful repulsion of the great siege of Malta (1565) ever occurred, Marlowe downplays the one achievement of the knights that might have endeared them to an English audience.[23]

Beyond these considerations, the actions of the knights speak for themselves. The play's plot is set into motion by the knights' seizure of Barabas's wealth, on pain of an enforced conversion to Christianity, in order to pay overdue tributes to the Ottoman prince Calymath. The theft is justified by the knights in religious terms, but Barabas's frank appeal and Ferneze's affected response reveal both the injustice and the hypocrisy of the whole procedure. Barabas questions the viability of punishing an individual for the sins of the collective creed to which he belongs (in the process stressing the tension between the individual and the multitude), when he remarks: "But say the tribe that I descended of / Were all in general cast away for sin, / Shall I be tried by their transgression?" (1. 2. 114–16). Barabas rightly perceives that the seizure of his wealth is justifiable, in the eyes of the knights, purely because of his "profession," or faith. In his response Ferneze attempts to establish that the seizure of Barabas's goods will be spiritually edifying for him: "Excess of wealth is cause of covetousness, / And covetousness, O, 'tis a monstrous sin" (1. 2. 124–5).

Ferneze's argument, already risible in its insincerity, becomes especially so when at the first opportunity he decides to fight the Turks and keep the money.[24] As Catherine Minshull has persuasively argued, it is one of the play's great ironies that Barabas, identified so explicitly with Machiavellian policy in the prologue, is beaten, along with the Turks, at his own game by the Christian knights.[25] In *The Jew*

---

[23] Emily Bartels, "Malta: *The Jew of Malta*, and the Fictions of Difference," in *Christopher Marlowe*, ed. Richard Wilson (London: Longman, 1999), 165.

[24] Tromly notes the hypocrisy of the play's Christians when it comes to avarice: "One of the play's pervasive jokes is that, covetous as Barabas may be, most of the Christians turn out to be worse, being at least as greedy and far less intelligent." *Playing With Desire*, 99. Whether Barabas in fact turns out to be more intelligent than Ferneze is questionable, a point that will be discussed below. Sanders similarly observes Marlowe's trick of investing Christian characters with supposedly "Jewish" vices: "the strongest tendency in the play is to assail the facile and hearty complacency of Christian anti-semitism with persistent inversions and permutations of the Jew-Christian antithesis." *The Dramatist and the Received Idea*, 41.

[25] See Minshull, "Marlowe's 'Sound Machevill.'" See also Sales, *Christopher Marlowe*, 91, and Tromly, *Playing With Desire*, 106.

of Malta, deception and hypocrisy are the norm of behaviour. As Greenblatt puts it, "Barabas's avarice, egotism, duplicity, and murderous cunning do not signal his exclusion from the world of Malta but rather his central place within it."[26]

Perhaps the only character in the play that could possibly lay claim to representing a moral guiding light is Barabas's unfortunate daughter, Abigail. Christopher Fanta argues that her virtue and spirituality are apt to incite approval:

> Like Olympia and the early Zenocrate, she preserves her chastity, symbol of maidenly honor, and dies in exemplary fashion. Because of her language and attitudes ... we come to associate her virtue with her Christian faith; and in this dramatic context we tend to approve of her conversion and escape from evil.[27]

Abigail's new faith in Christianity is, however, more indicative of naivety than of virtue. Immediately after Abigail utters her expiring words – "And witness that I die a Christian" (3. 6. 40) – we see the friar to whom she has just confessed lewdly remark "Ay, and a virgin, too; that grieves me most" (3. 6. 41). The same friar later goes on to attempt to use the information gathered in Abigail's confession as leverage with which to extort Barabas.[28] Abigail's association with Christianity, as it exists in *The Jew of Malta*, is hardly flattering, nor is it entirely convincing, since she has, of course, already made an insincere conversion in order to help her father recover his confiscated gold. As Julia Reinhard Lupton observes, "the doubling of conversions, like the doubling of boyfriends, sours the sentimental seriousness of Abigail's turn to Christianity."[29] Furthermore, the lines spoken shortly before her conversion – "But I perceive there is no love on earth, / Pity in Jews, nor piety in Turks" (3. 3. 47–8) – imply that her decision to convert derives from a lack of viable alternatives rather than from the onset of a religious epiphany. Undoubtedly the least corrupt of the play's characters, Abigail is nonetheless an accomplice in murder and theft, and is inconstant in her religious faith. The audience is denied the luxury of a moral "safe bet." Steane is correct when he writes that "Mercy,

---

[26] Greenblatt, "Marlowe, Marx, and Anti-Semitism," 146.

[27] Fanta, *Marlowe's "Agonists,"* 26. Other approving readings of Abigail come from Levin, who calls her "the single disinterested character in the play, who is characterized by the first four words she speaks: 'Not for my self ...,'" *The Overreacher*, 90–91; Steane, who argues that "the monster-farce does not extend to her, and her love ennobles Barabas dramatically, as Zenocrate's did Tamburlaine," *Marlowe: A Critical Study*, 182; and Lagretta Tallent Lenker, for whom Abigail represents "the quintessential 'innocent victim' who, despite her relatively brief appearance in the play, does offer a moral compass to serve as foil to the more emblematic character of her father," "The Hopeless Daughter of a Hapless Jew: Father and Daughter in Marlowe's *The Jew of Malta*," in *Placing the Plays of Christopher Marlowe: Fresh Cultural Contexts*, ed. Sara Munson Deats and Robert A. Logan (Aldershot: Ashgate, 2008), 70.

[28] Tromly notes that "An audience may ... find itself laughing at the hapless Abigail's credulity, for only someone who is other-worldly to a fault could trust such a scurvy excuse for a friar." *Playing With Desire*, 105.

[29] Lupton, *Citizen-Saints*, 63.

selflessness, affection, loyalty, beauty, warmth have no place" in Marlowe's Malta, as is Bevington when he contends that "Marlowe's world of chronicle is morally neutral. Ferneze, Calymath, and del Bosco are no better and no worse than Barabas; Ferneze's final victory is merely a fact."[30]

Religious Ambiguity

The diminishing of clear moral distinctions between the play's characters removes an obstacle to the notion of unity on Marlowe's Malta; the play manages to depict something akin to a community of like minds, however unsavoury the basis of their commonality may be. Central to the creation of this effect is the complex dramatization of the three religious faiths present on the island. Religion has the capacity to act simultaneously as a unifying and distinguishing category. Appeals for unity in contemporary pamphlets did not so much call for an all-encompassing unity, but for an alliance of co-religionists against the threat of a perceived enemy such as the Catholic Church or the Ottoman Empire.[31] In such discourse, the notion of unity relies upon difference for its meaning. Marlowe's play, however, serves to undermine as much as accentuate differences between faiths. While the play invests each of the denominations with stereotypical traits that were popularly applied to them – Jews obsess about money, Catholics are duplicitous, Turks are either slaves or empire builders – it also draws attention to the points at which they overlap, subtly promoting consideration of their common Abrahamic origins. Lupton has noted the fellowship that exists across cultures in the play, particularly among socially marginalized characters.[32] After being left for dead outside the city walls by Ferneze and the Christian knights, Barabas finds little difficulty in establishing a mutually beneficial relationship with Calymath. Similarly, upon losing his daughter to the convent, he strikes up a quasi-familial bond with his purchased slave Ithamore, referring to him as "My trusty servant, nay, my second self!" (3. 4. 15). Shortly afterwards he makes their attachment official, promoting his charge from the position of servant to that of companion and heir:

> O trusty Ithamore, no servant, but my friend!
> I here adopt thee for mine only heir.
> All that I have is thine when I am dead,
> And, whilst I live, use half; spend as myself.
> (3. 4. 42–5)

---

[30] Steane, *Marlowe: A Critical Study*, 167, and Bevington, "*The Jew of Malta*," 157.

[31] See, for example, Robert Hitchcock's warning that "Euen as discord in a cittie doth discouer and giues occasion to those that lye in waite to betray, to perform their practises well: so vnitie doth knit together the diuersities of opinions, and of many making one body alone keepe gouernments and States vncorrupted." Hitchcock, *The quintesence of wit*, Sig. D4v–E. Further examples of this kind of rhetoric are discussed in the Introduction to this volume.

[32] See Lupton, "*The Jew of Malta*."

The ease with which these alliances are established may be indicative of a contemporary suspicion that Jews often conspired with Muslims against Christian interests. It is certainly true that the geographical spread of the diaspora, and the network of contacts existing within it, made Jews useful allies in Mediterranean trade, for both Christians and Muslims.[33] Daniel Vitkus describes the relationship between Barabas and Ithamore as "darkly emblematic of the genuine cooperation that existed between Jews and Muslims in the eastern Mediterranean."[34] Complicity between Jews and Muslims is a particularly pertinent issue in relation to the play's setting: a number of Jews reportedly fought valiantly alongside the Knights Hospitaller during the great siege of Malta in 1565, but this, according to James Siemon, was not sufficient to stop rumours of a financially motivated Jewish-Muslim conspiracy in the conflict:

> The repulsed siege of Malta was not only known as a Christian victory over Islam, but it was also the subject of contemporary rumours about financial complicity between the Jews and the Turks, who were said to have joined forces because the aggressive raids of Malta's Knights had turned it into an infamous market for enslaved captives.[35]

The unity between Barabas and the play's Islamic characters is solidified by a common opposition to Christianity; by the time he joins forces with Calymath both groups share an open enmity with Ferneze. In the case of his relationship with Ithamore, their common experience is social marginalization at the hands of Christians. Furthermore, a practice shared by Jews and Muslims is highlighted by Barabas as a mark of difference from their oppressors, when he says to Ithamore "Both circumcisèd, we hate Christians both" (2. 3. 216). Marlowe's penchant for suggestive naming comes into play here also, with "Ithamore" being a portmanteau of "Ithamar," son of Moses's high priest Aaron, and the common term for North African Muslims, "moor."

The play suggests a similar commonality between Christianity and Judaism. The ease of Abigail's multiple conversions between Judaism and Christianity, whatever they indicate about her morally, bespeak an openness of exchange between the two faiths. Again, this connection is accentuated by Marlowe's use of names, and by his selection of the play's setting. Barabas shares his name with the condemned thief of the New Testament whom the Jewish populace spare instead of Jesus. This discomfiting proximity between Barabas and Jesus is further suggested by the mock resurrection that Marlowe's protagonist undergoes in the latter stages of the play. The Knights of St John of Jerusalem are named after a Jew who

---

[33] Levin notes that "There seems to be little doubt that Jewish moneylenders, whose international connections enabled them to organize some of the earliest stock exchanges, performed an indispensable function in the developing European economy." *The Overreacher*, 85.

[34] Vitkus, "Turks and Jews in *The Jew of Malta*," 67.

[35] Siemon, introduction to *The Jew of Malta*, xii.

converted to Christianity, and the religious significance of the setting of Malta is outlined by Lisa Hopkins: "Malta owes much of its fame, some of its place-names, its distinguished Christian ancestry and, legend avers, its freedom from snakes, all to one very famous Jew: St Paul."[36] *The Jew of Malta*, then, portrays a level of exchange and association between the three faiths, and a similarity of behaviour between their adherents, that make the differences between them seem nominal.

Marlowe's illustration of the fluidity of religious thought and exchange is to a large extent facilitated by his choice of both a protagonist and a setting that occupy a markedly interstitial position. As mentioned above, the Mediterranean-wide diaspora of Jewish refugees that resulted from the Iberian Inquisition meant that many Jews had access to networks of connections spanning from London to Constantinople, and were thus ideal as intermediaries in trade or intelligence operations involving nations of different religio-political beliefs. It is precisely the position of the Jew – nowhere a full citizen, but in so many places a tolerated outsider – that makes him so useful, and it is also this position that prompts Barabas's indifference to whether Malta is run by Christians or Arabs. Similarly, Malta, situated in the middle of the Mediterranean (itself taking its name from its position in the middle of the classical world), is geographically ideal in a play dealing with the meeting of cultures. As Richard Wilson observes, "Malta was exactly located to subvert the dichotomies of Renaissance ideology."[37] As important as Malta's geographical position is its claustrophobically small scale. We witness first hand intercultural machinations between characters whose faiths oppose one another but whose topographical situation dictates that they encounter one another frequently.[38] By focusing on this interstitial microcosm, Marlowe is able to present the audience with a variety of manifestations of alienness, and to invite consideration of the notion that the difference between the alien and the familiar is not as significant as it is commonly imagined to be.

Malta, then, makes a perfect location for a dramatic examination of how religion, across different particular faiths, works, or perhaps more pertinently, how it is put to use by heads of state in order to conceal or to manipulate. Religion in Marlowe's Malta has a predominantly political function; it is generally used to cloak the ambitious motivations of individuals, particularly when those interests run contrary to those of others. It is to these politics, and the conflicting interests of the island's tirelessly enterprising individuals, that the rest of this chapter will devote its focus.

Unity: Religion, the Individual and the Multitude

From close to its very beginning, *The Jew of Malta* prompts its audience to consider the relationship between the individual and the multitude, and more particularly

---

[36] Hopkins, *Christopher Marlowe: A Literary Life*, 89.
[37] Wilson, "Another Country: Marlowe and the Go-Between," 188.
[38] See Hopkins, *Christopher Marlowe: A Literary Life*, 86.

the value of unity. When he first appears on stage, Barabas, surrounded by his mountains of gold, laments the necessity of "Wearying his fingers' ends" counting the coins with which his "steel-barred coffers are crammed full" (1. 1. 16, 14). The better thing to do, to avoid all of this toil, would be to trade with merchants whose traffic is "metal of the purest mould" (1. 1. 20), or in

> seld-seen costly stones of so great price
> As one of them, indifferently rated
> And of a carat of this quantity,
> May serve in peril of calamity
> To ransom great kings from captivity.
> (1. 1. 28–32)

This ideal of untold wealth compressed into the smallest of sizes is encapsulated in the memorable lines in which Barabas imagines the enclosure of "Infinite riches in a little room" (1. 1. 37). Barabas's riches, in their multiform manifestations, are not only tiresome to count, but are also unruly: they threaten to grow beyond his control and burst the walls of his "crammed full" counting house. In contrast, equivalent wealth enclosed in the space of a single gem or diamond is entirely manageable – a unified entity which can be carried, stored or watched with ease. While this scene serves primarily to demonstrate the enormity of Barabas's wealth, it also foreshadows the play's concern with political notions of unity. Ferneze, and heads of state in general, have a similar problem to Barabas. A state with a multivalent and unruly populace is like a counting house bursting with small change; the boundaries which define it are stretched to breaking point. Conversely, a state with a people that are of one mind – that act together as a multitude – will have a Prince that is fully in control of his territory.

The focus on the complex relationship between the individual and the multitude becomes explicit in the following scene, in which Barabas, having been summoned to the Maltese senate house, argues with Ferneze over the absorption of his fortune. Barabas's initial response to Ferneze's demand is to accentuate his status as an outsider, asking pointedly, "Are strangers with your tribute to be taxed?" (1. 2. 59). Barabas's logic is turned against him by the Second Knight, who reminds him of the freedom he has been given to earn his wealth: "Have strangers leave with us to get their wealth? / Then let them with us contribute" (1. 2. 60–61). Barabas, neither welcome enough on Malta to be considered anything other than a stranger to it nor sufficiently outcast to act independently of its customs, is caught in an impossible situation. Ferneze is ultimately able to justify the seizure by adopting a characteristically pious tone:

> BARABAS: Will you then steal my goods?
>   Is theft the ground of your religion?
> FERNEZE: No, Jew, we take particularly thine
>   To save the ruin of a multitude;
>   And better one want for a common good
>   Than many perish for a private man.
> (1. 2. 95–100)

Barabas's attempt to attribute Ferneze's individual act of theft to all of Christianity backfires, as Ferneze follows Barabas's lead by shifting attention away from the level of the individual to that of the multitude, justifying the seizure on the basis of its benefit to the society at large. As Troni Grande has noted, Ferneze's argument calls to mind the account in John 18:14 of Caiaphas's condemnation of Jesus, on the basis that "it was expedient that one man should die for the people," in turn ironically situating Barabas in the position of Christ.[39] This scene suggests not just a distinction between the individual and the multitude, but a more open conflict of interests between them. Where the concept of the common good is evoked, it is simultaneously undermined by the insistence upon an individual to whom that commonality does not apply.

Just as it allows for an intermediate positioning of the play between Christianity and Islam, the casting of a Jewish protagonist is ideal for a play which explores the contradictions of the relationship between the individual and the multitude. For an Elizabethan audience Jews are, officially speaking, quite literally external to the community, since their expulsion from England was still in full effect, and a large number of Jews across Europe, North Africa and the Eastern Mediterranean had relocated after being cast out of the Iberian peninsula by the Inquisition. In the regions where Jews were tolerated, they were rarely seen as full members of society, often living in walled ghettos which marked their separation from the gentile populace. This liminal state of residence is highlighted by the comments of theologian Andrew Willet, who in 1590 stated that "A Jew ... whether he journeys into Spain, or France, or into whatever other place he goes to, declares himself not a Spaniard or a Frenchman, but a Jew."[40] Willet's comment highlights the independence of Jews, yet also implies a community of sorts: in eschewing the identity of their host nation, Jews retain membership of another, less geographically defined group. Similarly, by marking out a recognizable group as distinct from the community, one makes a smaller community with autonomy of its own; the walls around a ghetto like the one in Venice keep the Jews out of the larger community, but also mark the boundaries of what is effectively a state within a state. Lupton argues that this was the case in early modern Malta, where Jews "functioned as a semi-autonomous, self-regulating body within the larger political order of Malta."[41] At stages the play seems to reflect this: when the First Jew and Second Jew take the stage Barabas describes them as flocking in multitudes, and when he calls them his countrymen, he doubtless means of Israel, rather than of Malta (1. 1. 141). As such, while ostensibly positioning Barabas as marked out from the multitude, the play offers at least the potential of belonging to a unified micro-community.

The idea of a Jewish community with a collective mindset is soon put under strain, however. Later in his conversation with his fellow Jews, Barabas's gestures of communality are flatly contradicted in his sardonic asides to the audience: promising to attend the meeting with Ferneze, he assures his "countrymen" that

---

[39] See Grande, *Marlovian Tragedy*, 147.
[40] Cited in Vitkus, *Turning Turk*, 165.
[41] Lupton, "*The Jew of Malta*," 145.

"If anything there shall concern our state, / Assure yourselves I'll look – (*aside*) unto myself" (1. 1. 170–71). After the meeting, in which he declares himself a stranger to the general Maltese society, Barabas also openly marks himself as separate from the Jewish community, when complaining to the other Jews:

> Why did you yield to their extortion?
> You were a multitude, and I but one,
> And of me only have they taken all.
> (1. 2. 178–80)

After these early exchanges, the play's other Jews (with the exception of Abigail, who in any case converts to Christianity) make no more appearances, and Barabas does little to suggest any kind of affinity to a religious community, reminding the audience of his Jewishness only when it serves to further his plots or to satirize anti-Semitic stereotypes.

Yet despite Barabas's individualism and his apparent position of separation from both the Maltese community and the smaller Jewish one, it is clear that, on certain levels, he is able to operate in something resembling a community. He is, after all, the Jew *of Malta*, and he interacts with characters from the very top to the very bottom of the social scale, who, although indulging in varying degrees of religious and racial prejudice, do not deny him his place on the island.[42] He may be disenfranchised, classed as a stranger by the powers running the island, but then so are the majority of the individuals in Malta, the play implies. This ambiguous state of belonging is described by Lupton, who makes a distinction between civic and civil contributions to a society, characterizing the latter as belonging to "the realm of informal affiliation and negotiation that shapes the give and take of both the stock market and the coffee house, the university and the brothel."[43] Denied access to civic processes, Barabas flourishes in civil society; he is allowed to interact with Maltese society because his individualistic pursuits in international capitalist trade make him a financial asset to Malta, an asset whose potential is realized early in the play when his wealth is called upon to bail the state out of its debt to the Turks. The Jews are considered as outsiders, alien and even dangerous, but the same perceived self-interest for which Christian society condemns the Jews is what makes them valuable and renders their presence acceptable.

Again, the ostensible values of the ruling Christians are undercut by more cynical motivations: Ferneze is prepared for his populace to accommodate "infidels" in exchange for the accordant financial benefits. A preoccupation with wealth, far from being the unique preserve of an avaricious Jew, filters from the top to the bottom of the Maltese social scale and is exhibited by almost every character

---

[42] Tromly notes the irony implicit in the incongruity of Barabas's individualism and his apparent attachment to Malta: "In increasingly ironic ways, the play reveals him to be truly the Jew *of* Malta. When his supposedly lifeless body is dumped outside the walls, he immediately burrows his way back into the city, which suggests that he cannot conceive of himself as a Jew *off* Malta." *Playing With Desire*, 107.

[43] Lupton, *Citizen-Saints*, 53.

in the play (Abigail is a possible exception, although she is instrumental in her father's plans to steal back his gold). Bellamira complains of her lack of wealth since the Turkish siege began and, together with Ithamore and Pilia-Borza, plans to extort it from Barabas; the avarice of the friars Barnardine and Jacomo allows them to be played off against one another with laughable ease; and when Callapine arrives at Malta to collect on his bargain with Ferneze, he quite openly states that he has been hurried forth by "The wind that bloweth all the world besides: / Desire of gold" (3. 5. 3–4). Far from exhibiting an investment in the "common good" alluded to by Ferneze early in the play, the inhabitants of Malta are driven by entirely individualistic and acquisitive motivations, a point which is implied when, at Del Bosco's slave market, the Second Officer chillingly states that "Every one's price is written on his back" (2. 3. 3). The fragmented society of Marlowe's Malta reflects the contemporary anxieties regarding the discordant state of England that appeared in the years leading up to the play's composition. It is a world in which the kind of exhortations to unity published by writers like Averell, Hitchcock and Wither[44] would be patently futile, and one much like that bemoaned in the anonymous verse piece *Mar-Martine*, a response, sometimes dubiously attributed to Marlowe's associate Thomas Nashe, to the Marprelate tracts:

> *Our England, that for vnitie hath beene,*
> *A glasse for* Europe, *hath such monsters bread,*
> *That raile at Prelats, and oppugne their Queene,*
> *Whole common wealthes, each beareth in his head.*[45]

In Marlowe's Malta the allegiance of individuals extends only to the commonwealth they bear in their heads. Indeed, exactly what commonwealth they might be expected to show allegiance to is unclear; as Bartels has shown, the majority of the inhabitants of the island are aliens of some kind. Even the governing knights represent a recently imported regime.

Similarly, while the play's undermining of religious distinctions and stereotypes may facilitate a degree of exchange and fellowship, it also reveals the entirely individualistic motivations of characters unencumbered by any monolithic group identity. Ironically, the thing that most unites the inhabitants of Marlowe's Malta is their resolute individualism. Barabas, in particular, is introduced as an entity operating independently from, and, it might be suggested, in competition with, the society of Malta; his self-sufficiency is spelled out in the opening scene both by lengthy accounts of the reach of his argosies, and by his quotation of Terence in response to the news of the Turkish threat to the Maltese state: "*Ego mihimet sum semper proximus*" [no man is nearer friend to myself than I am] (1. 1. 187).

---

[44] See Introduction.

[45] Anon, *Mar-Martine* (London, 1589), STC (2nd ed.) / 17461, Sig. A4. See also another anonymous text misattributed to Nashe, *A Myrror for Martinists* ... (London, 1590), STC (2nd ed.) / 23628, particularly 29/C–30/Cv. On the authorship of these tracts see *The Works of Thomas Nashe*, ed. R. B. McKerrow (London: Sidgwick & Jackson, 1910), 5:34–65.

Similarly, he asserts his status as an individual existing outside of the multitude when he questions Ferneze's right to seize his assets, asking "Are strangers with your tribute to be taxed?" (1. 2. 59). His initial indifference to the identity of the island's governors later turns to opposition when he has sufficiently recovered his wealth to once again buy property:

> I have bought a house
> As great and fair as is the governor's;
> And there in spite of Malta will I dwell.
> (2. 3. 13–15)

As Andrew Hiscock states, "Barabas' aim is to maintain his authoritative difference through acquisition. Moreover, he needs to ensure his liminal status in order to avoid the dangers of allegiance to any one ruling caste."[46] This sense of isolation from the commonweal is shared by many of the play's other characters. Like Barabas, Bellamira is concerned with matters of state significance only insofar as they impact upon her own individual financial well-being:

> Since this town was besieged, my gain grows cold.
> The time has been that but for one bare night
> A hundred ducats have been freely given;
> But now against my will I must be chaste.
> (3. 1. 1–4)

The courtesan describes the fallout of the Turkish siege in entirely personal terms – Malta's plight affects her only indirectly. The nuns live a life of separation from the wider multitude, and the friars in particular display a lasciviousness that sets them apart from the ostensible moral code of the religious community in which they operate. The play's individualistic, multicultural and competitive environment flies directly in the face of the idealized concept of a unified multitude. Indeed, it is closer to the world described by Machiavelli, in which it is safest to assume that every individual is preoccupied with personal gain, and will willingly perform any kind of betrayal in order to remove obstacles to achieving it. In *The Jew of Malta*, the macro-level view of the multitude as a unified entity is undermined on the micro level by the competitive and self-seeking nature of the individuals that form it. The play suggests that a fully unified multitude is an impossibility; in line with the thinking of the speaker of its prologue, it presents the world on the level of the individual as a site of self-seeking ambition and competition.

The Jew of Malta does not dispense with the idea of unity altogether, however. Rather, it demonstrates the deployment of the idea of unity, and in particular religious unity, as an expedient fiction. Marlowe's Machevil misrepresents Machiavelli when he states in the play's prologue that he "counts religion but a childish toy" (Prologue. 14). In fact, Machiavelli, particularly in his *Discourses on Livy*, places emphasis on its use as an instrument of state control. In a discussion of

---

[46] Hiscock, *The Uses of This World*, 59.

the rule of Numa Pompilius, the successor to Romulus, Machiavelli reflects on the effectiveness of religion in reducing a multitude to order, stating that

> whoever runs through the vast number of exploits performed by the people of Rome as a whole, or by many of the Romans individually, will see that its citizens were more afraid of breaking an oath than of breaking the law, since they held in higher esteem the power of God than the power of man.[47]

One is reminded of the remark attributed to Marlowe by Richard Baines, that religion was an invention designed "only to keep men in awe."[48] Machiavelli's coolly pragmatic account of the unifying power of religion is of a piece with its representation in *The Jew of Malta*. When Ferneze, whom Minshull has shown to be the play's most authentic Machiavellian, finally quashes all resistance to his rule, he brings proceedings to a close with the politically astute couplet "So, march away, and let due praise be given / Neither to fate nor fortune, but to heaven" (5. 5. 122–3). The accreditation of his victory to God represents a move by Ferneze to re-establish an image of social unity: the triumph is not Ferneze's but heaven's, a statement that not only implies the divine sponsorship of his rule, but also demands the complicity of all of the island's religious citizens.

Ferneze's proclamation obscures the fact of his *realpolitik* behind the carapace of religious unity. It is a piece of stagecraft, designed to elicit precisely the unifying effect that Stephen Gosson feared the theatre was capable of producing and at which Barabas has also shown himself to be highly adept.[49] It is only an image, but the fact that the play ends with it is significant. Indeed, the final couplet is just the last of a number of instances in the play in which religion is associated with that which is unseen, and references to it are persistently marked with a language of concealment. Religion, Barabas says to Abigail, "Hides many mischiefs from suspicion" (1. 2. 282–3), and we are given plenty of evidence to support his claim. Ferneze calls upon theological rhetoric in order to justify his hijacking of Barabas's wealth, and in return Barabas has his daughter imitate religious conversion in order to steal some of it back (from its hiding place under a floorboard marked, fittingly enough, with a cross). The poisoning of the broth at the nunnery is made possible by the fact that Maltese ceremony demands that on Saint Jacques' Eve alms must be delivered anonymously to the dark entry of the building (3. 4. 76–82); the Abbess tells Abigail upon her first "conversion" that the nuns "love not to be seen" (1. 2. 307); and when moments later Abigail appears at the convent's window with her father's treasure, she proudly urges us to "behold, unseen, where I have found / The gold, the pearls, and jewels which

---

[47] Niccolò Machiavelli, *The Discourses*, ed. and trans. Bernard Crick (Harmondsworth: Penguin, 1970), 139.

[48] From "The Baines Note," cited in A. D. Wraight and Virginia F. Stern, *In Search of Christopher Marlowe* (London: Macdonald, 1965), 308–9.

[49] For a reading which posits Barabas and Ferneze as rival dramatists, see Sales, *Christopher Marlowe*, 53–5.

he hid" (2. 1. 22). Ferneze's attribution of his final victory to the will of God, then, is the last in the play of a series of con tricks which are facilitated by the cover of piety. Religion in Marlowe's Malta has a predominantly political function: it serves to cloak the ambitious motivations of individuals, particularly when those motivations might be seen to run contrary to those of the wider society.

The individuals of Malta are engaged in incessant competition, and their relationships with each other and with the state, which itself changes hands three times in the play, are in a constant process of renegotiation. Thus, paradoxically, the state must, in its own interests and in competition with the interests of many of the individuals over whom it rules, conduct an ongoing campaign of suppression of competing ideals in order to keep alive the impression of a common interest – to contain infinite riches in a little room.

The Massacre at Paris

The Massacre at Paris, truncated as it is in its extant form, is a notoriously difficult text to make sense of. Yet despite being narrower in scope and somewhat clumsier in execution, the play has much in common with *The Jew of Malta*. What appears at first to be a crude piece of anti-Catholic polemic eventually develops into a depiction of a morally complex world in which the distinction between Papist and Huguenot is elided. Like his Malta, Marlowe's France is a place in which collective endeavour collides with individual interests, and in which religious rhetoric and religiously informed action serve cynical political purposes.

The Massacre at Paris has, generally speaking, been Marlowe's most ignored play. Despite apparently having been a financial success in its early performances, it has barely seen the stage in succeeding centuries, and has tended to be overlooked in critical studies of Marlowe's work up to the present day.[50] The predominant reason for this is undoubtedly what Paul H. Kocher describes as "its feeble quality and bad text," although he is uncharitable to refer to these as separate issues.[51] As well as appearing to be significantly truncated (it is roughly half the length of Marlowe's other plays), the text is beset with repetition and contains passages which reproduce in mangled form passages from other plays. This, together with the fact of the existence of the Collier leaf, which offers a tantalizing if not entirely reliable suggestion of what the play might have looked like, leads Joseph Q. Adams to suggest that the text "gives us little more than a synopsis."[52] H. J. Oliver stated in the introduction to his 1968 edition of the play that "All the evidence points ... to the probability that the Octavo *Massacre at Paris* is a corrupt text put together

---

[50] On the play's takings at the Rose Theatre in 1593, see Roger Carter Hailey, "The Publication Date of Marlowe's *Massacre at Paris*, with a Note on the Collier Leaf," *Marlowe Studies: An Annual* 1 (2011): 26.

[51] Paul H. Kocher, "François Hotman and Marlowe's *The Massacre at Paris*," *PMLA* 56, no. 2 (1941): 349.

[52] Joseph Q. Adams, "The *Massacre at Paris* Leaf," *The Library* 14 (1934): 447.

by memorial reconstruction," and that seems to have remained, broadly speaking, a consensus view. Mark Thornton Burnett reasserts the thesis in his 1999 *Complete Plays*, suggesting that the text seems to have been reconstructed from memory by a touring group of actors, some of whom had a firmer grasp of their characters' lines than others, and who substituted lines or phrases from other plays in the touring repertoire when memory failed them.[53]

With these textual problems in mind, many critics have considered the play too problematic to warrant serious critical consideration. Its incompleteness and its obvious textual contamination mean that any sustained attempt at interpretation must be conducted with an unsure footing. The situation has not been helped by the fact that, of the critics that have made a sustained attempt at making sense of the play, several have dismissed it as an exercise in one-dimensional jingoism. Douglas Cole, for example, asserts that *Massacre* represents "a crude spectacle of sensationalist propaganda," while Wilbur Sanders vividly describes it as "a chaos of religious platitudes and nationalist war-cries, gigantic self-assertions of gigantic non-entities, resounding in a poetic void."[54] Such accounts of the play build on Kocher's work in identifying anti-Catholic pamphlets, particularly François Hotman's *A true and plaine report of the Furious outrages of Fraunce*, as sources for the play, and tend to note the contrast between the exaggerated villainy of the Catholic Guise and the spotless virtue of the Protestant Navarre as a symptom of a literary work prostituted to purely political ends.[55]

Even among those critics who have dismissed the play as jingoistic, however, some have been less convinced of its clear division of sympathies. Despite reading the play as exhibiting "rousing but safe politics," J. B. Steane observes that the Huguenot faction does not represent an unproblematic alternative to their Catholic enemies. "What triumphs," he suggests, "is a 'good' (as opposed to Machiavellian) political realism, and it is a hard and not idyllic re-establishment of order."[56] Even Sanders, in tension with his overall dismissal of the play as anti-Catholic diatribe, recognizes a moral ambiguity in its treatment of Anjou/Henry III, which he explains by stating that "Marlowe's indiscriminate appetite for vice garners it from any source."[57] There may be some moral ambiguity in the play, the argument goes, but this is more owing to the flawed artistry (or indeed character) of the dramatist than it is to any artistic design. More recently, however, critics have

---

[53] See H. J. Oliver, introduction to *Dido Queen of Carthage and The Massacre at Paris*, by Christopher Marlowe (London: Methuen, 1968), lix, and Mark Thornton Burnett, introduction to *The Complete Plays*, by Christopher Marlowe (London: Everyman, 1999), xxv.

[54] See Cole, *Suffering and Evil*, 155, and Sanders, *The Dramatist and the Received Idea*, 32.

[55] See Kocher, "François Hotman and Marlowe's *The Massacre at Paris*" and "Contemporary Pamphlet Backgrounds for Marlowe's *Massacre at Paris*," *MLQ* 8, no. 2 (1947): 151–73 [part one] and *MLQ* 8, no. 3 (1947): 309–18 [part two].

[56] Steane, *Marlowe: A Critical Study*, 244.

[57] Sanders, *The Dramatist and the Received Idea*, 27.

seen fit to challenge this view of the play as itself a crude and simplified account. Julia Briggs, in particular, takes aim at Kocher and Sanders, undermining a central foundation of both of their arguments by showing that events in the play which they asserted to have been invented by Marlowe to appeal to anti-Catholic fervour (particularly Henry III's dissolution of his council and the subsequent prominence of Epournon) were in fact based on contemporary historical accounts.[58] Rather than reading the play as a unilateral anti-Catholic hatchet job, Briggs offers an account of its structure as comprising two distinctly opposed sections: the first (scenes 1–12) deals with the events of the St Bartholomew's Day massacre of 1572, and the second (scenes 13–24) dramatizes the political machinations of the late 1580s. The first of these sections, Briggs suggests, draws primarily from anti-Catholic pamphlet sources, while the second draws from sources more sympathetic to the Catholic League, the overall effect being an invitation to audiences to recognize a parallel between the conduct of the Catholic League and that of the Huguenot faction when in a position of ascendancy: "by paralleling the murder of the Guise brothers with St. Bartholomew's Day, Marlowe can bring out the extent to which personal spite motivated both actions, even as their protagonists exploited the more impersonal forces of the two opposed religious faiths."[59] More recent critiques have followed in Briggs's footsteps. Troni Grande suggests that "In *The Massacre at Paris*, the difference between Catholic and Protestant, the heretic and the faithful, becomes ironically blurred in the Protestants' final vow of bloody revenge," while Rick Bowers characterizes the play as one in which "Catholic murderousness shades into Protestant murderousness."[60]

If one accepts Briggs's interpretation of the play's structure, and I find it a persuasive one, then not only does the play become more interesting, but it also begins to resemble *The Jew of Malta* in its manipulation of audience sympathies. Just as that play does, *The Massacre at Paris* presents its audience with clear moral outrages perpetrated by recognizable "others" – in this case the French Catholic League – but ultimately goes on to invite consideration of the possibility that those moral outrages are equally capable of being performed by the figures in the play with whom the audience would presumably be inclined to associate themselves, namely the Huguenot Protestants. Like his Malta, Marlowe's France becomes a moral vacuum, in which no cause exists separately from private interests. As with *The Jew of Malta*, this moral indeterminism prepares the ground for the play's interrogation of notions of unity or collective purpose. The first few lines of the play, in which the Catholic King Charles reflects on the marriage of his daughter Margaret to the Huguenot King of Navarre, bring these ideas to the foreground:

---

[58] Julia Briggs, "Marlowe's *Massacre at Paris*: A Reconsideration," *The Review of English Studies* 34, no. 135 (1983): 261–2.

[59] Ibid., 269.

[60] See Grande, *Marlovian Tragedy*, 158, and Rick Bowers, "*The Massacre at Paris*: Marlowe's Messy Consensus Narrative," in *Marlowe, History and Sexuality: New Critical Essays on Christopher Marlowe*, ed. Paul Whitfield White (New York: AMS Press, 1998), 137.

> I wish this union and religious league,
> Knit in these hands, thus join'd in nuptial rites,
> May not dissolve till death dissolve our lives.
> (1. 3–5)[61]

The play thus begins with a double act of unification: on an individual level a union between Margaret and Navarre, and, more significantly, a religious league between the Catholic and Protestant elements at the forefront of 1570s French politics. Charles's lines linger on the idea of unity, but do so in a way which underscores its fragility at the same time as celebrating it; by uttering with repeated emphasis his wish that the union may not be "dissolved," Charles simultaneously asserts that Margaret and Navarre have become a single entity and emphasizes the possibility of that entity's dissipation. This possibility is not lost on Catherine, who only a few lines later responds to her son's invitation to "honour this solemnity" by uttering an aside to the audience: "Which I'll dissolve with blood and cruelty" (1. 25). Catherine's appropriation of her son's language capitalizes on its ambiguity, turning the possibility of dissolution into a certainty. As in *The Jew of Malta*, the prospect of political and social unity is offered up with one hand and taken away with the other; the ceremonial optimism of the union is almost immediately made to appear a naive fantasy that cannot withstand the will of powerful individuals.

This undermining of the appearance of unity with the frank unveiling of personal interests is seen most clearly in the figure of the Guise. Shortly after having put into motion the plans for the play's first two murders, the Guise delivers the play's most sustained (and most Marlovian) set piece, in which, like Machevil in the prologue to *The Jew of Malta*, he aligns himself with the Catholic enemies of Elizabethan England. In it, he makes clear his individualistic credo:

> Oft have I levell'd, and at last have learn'd
> That peril is the chiefest way to happiness,
> And resolution honour's fairest aim.
> What glory is there in a common good
> That hangs for every peasant to achieve?
> That like I best that flies beyond my reach.
> (2. 34–9)

As in the early scenes of *The Jew of Malta*, a conflict is set up between the notion of a common good and the desire for personal advancement. Even the term "resolution," which upon first encounter appears to carry the same sense as in Faustus's desire to be resolved of all ambiguities, can be read as connoting disintegration: the *OED* offers a definition of the word, now rare but current in Marlowe's time, as signifying "The reduction or separation of an object or substance into constituent

---

[61] Marlowe, *Dido Queen of Carthage and The Massacre at Paris*, ed. H. J. Oliver. All subsequent quotations from the play are from this edition.

parts or elements; decomposition, disintegration, dispersion."[62] Understood in this sense the line becomes consistent with the dismissal of the common good that follows it; for the Guise, the truly honourable pursuit is in the disintegration of common interests in favour of personal, individual ambition. Like all of Marlowe's Machiavellians, however, the Guise is able to assume the appearance of belief in a common cause. This is nowhere more evident, ironically enough, than when he persuades Charles to pursue fully the massacre of the Huguenots:

> Methinks, my lord, Anjoy hath well advis'd
> Your highness to consider of the thing,
> And rather choose to seek your country's good
> Than pity or relieve those upstart heretics.
> (4. 17–20)

Using rhetoric that chimes closely with that used by the barons in *Edward II*, the Guise demonstrates his capacity to employ the notion of a common cause in order to persuade those around him; the emptiness of this rhetoric is all too apparent to an audience that has already been informed of the Guise's philosophy of individualism, though.

As with *The Jew of Malta*, however, the possibility of commonality is suggested in the most unusual of places; nowhere does this play more clearly demonstrate togetherness than in its series of ritualistic murders. The Catholic perpetrators of the massacre demonstrate a degree of coordination that is unusual in Marlowe's plays, where scenes in which orders are given or in which courses of action are discussed tend to be precursors to acts of disobedience or betrayal (cases in point include Aeneas's plans to build another Troy in Carthage, Mycetes's discussions with Cosroe, Faustus's advice to the horse-courser and Mortimer's instructions to Lightbourn). Here, orders are distributed onstage and carried out, if not always with entirely successful results, to the letter. This sense of co-operation is given a visual dimension by the Guise's stipulation that

> They that shall be actors in this massacre
> Shall wear white crosses on their burgonets,
> And tie white linen scarfs about their arms.
> (4. 29–31)

This order ensures that the "actors" of the massacre can be distinguished from its intended victims, but also means that, for the audience, they are less likely to be distinguishable from one another. The uniformity of appearance signifies the unity of the group. For Bowers, the wearing of white costume by the killers also lends the massacre a ritualistic significance which is itself unifying: "the Guise costumes his cohorts in ceremonial purity to effect a mental distance from the atrocity to ensue, but also to intensify that same atrocity as meaningful

---

[62] "resolution, n.1, 1a," *OED Online*, June 2014, Oxford University Press, <http://www.oed.com/view/Entry/163721> (accessed 26 June 2014).

and unifying."[63] The Guise's "actors in the massacre" thus carry out a performance of unity: in adorning themselves with symbols of ritualistic significance and marking themselves as visually distinct from their victims they assert both the legitimacy and the togetherness of their actions.

The performance of unity by the Catholic League's killers is reinforced by the diminishment of the opposing forces. This is ensured not just through the murders of the Huguenots, but by the pointed refusal to allow them the opportunity to speak. The Admiral, discovered in his bed, is the first to be mockingly silenced:

> GONZAGO: Where is the Admiral?
> ADMIRAL: O let me pray before I die!
> GONZAGO: Then pray unto our Lady; kiss this cross.   *Stab Him*
> (5. 26–8)

Each of the murders contains an equivalent exchange; a few scenes later, for example, Seroune is denied recourse to prayer with similar contempt:

> SEROUNE: O let me pray before I take my death!
> MOUNTSORRELL: Dispatch then, quickly.
> SEROUNE: O Christ my Saviour!
> MOUNTSORRELL: Christ, villain? Why dar'st thou to presume to call on Christ, without the intercession of some saint? *Sanctus Jacobus*, he was my saint; pray to him.
> SEROUNE: O let me pray unto my God!
> MOUNTSORRELL: Then take this with you.   *Stab him*.
> (8. 8–15)

In each of these cases the momentary permission to pray seems to be granted the victim only in order to facilitate a barbaric jest.[64] Yet the prohibiting of speech in each of the murders serves a political purpose by pre-emptively obviating any narrative that runs counter to that of the state's perpetrators. It is noticeable in these two cases that the Protestant plea for the right to prayer is denied through ironic reference to specifically Catholic modes of worship. The official narrative is reinforced in the same moment that the counter-narrative is silenced. Moreover, Kristen Poole has argued that this silencing also denies the victims the status of martyrs, since in both contemporary pamphlet accounts of the massacre and in martyrdom narratives like Foxe's *Actes and Monuments* it is the subversive potential of the verbal assertion of faith in the moment of death which transform murder into martyrdom.[65] Through the closing down of multiple perspectives, the Guise's faction attempt to establish a reductive univocality that will ensure political supremacy.

---

[63] Bowers, "*The Massacre at Paris*: Marlowe's Messy Consensus Narrative," 135–6.

[64] On the humour of the play's murders, see Clayton G. Mackenzie, "*The Massacre at Paris* and the *Danse Macabre*," *Papers on Language and Literature* 43, no. 3 (2007).

[65] Kristen Poole, "Garbled Martyrdom in Christopher Marlowe's *The Massacre at Paris*," *Comparative Drama* 32, no. 1 (2008).

This reductive performance takes on an ironic dimension, however, with the murder of Peter Ramus. More than any of the other victims of the massacre, he is given both a reason for his murder and an opportunity, albeit a severely limited one, to respond:

> RAMUS: O good my Lord, wherein hath Ramus been so offensive?
> GUISE: Marry, sir, in having a smack in all
>   And yet didst never sound anything to the depth.
>   Was it not thou that scoff'dst the *Organon*
>   And said it was a heap of vanities?
>   He that will be a flat dichotomist
>   And seen in nothing but epitomes
>   Is in your judgement thought a learned man.
> (9. 23–30)

The Guise's complaint at Ramus's superficiality – at his "having a smack in all" without achieving mastery in any one discipline – reflects contemporary criticisms of the historical Ramus's conflation and simplification of the disciplines of dialectic and rhetoric, which was particularly influential in European universities – not least Marlowe's Cambridge – in the latter part of the sixteenth century. This simplification is the root of the accusation that Ramus scoffed at the *Organon*, Aristotle's treatises on logic; indeed, Peter Mack, in an essay whose overall aim is to recuperate Ramus's reputation, admits that "Ramist teaching could promote an unsympathetic, reductive and impoverished understanding of Aristotle."[66] For the Guise, then, Ramus is a debaser of academic standards who considers learned any petty scholar who reduces all argument to simplistic dichotomies or epitomes. The complaint is reminiscent of Faustus's frustration with logic, the only apparent aim of which was to "dispute well."[67] Uniquely amongst the murders, the victim in this case does not seek permission to pray, but defends himself against the Guise's charges of superficiality:

> Not for my life do I desire this pause,
> But in my latter hour to purge myself,
> In that I know the things that I have wrote,
> Which, as I hear, one Sheckius takes it ill,
> Because my places, being but three, contains all his.
> I knew the *Organon* to be confus'd
> And I reduc'd it into better form.
> (9. 40–46)

---

[66] Peter Mack, "Ramus and Ramism: Rhetoric and Dialectic," in *Ramus, Pedagogy and the Liberal Arts: Ramism in Britain and the Wider World*, ed. Steven J. Reid and Emma Annete Wilson (Farnham: Ashgate, 2011), 7.

[67] For a useful discussion of this scene in relation to *Faustus*, see Sarah Knight, "Flat Dichotomists and Learned Men: Ramism in Elizabethan Drama and Satire," in *Ramus, Pedagogy and the Liberal Arts*, ed. Reid and Wilson, 55–60.

Ramus does not deny the charge of reduction, but rather asserts it as a virtue. Rather than his own work being too simplistic, Ramus argues, it is the work of his rivals and predecessors that is too baggy. Yet there is as much of Faustus's arrogance in Ramus's response as there is of his frustration in the Guise's challenge. Ultimately, this rather incongruous exchange is one from which neither party emerges with a great deal of credit. The Guise, in the midst of a reductive campaign of aggression, attacks Ramus for his reductiveness; his objection may be hypocritical, but it has a sound foundation in contemporary scholarly argument: as Sarah Knight has noted, "Guise is a raging murderer, certainly, but his attack on the foundations of Ramism ... is echoed by other, saner, real-life thinkers."[68] Ramus's response is boastful without being convincing, and is comically deflated by what follows it:

> GUISE: Why suffer you that peasant to declaim?
>   Stab him, I say, and send him to his friends in hell.
> ANJOY: Ne'er was there collier's son so full of pride. *Kill him.*
> (9. 53–5)

Fittingly, the exchange is immediately followed by the most brutally reductive act of the entire play, as the Guise orders the murder of one hundred Protestants who have been corralled into the Seine.

Ultimately, the Guise is able to successfully manufacture a unity of sorts, to the extent that, after his death, King Henry (Anjou) worries that the remaining members of his family "will make one entire Duke of Guise" (21. 131). But, as the Guise's overblown soliloquy earlier in the play has demonstrated, this unity in no way serves the interest of a common good; the play makes clear that, like Ferneze in *The Jew of Malta*, the Guise promotes a sense of unity among his people in order to service his personal political ambitions. Yet, as has already been suggested, the Guise is not the root of all the play's evil. The unflattering representation of Ramus, a figure strongly associated with the Protestant cause, is indicative of the way in which this play refuses to reduce to simplistic jingoism.[69] As Julia Briggs has convincingly shown, Anjou and Navarre, once in positions of power, begin to look less like viable alternatives to the Guise's *modus operandi* and more like reiterations of it. After the murder of the Duke Joyeux, Navarre also sounds a great deal like Ferneze, when he proclaims

> The Duke is slain and all his power dispers'd,
> And we are grac'd with wreaths of victory.
> Thus God, we see, doth ever guide the right,
> To make his glory great upon the earth.
> (18. 1–4)

Navarre makes clear to his audience, both offstage and onstage, that God's approval of the murder should be met with their own. Yet the assertion rings hollow, given

---

[68] Knight, "Flat Dichotomists," 59.

[69] On Ramus and Protestantism, see Knight, "Flat Dichotomists," 47–55.

the similarity of the act to those successfully carried out by the Guise's men in the first half of the play: if success implies divine approval, then it follows both that the Guise has also been the subject of divine approval and that divine approval is temporary. A similar ambiguity is produced at the end of the play, when both a dying Henry III and his successor, Navarre, proclaim their enmity to Rome and their allegiance to Elizabeth's England. First, as his fatal wound is being searched by a surgeon, Henry delivers a sonorous anti-Catholic message to the English agent who has mysteriously joined proceedings:

> Agent for England, send thy mistress word
> What this detested Jacobin hath done.
> Tell her, for all this, that I hope to live,
> Which if I do, the papal monarch goes
> To wrack, and antichristian kingdom falls.
> These bloody hands shall tear his triple crown
> And fire accursed Rome about his ears.
> (24. 55–61)

These lines have provided plentiful ammunition for critics who dismiss the play as simplistic anti-Catholic propaganda, and, on the face of it, it is easy to see why; it seems intuitive to assume that the sentiments expressed here would have been met with popular approval in the same way that similar passages in *Doctor Faustus* and *Edward II* most probably were. Yet the context of the speech renders it problematic. Firstly, Henry, it is abundantly clear, is *not* going to live. In this, his most assertive moment, he is making a series of bombastic promises which he will never have to keep. Like Ramus's retort to the Guise, Henry's rhetoric undergoes a bathetic deflation when the surgeon reveals within the space of a few lines that the wound is fatal. Secondly, while the content of the speech is of an ostensibly agreeable nature to an Elizabethan post-Armada audience, its declamatory style is distinctly Guise-like. The point at which Henry is delivering his most vehement anti-Catholic rhetoric is also the point at which he sounds most like the play's Catholic villain. Navarre sounds a note of optimism upon Henry's death, swearing that Rome "Shall curse the time that e'er Navarre was king, / And rul'd in France by Henry's fatal death!" (24. 110–11), but by now even the most partisan of audiences must have learned to be suspicious of such promises (even if they weren't aware of the historical Henry IV's conversion to Catholicism around the time of the play's early performances).

Whatever the reasons may be, *The Massacre at Paris* lacks the complexity of *The Jew of Malta*, but it shares some of its concerns. Like *The Jew*, it manipulates audience preconceptions, destabilizing ostensibly clear distinctions between opposing religio-political groupings. It dramatizes the ways in which both the use and the prohibition of language can be used to manufacture a sense of unity, but crucially, like *The Jew*, it always prompts its audience to consider in whose private interests that sense of unity is being manufactured.

Chapter 5
True Contraries:
Edward II

Edward II is in many ways the most genuinely ambiguous of Marlowe's plays. It focuses on and shifts between two factions, without offering centre stage to any one dominant character; the restraint and dramatic balance for which the play is often judged as superior to Marlowe's earlier work means that no Tamburlaine, Barabas or Faustus is given the opportunity to attempt at length to win himself into our sympathies. So finely balanced is the play's depiction of the competing factions that the audience is denied the liberty of sympathizing predominantly with one or the other. Critical responses to the play have mirrored this equipoise by diverging on a number of issues, including the extent to which the play's concerns are political or personal, and whether Edward's sexuality is a central issue or a subordinate concern to his disruption of the social order. Yet ultimately, I will argue, personal, political, sexual and social concerns converge in each faction's discourse, informing two incompatible hierarchical world views which are articulated by their adherents in terms of nature; disharmony between king and realm, disunity among the nobility and subversion of hierarchical and sexual norms are all repeatedly figured by participants in terms of fissures in the natural cosmological order. Yet, by virtue of the incompatibility of the play's competing hierarchical orders, *Edward II* undermines the validity of the concept of unitary natural order, instead presenting us with an environment, like those of *The Jew of Malta* and *The Massacre at Paris*, in which the concept of unitary order is deployed as politically expedient propaganda which serves a very particular interest.[1]

Moral Ambiguity

As I have suggested elsewhere in this book, the lack of a moral compass is a standard feature of Marlovian drama, but *Edward II* is perhaps unique in that, as well as failing to establish a morally sound position, none of its characters achieves anything admirable. Where they are not repulsive, they are unimpressive, particularly in relation to vaunting Marlovian stars like Tamburlaine, Faustus and Barabas, to whom "other characters are so subordinate as to be almost negligible."[2]

---

[1] My reading of *Edward II* is indebted to that of Sara Munson Deats, in her *Sex, Gender and Desire*, 162–201. While Deats's reading differs from mine by ultimately focusing on gendered subjectivity, her account of the play's ambiguity – which includes the assertion that, within both the play and the culture that produced it, "contrarieties frequently co-existed as 'true'" (163) – anticipates my own.

[2] J. M. Berdan, "Marlowe's *Edward II*," *Philological Quarterly* 3 (1924): 197.

The lack of a dominant figure in *Edward II* has been put down to its having been written for Pembroke's rather than Strange's Men, Marlowe's usual company, and therefore without the forceful stage presence of Edward Alleyn in mind.[3] It is noteworthy that the closest play to *Edward II* in this respect, *Dido, Queen of Carthage*, was also written for a company other than Strange's Men. Practical reasons aside, however, I will suggest that this even distribution of attention amongst the play's cast of characters is entirely appropriate to the themes with which it deals; the play's fine balance – between competing factions and competing ideologies – requires that there be no single dominant force on the stage.

In the words of Clifford Leech, "it can be said that, at the beginning of the play, no one in *Edward II* makes a good impression on us."[4] Similarly, and still more directly, J. B. Steane asserts that "the people of the play are on the whole most unlikeable."[5] It is certainly the case that Marlowe, by beginning the play with a homoeroticized statement of Machiavellian intent from Gaveston, ensures the arousal of the audience's suspicion from the start. Carrying a letter from the king filled with "amorous lines" (1. 1. 6),[6] the newly returned favourite ominously soliloquizes:

> I must have wanton poets, pleasant wits,
> Musicians that, with touching of a string,
> May draw the pliant king which way I please.
> Music and poetry is his delight;
> Therefore I'll have Italian masques by night,
> Sweet speeches, comedies, and pleasing shows.
> (1. 1. 50–55)

Gaveston, whatever the sincerity of his attachment to King Edward (more on this later), is shown here to be tellingly aware of the opportunities his closeness with the king affords him. His intentions would strike an Elizabethan audience as problematic on two counts: firstly in that he means to bend the will of a "pliant king" of England to his own purposes, and secondly, for the more puritanically minded at least, in that he means to do so with the employment of effeminate pastimes – music, poetry, masques, comedies – which can only serve to distract a head of state from his divinely ordained duty. Philip Stubbes, for example, is unequivocal about

---

[3] See L. J. Mills, "The Meaning of *Edward II*," *Modern Philology* 32 (1934): 28, and Levin, *The Overreacher*, 108. For an alternative view see Roslyn L. Knutson, "Marlowe, Company Ownership, and the Role of Edward II," *Medieval & Renaissance Drama in England* 18 (2005). Knutson argues that the distribution of lines between the play's characters suggests that the play may have been written with Alleyn and Strange's Men in mind and may have subsequently ended up in the ownership of Pembroke's Men.

[4] Clifford Leech, "Marlowe's 'Edward II': Power and Suffering," *Critical Quarterly* 1 (1959): 187.

[5] Steane, *Marlowe: A Critical Study*, 213.

[6] Christopher Marlowe, *Edward II*, ed. Charles R. Forker (Manchester: Manchester University Press, 1994). All subsequent quotes from the play will be from this edition.

the effect of the kind of entertainments Gaveston proposes on the constitution of the recipient. In *The Anatomie of Abuses*, Stubbes's raisonneur, Philoponus, asserts the danger of music used for purposes other than the glorification of God: "But being used in publique assemblies and private conventicles as directories to filthie dancing, thorow the sweet harmonie & smoothe melodie thereof, it estraungeth the mind stireth up filthie lust, womannisheth the minde rauiseth the hart, enflameth concupisence, and bringeth in uncleannes."[7] Gaveston's musical entertainments foreshadow the effeminacy that the audience will soon see in the "pliant king." They will also, according to Stubbes's reasoning, make the king *more* pliant, helping to create the conditions for further manipulation. At the beginning of the play, at least, Gaveston is marked out at as a dangerous man.

Spencer, who eventually fills the executed Gaveston's role as Edward's favourite and companion, is introduced in a similar manner.[8] In a discussion with Baldock regarding which of the disputing factions he wishes to support now that his patron, Gloucester, has passed away, Spencer reveals the rationale behind his decision to support the king to be based on *realpolitik* rather than on moral conviction:

> Baldock, learn this of me: a factious lord
> Shall hardly do himself good, much less us;
> But he that hath the favour of a king
> May with one word advance us while we live.
> The liberal Earl of Cornwall is the man
> On whose good fortune Spencer's hope depends.
> (2. 1. 6–11)

Baldock exhibits similar policy when, in the same discussion, he hears that Gaveston is likely to marry the late Earl of Gloucester's daughter and says, "Then hope I by her means to be preferred, / Having read unto her since she was a child" (2. 1. 29–30). A principal hazard of Edward's reign, then, is a king's capacity to attract acquaintances whose interests would seem to lie in their own furtherance rather than in the welfare of the realm or of the king. "It is obvious," writes L. J. Mills, "that King Edward does not have the ability to distinguish between worthy and unworthy companions."[9] However slow Edward may be to perceive the relative worth of his associates, Gaveston and the duo of Spencer and Baldock would be recognized by the audience, from their respective introductions alone, as flatterers.

The influence of flatterers on the monarch is evidently the point of concern which leads to the uprising of the "factious" lords mentioned by Spencer.

---

[7] Philip Stubbes, *The Anatomie of Abuses* (London: 1583), STC (2nd ed.) / 23376, Sig. D4v.

[8] In this chapter I shall abbreviate "Spencer Junior" and "Mortimer Junior" to "Spencer" and "Mortimer" respectively. Their respective father figures will be referred to in full as "Spencer Senior" and "Mortimer Senior."

[9] Mills, "The Meaning of *Edward II*," 25.

Their complaint might well be seen as just, yet the manner in which they pursue their cause, particularly as the play draws on, cannot be said to have been given a sympathetic depiction by Marlowe. The sinister inhumanity of the treatment of Edward during his captivity, of which Marlowe's account is drawn out to a length that is disproportionate to the frenetic pace of the rest of the play, is alone damning of his jailors and their sponsor, Mortimer. Leech describes the visceral quality of this part of the play:

> The barbarity of these latter scenes makes them painful to read or to see or to speak of. No other tragic figure in Elizabethan or Jacobean times is treated in the degrading way that Mortimer permits for Edward ... The Jacobean playwrights could think of strange ways of torment and murder, but they never tear at our nerves as Marlowe does in this play.[10]

Everything about the treatment of Edward, from his psychological torture, to his murder, ironically performed by anal penetration (described in Holinshed, implied in the play), to Mortimer's double-crossing of the murderer, seems calculated to excite distaste for its devisers.[11] Mortimer in particular, despite being the figurehead of the rebellion, begins to exhibit the kind of behaviour against which he initially claims to be rebelling; when instructing Gourney on how to break Edward's resolve, he appeals, in hubristic language reminiscent of that of Tamburlaine, to

---

[10] Leech, "Power and Suffering," 194.

[11] Before Edward's murder, Lightborn commands Matrevis to "get me a spit, and let it be red hot" (5. 5. 30), but the spit is not mentioned again. Editors, directors and critics have tended to accept that this is a textual omission, and that the climactic scene was intended to play out in the same way as it does in Holinshed, where it is described in gruesome detail: "they came suddenly one night in into the chamber where he lay in bed fast asleep, and with heavy featherbeds or a table (as some write) being cast upon him they kept him down and withal put into his fundament an horn, and through the same they thrust up into his body an hot spit, or (as others have) through the pipe of a trumpet, a plumber's instrument of iron made very hot, the which passing up his entrails, and being rolled to and fro, burnt the same, but so as no appearance of any wound or hurt outwardly might be once perceived." Thomas and Tydeman, *The Plays and Their Sources*, 369, lines 713–21. Stephen Orgel, however, contends that critics who envisage the play's murder happening in the same way as the chronicle are misguidedly "'correcting' Marlowe in reference to Holinshed." *Impersonations: The Performance of Gender in Shakespeare's England* (Cambridge: Cambridge University Press, 1996), 47. Logan concurs, positing that "nothing is mentioned to suggest that the punishment fits a sexual crime." *Shakespeare's Marlowe*, 96. Both Orgel and Logan are understandably resistant to the notion that Marlowe might have been inclined to suggest that homosexual sex deserved such brutal retribution. My own sense is that Edward's murder *is* carried out as in Holinshed; I can see no convincing reason why the spit would be mentioned otherwise. This does not mean, however, that Marlowe or the play passes judgement on Edward's sexuality at this moment; rather, it seems to me, the method and rationale of the murder reveals the cruelty of Mortimer and his faction.

the same ambition in his colleague to which he previously objected so strongly in both Gaveston and Spencer:

> As thou intendest to rise by Mortimer,
> Who now makes Fortune's wheel turn as he please,
> Seek all the means thou canst to make him droop,
> And neither give him kind word or good look.
> (5. 2. 51–4)

Mortimer goes on, once he has fully assimilated the powers of a king, to espouse an explicitly Machiavellian political stance, stating: "Feared am I more than loved; let me be feared, / And when I frown, make all the court look pale" (5. 4. 50–51).[12] The degeneration of Mortimer's initially proclaimed principles is observed by Marie Rutkoski: "As the play progresses, Mortimer Jr. becomes less a foil to Edward and more a doppelganger as he takes Isabella as a lover, wins paternal control over Edward III, and gains the power of a king."[13] Yet Edward himself, despite being the victim of horrifying cruelty and being subjected to the humiliation of usurpation at the hands of his own subjects, is far from a passive vessel for audience sympathy. Throughout the play, with the encouragement of Gaveston during the earlier part, he is churlish and spiteful in his conduct towards his wife Isabella, and harbours suspicions about her relationship with Mortimer which, although prophetic, are arguably the effective cause of her eventual unfaithfulness:

> ISABELLA: Whither goes my lord?
> EDWARD: Fawn not on me, French strumpet; get thee gone.
> ISABELLA: On whom but on my husband should I fawn?
> GAVESTON: On Mortimer; with whom, ungentle queen –
>   I say no more; judge you the rest, my lord.
> (1. 4. 144–8)

Edward subordinates Isabella to his male favourite to an insulting degree, as she herself, in one of the passages of the play most explicitly suggestive of a sexual relationship between the king and Gaveston, complains to Mortimer:

> For now my lord the king regards me not,
> But dotes upon the love of Gaveston.
> He claps his cheeks and hangs about his neck,
> Smiles in his face and whispers in his ears,
> And when I come, he frowns, as who should say

---

[12] Machiavelli includes in *The Prince* a chapter entitled "Of cruelty and clemency, and whether it is better to be loved than feared." Machiavelli's conclusion is more equivocal than it is often characterized as being, but nonetheless he does state that "A prince ... should not mind the ill repute of cruelty, when he can thereby keep his subjects united and loyal." *The Prince*, 64.

[13] Marie Rutkoski, "Breeching the Boy in Marlowe's *Edward II*," *Studies in English Literature, 1500–1900* 46, no. 2 (2006): 295.

'Go wither thou wilt, seeing I have Gaveston'.
(1. 2. 49–54)

Edward's neglect of Isabella is mirrored, and magnified, in his negligent approach to statecraft: the king displays a petulant lack of regard for the interests of his subjects, explicitly declaring state concerns to be subordinate to his own desire to enjoy the private company of favourites. When the nobles petition Edward for the banishment of Gaveston, his response is to suggest the disintegration of the nation state into baronial regions, if it will allow him to keep his minion:

> If this content you not,
> Make several kingdoms of this monarchy,
> And share it equally amongst you all,
> So I may have some nook or corner left
> To frolic with my dearest Gaveston.
> (1. 4. 69–73)

Edward exhibits the same order of priorities when news of enemy advances is brought to him during preparations for Gaveston's triumphal return from exile:

> EDWARD: How now, what news? Is Gaveston arrived?
> MORTIMER JUNIOR: Nothing but Gaveston! what means your grace?
>   You have matters of more weight to think upon;
>   The king of France sets foot in Normandy.
> EDWARD: A trifle! We'll expel him when we please.
> (2. 2. 6–10)

Later in the same scene, the results of Edward's manifestly poor political, martial and economic leadership are related to him in stark terms by Mortimer and Lancaster, in an account which condenses the events of several years of the historical Edward's reign into a catastrophic and simultaneous collapse of national order:

> MORTIMER JUNIOR: The idle triumphs, masques, lascivious shows,
>   And prodigal gifts bestowed on Gaveston
>   Have drawn thy treasure dry and made thee weak;
>   The murmuring commons overstretchèd hath.
> LANCASTER: Look for rebellion, look to be deposed.
>   Thy garrisons are beaten out of France,
>   And, lame and poor, lie groaning at the gates;
>   The wild O'Neill, with swarms of Irish kerns,
>   Lives uncontrolled within the English pale;
>   Unto the walls of York the Scots made road
>   And unresisted drave away rich spoils.
> MORTIMER JUNIOR: The haughty Dane commands the narrow seas,
>   While in the harbour ride thy ships unrigged.
> (2. 2. 156–68)

As Thomas and Tydeman have noted, indiscretions that took place over a long historical reign are condensed into a few lines of verse, lending an exaggerated credence to the barons' complaints.[14]

As has been discussed, however, the barons act on their grievance with repugnant cruelty and ambitious opportunism. Similarly, while Edward's devotion to Gaveston at the expense of his subjects is likely to have attracted opprobrium, his plight at the hands of his ruthless enemies surely would have earned him pity. The indeterminate morality of the play is highlighted by Roma Gill, who states that

> The barons are admirable in their defence of the realm, but a personal vindictiveness tarnishes their patriotism. That Edward is at fault there is no doubt: he neglects the kingdom, disparages the earls, cruelly insults his queen, and is all the time besotted with his Gaveston. Yet the younger Mortimer's aggressive inferiority, the vanity of Lancaster, and Warwick's unscrupulous murdering of Gaveston "flatly against the law of arms" (III. ii. 121), all confuse the emotions.[15]

Several critics have in fact noted a symmetry in the play around a centre point at which the audience's sympathies undergo a change. Levin, for example, identifies at the middle point of the play a "watershed which divides our sympathies": "Up to that point, Edward's follies alienate us, and afterward his trials win us back; while Isabell [sic], who starts by being ungallantly abused, ends by justifying his antipathy."[16] J. B. Steane makes a similar observation: "A remarkable feature of the construction is its symmetry. At a performance one has the impression that there are really two plays: in the first half the subject is the homosexual king and his favourite; in the second it is the rise of Mortimer and the fall of Edward."[17] The play is ambiguous, then, in its structural makeup: around the time of Gaveston's execution the play appears to encourage a switch of sympathies from the aggrieved nobles to the powerless king. Indeed, as Ian McAdam has noted, it is possible to map the audience's changes of allegiances onto those of Kent, who acts as a "moral weathervane" (a rare thing in Marlowe's work).[18]

It would be simplistic, however, to suggest that Marlowe simply flips the coin at the halfway point. While the symmetrical structure provides a useful account of the overarching trajectory of the play, subtle ambiguities are at work in

---

[14] Thomas and Tydeman, *The Plays and Their Sources*, 348.

[15] Roma Gill, introduction to *Edward II*, by Christopher Marlowe (Oxford: Oxford University Press, 1967), 21.

[16] Levin, *The Overreacher*, 121.

[17] Steane, *Marlowe: A Critical Study*, 204–5. Steane goes on to extend his model of the play's structure to three parts, perceiving a middle section in which "the king is for a short time strong, determined and victorious" (205). His proposed structure remains symmetrical, however. Elsewhere, Sara Munson Deats characterizes the structure of the play as a "dramatic chiasmus." "Marlowe's Fearful Symmetry in *Edward II*," in *"A Poet and a Filthy Playmaker": New Essays on Christopher Marlowe*, ed. Kenneth Friedenreich, Roma Gill and Constance B. Kuriyama (New York: AMS, 1988), 241.

[18] McAdam, *The Irony of Identity*, 224.

characterization and manipulation of chronicle sources from the start of the play to its finish. While Kent may be seen as a guide to an audience's moral sympathies, he nonetheless proves to be "ineffectual as an actor."[19] Early in the play, when, according to the symmetrical model, we are supposed to find Edward's actions reprehensible, the following set piece occurs after Edward has been cornered into signing the warrant for Gaveston's banishment by the Catholic Bishop of Coventry:

> Why should a king be subject to a priest?
> Proud Rome, that hatchest such imperial grooms,
> For these thy superstitious taper-lights,
> Wherewith thy antichristian churches blaze,
> I'll fire thy crazèd buildings and enforce
> The papal towers to kiss the lowly ground,
> With slaughtered priests may Tiber's channel swell,
> And banks raised higher with their sepulchres.
> (1. 4. 96–103)

This proto-Protestant outburst by Edward, although manifestly an empty threat, is nonetheless a crowd-pleaser in the same vein as Faustus's japery at the expense of the Pope. The references to "superstitious taper-lights" and "antichristian churches" appeal to the same kind of religious partisanship as the iconoclastic Protestant invective that was so commonly to be found in broadsides and pamphlets in post-Armada London.[20] The passage's patriotic appeal bears a striking similarity to Henry of Anjou's message to Queen Elizabeth, which, despite being deflated by his death almost immediately afterwards, represents Anjou's most heroic moment in *The Massacre at Paris*:

> Tell her, for all this, that I hope to live,
> Which if I do, the papal monarch goes
> To wrack, and antichristian kingdom falls.
> These bloody hands shall tear his triple crown
> And fire accursed Rome about his ears.
> I'll fire his crazed buildings, and incense
> The papal towers to kiss the holy earth.
> (24. 57–63)[21]

---

[19] Ibid., 224.

[20] Typical of this is John Bale's *The Pageant of Popes*, in the preface to which Bale invites the reader to "Behold what monsters Popery hath nourished throughout England in abbeyes and colleges. Are not these foule birdes most justlye banished with their most filthye Pope, the Romishe Idoll? In all other places as well in congregations as colleges the like things are committed and done, the which were to longe or rather to shameful thoroughly to declare, for they gate unto them in most places through this Popishe Religion, either the French pockes or the Spanish decease." *The Pageant of Popes, Contayning the lyues of all the Bishops of Rome, from the beginninge of them to the yeare of Grace 1555* (London: 1574), STC (2nd ed.) / 1304. The passage quoted here is from "Bale's Epistle to the Reader," Sig. C3.

[21] Marlowe, *Dido Queen of Carthage and The Massacre at Paris*, ed. H. J. Oliver.

Before we come to pity Edward for his cruel misfortune, then, and despite his childlike petulance, we are at least invited to admire his religious leanings and his choice of enemies.[22]

Similarly, Claude Summers has countered the much-levelled criticism that Isabella's metamorphosis from virtuous and wronged wife to adulterous and ambitious harpy is dramatically implausible, arguing that she is in fact a schemer from the start. Summers cites her apparent influencing of Mortimer, delivered in private whispers, to agree to the repeal of Gaveston's banishment in order to present the nobles with the opportunity to assassinate him.[23] From very early in the play, then, there is both a suggestion of Isabella's capacity to double-deal and "a hint of a special relationship between the Queen and Mortimer."[24] These are no more than suggestions or hints; an audience's impression of Isabella's moral trajectory is based on scant evidence.

Members of the baronial faction also confound the neat symmetrical model. In the latter part of the play, in which their conduct is marked by its cruelty, they nonetheless exercise mercy towards their enemies: Maltravers, Lancaster and Pembroke all argue for the acquiescence to Edward's request that he see Gaveston a final time before his execution (2. 5. 32–110), and Leicester later exhibits sympathy and kind-heartedness to Edward when he acts as his jailor:

> LEICESTER: Be patient, good my lord, cease to lament.
>   Imagine Killingworth Castle were your court,
>   And that you lay for pleasure here a space,
>   Not of compulsion or necessity.
> EDWARD: Leicester, if gentle words might comfort me,
>   Thy speeches long ago had eased my sorrows,
>   For kind and loving hast thou always been.
> (5. 1. 1–7)

Even the king's favourites, despite arguably representing the root cause of the political fracture dealt with in the play, are not depicted as negatively by Marlowe as they might have been. Spencer is given a dubious character assessment in the chronicles of Holinshed, Marlowe's primary source:

---

[22] See Berdan, "Marlowe's *Edward II*," 201–2, and Leech, "Power and Suffering," 188.

[23] Claude J. Summers, "Isabella's Plea for Gaveston in Marlowe's *Edward II*," *Philological Quarterly* 52 (1973). For a similar line of argument see Kathleen Anderson's "'Stab as Occasion Serves': The Real Isabella in Marlowe's *Edward II*," *Renaissance Papers* (1992). For an example of an argument which derides the apparent immediacy of the transition in Isabella's character, see Sanders, *The Dramatist and the Received Idea*, 131–2. Levin comments on the suddenness of the alteration in Isabella's character, remarking that "the transition is abruptly made in two brief soliloquies which stand no more than a page or a scene apart," *The Overreacher*, 121; and while Leech sees the shift as "one of the most perceptive things in Marlowe's writing," he does so because the dramatist "knew a woman's frustrated love could turn rancid," "Power and Suffering," 191.

[24] Leech, "Power and Suffering," 188.

> King Edward now after that the aforesaid Piers Gaveston, the Earl of Cornwall, was dead, nothing reformed his manners, but as one that detested the counsel and admonition of his nobles, chose such to be about him, and to be of his privy council, which were known to be men of corrupt and most wicked living (as the writers of that age report); amongst these were two of the Spencers, Hugh the father, and Hugh the son, which were notable instruments to bring him unto the liking of all kind of naughty and evil rule.[25]

A similarly damning account is provided by John Stow's *Annals of England*, another of Marlowe's sources, in which Spencer is described as being "in body very comely, in spirit proud, and in action most wicked, whose covetousness and ambition, by the disheriting of widows and strangers, wrought the death of the nobles, the fall of the king, with the utter destruction of himself and his father."[26] As has been argued above, Marlowe's introduction of Spencer and Baldock does suggest a degree of Machiavellian policy in their decision to back the king's faction, but once they have made that decision they remain his staunch and loyal supporters to the point of their deaths. This much is demonstrated by Spencer's final words in the play, after Edward has been seized and before he is led to his own execution:

> O is he gone? Is noble Edward gone?
> Parted from hence, never to see us more?
> Rend, sphere of heaven, and fire, forsake thy orb,
> Earth, melt to air; gone is my sovereign,
> Gone, gone alas, never to make return.
> (4. 7. 100–104)

Similarly, while it would be difficult to present a positive overall case for Edward's more notorious favourite, some critics have found redeeming features in Gaveston's character. Mills, for example, suggests that, "although Marlowe makes clear Gaveston's unworthiness, he pictures him as less crass and ignoble than Holinshed does."[27] Interlaced with his divulgence to the audience of his Machiavellian ambitions at the opening of the play are suggestions of genuine affection for and devotion to Edward – he may wish to "draw the pliant king" which way he pleases, but it is the same king "upon whose bosom" he wishes to die (1. 1. 52, 14). Gaveston's desire to see his "Sweet sovereign" for a final time on the eve of his execution also seems to be genuine enough; his final line in the play, delivered as he is seized by Warwick, speaks of this concern: "Treacherous

---

[25] Reproduced in Thomas and Tydeman, *The Plays and Their Sources*, 356, lines 201–9.
[26] Ibid., 375, lines 77–81.
[27] Mills, "The Meaning of *Edward II*," 14. Holinshed's description of Gaveston is reminiscent of the famous speech early in the play by Marlowe's version of the character. However, Holinshed's account, of course, denies Gaveston the opportunity to introduce himself, and condemns him for, among other things, "filthy and dishonorable exercises." See Thomas and Tydeman, *The Plays and Their Sources*, 352, lines 31–44.

earl! Shall I not see the king?" (2. 6. 15). As Leech suggests, "Gaveston is allowed no eloquent last words, yet Marlowe suggests that he has a genuine desire to see Edward once more."[28]

It is the apparent sincerity of Gaveston's devotion to Edward, and perhaps more so of Edward's to Gaveston, which prevents him from becoming a mere caricature, a fact observed by Leonora Leet Brodwin, who argues that the relationship between Edward and Spencer "is totally lacking in that poetry which redeemed Edward's love for Gaveston."[29] The poetry of this love, however, also gives rise to one the most ambiguous elements of the play, which has divided critics since modern study of *Edward II* began: what exactly is the nature of the relationship between these two men?

Sexual Ambiguity

Despite the apparent consensus among modern theatre directors that *Edward II* is a play about a homosexual king,[30] there has been some divergence in critical opinion on whether Edward and Gaveston's relationship is a sexual one, and considerable variation on the extent to which the sexuality of the relationship is considered central to the play. While a number of early twentieth-century critics either avoided or overlooked the topic of sexuality in their accounts of the play, Mills is an early critic who stands out in addressing the issue, albeit to argue that there is no suggestion of homosexuality in the play, but rather of a classical sensibility of male friendship with which modernity has lost touch: "The endearing terms in friendship stories result from the glorification of the passion in philosophy and literature; Marlowe has merely borrowed from such literature that means of presenting Edward and Gaveston as devoted friends; and Elizabethans understood the method better than most readers of Marlowe do today."[31] Mills does not have a great deal of company in claiming that no homosexual relationship exists in the play, but several early to mid-twentieth-century critics who believed that there was one were able nonetheless to dismiss the importance of it. Berdan, for instance, remarks, "That … sexual perversion occurs in the play is plainly stated, more plainly than in Fabian or Holinshed. Yet the play is by no means a study of sexual perversion. It is quite possible that we of today emphasize a trait that was

---

[28] Leech, "Power and Suffering," 191.

[29] Leonora Leet Brodwin, "*Edward II*: Marlowe's Culminating Treatment of Love," *English Literary History* 31, no. 2 (1964): 153.

[30] See Hopkins, *Christopher Marlowe, Renaissance Dramatist*, 66–74, for an account of the recent performance history of the play. Of particular interest with regard to sexuality in stage or screen versions is Derek Jarman's 1991 film adaptation, and his accompanying book, *Queer Edward II* (London: British Film Institute, 1991). Jarman, in his own words, "violates" a "dusty old play" in order to make an explicit and provocative attack on contemporary British attitudes towards homosexuality (10).

[31] Mills, "The Meaning of *Edward II*," 16.

somewhat casual in the Renaissance."[32] Douglas Cole, while acknowledging that Gaveston's affection for the king is not "free from overtones of homosexuality," relegates his discussion of it to a footnote,[33] and the matter is brushed over with similar brevity or avoided completely in important discussions of the play by critics such as Leech, Ribner and Steane.[34]

Of course, these approaches to the issue of homosexuality in the play say as much about the time in which they were taken as they do about the play itself. As homosexuality very gradually became less taboo as a subject of academic or artistic consideration through the latter half of the century, initially tentative but increasingly frank discussions of Edward and Gaveston's relationship began to appear alongside productions of the play, such as that directed by Tony Robertson in 1958, that foregrounded its homoeroticism.[35] In 1957 Harold Levin suggested that "to ignore the presence of such [homoerotic] motivation in *Edward II*, as most of its critics discreetly tend to do, is to distort the meaning of the play,"[36] while ten years later Roma Gill stated more forcefully that "A nice discretion has usually turned the eyes of critics away from the homosexual heart of *Edward II*, but it is this that gives the play its meaning and this, most probably, that prompted Marlowe's choice of Edward's reign for the subject of his tragedy."[37] The centrality of homosexuality to the play proposed here by Gill is representative of the modern critical consensus to the extent that it is difficult to find critical writing on *Edward II* from the last thirty years that does not discuss it.

While the play stops short of making explicit reference to a sexual relationship between Gaveston and the king, there is strong suggestion of it from the very beginning of the play. Upon reading Edward's letter in the first scene, Gaveston joyously soliloquizes:

---

[32] Berdan, "Marlowe's *Edward II*," 199.

[33] Cole, *Suffering and Evil*, 163, n. 3.

[34] In "Power and Suffering," Leech mentions that Gaveston intends "to exploit Edward's homosexual leanings," but this is the extent of the discussion of the issue (187). Irving Ribner's "Marlowe's *Edward II* and the Tudor History Play," *English Literary History* 22, no. 4 (1955) makes no mention of sexuality whatsoever. In *Marlowe: A Critical Study*, Steane's discussion of sexuality in the play extends to acknowledging that the first half of it deals with "the homosexual king and his favourite," and stating of Edward and Gaveston's relationship that "the thing is seen as a degenerating force" (205, 234).

[35] For a brief and useful account of the development of critical discussions and theatrical representations of homoeroticism in *Edward II*, see Alan Stewart, "*Edward II* and Male Same-Sex desire," in *Early Modern English Drama: A Companion*, ed. Garrett A. Sullivan Jr., Patrick Cheney and Andrew Hadfield (Oxford: Oxford University Press, 2006), 82–6.

[36] Levin, *The Overreacher*, 116.

[37] Gill, introduction, 28. Around the same time articles began to appear which specifically discussed sexuality and homoeroticism in the play. Examples of these are Brodwin's "Marlowe's Culminating Treatment of Love" and Purvis E. Boyette's "Wanton Humour and Wanton Poets: Homosexuality in Marlowe's *Edward II*," *Tulane Studies in English* 22 (1977).

> What greater bliss can hap to Gaveston
> Than live and be the favourite of a king?
> Sweet prince, I come. These, these thy amorous lines
> Might have enforced me to have swum from France,
> And, like Leander, gasped upon the sand,
> So thou wouldst smile and take me in thy arms.
> (1. 1. 4–9)

While the epithet "sweet" is not uncommon between male friends in Marlowe's work – it appears in this context in both *Dido* and *Tamburlaine* – Gaveston's description of Edward's letter as "amorous" and the erotically charged image of a glistening Leander panting on the beach (an image which prefigures Edward's lack of traditionally masculine leadership qualities by analogously gendering him as the female partner in a heterosexual relationship) establishes a highly suggestive set of associations which informs all further reference to their relationship. As we have seen, Isabella's expression of her grievance with her husband is similarly suggestive of a sexual relationship taking place between him and Gaveston:

> For now my lord the king regards me not,
> But dotes upon the love of Gaveston.
> He claps his cheeks and hangs about his neck,
> Smiles in his face and whispers in his ears,
> And when I come, he frowns, as who should say
> 'Go whither thou wilt, seeing I have Gaveston'.
> (1. 2. 49–54)

Later, Isabella accentuates this suggestion by alluding to Jupiter's pederastic relationship with his young cup-bearer, lamenting that "never doted Jove on Ganymede / So much as he on cursèd Gaveston" (1. 4. 180–81). Nevertheless, Mills suggests that such a consideration of lines like these is anachronistic:

> The use of such endearing terms seems extravagant and unreal to modern readers; but it is unnecessary to find any other explanation for them than the background furnished by the friendship literature previous to Marlowe. Passionate actions and terms are used to portray devoted friendships; the type of language associated today with love and lovers appears in sixteenth-century friendship situations. The origin of the fact is to be found in Greek philosophy.[38]

Mills's friendship model is undermined by the fact that the precedents by which it claims authority are themselves homoerotic. Mills in particular singles out Plato, whose *Symposium* comprises several discourses on male-male love, of which, it is taken for granted, sex is a part: genuine male friendship evolves out of an initially pederastic relationship between a mature and knowledgeable man and an adolescent beloved. In this case the discussion is brought to life when a drunken Alcibiades arrives at the Symposium and chastises Socrates out of sexual jealousy

---

[38] Mills, "The Meaning of *Edward II*," 15–16.

before giving an account of his first attempts to seduce him.[39] The episode between Alcibiades and Socrates is a particularly apt example, given that their relationship is one of those cited by Mortimer Senior as a noble precedent for that enjoyed by Edward and Gaveston. The affectionate language exchanged between the king and his favourite may be derived from a noble tradition of male friendship discourse, but that discourse is itself bound up with homoeroticism; the citation of Plato as a precedent strengthens rather than undermines the case for the interpretation of Edward and Gaveston's relationship as sexual. Ultimately, there seems to be too much suggestion in the play for one not to take that interpretative step; like the method of Edward's murder, itself a barbaric parody of sexual pleasures in which he has indulged, the sexual nature of the relationship is never explicitly stated, but is so heavily implied as to be beyond reasonable doubt.

What is perhaps more interesting, and certainly more difficult to resolve, is the extent to which the apparent homosexuality of Edward and Gaveston's relationship is central to the play, and what kind of response it would have provoked from a contemporary audience. Indeed, central to these questions is a further one: was there such a thing as an early modern homosexual? A groundswell of intellectual opinion, largely since the publication of Michel Foucault's *The History of Sexuality*, the first volume of which appeared in 1976, suggests that there wasn't; while the homosexual act has been in existence since time immemorial, homosexuality as a defining category, Foucault suggests, does not emerge until the nineteenth century. At the time Marlowe wrote *Edward II* (and in the time the play depicts), male-male sex was a sin, but not one which constituted a separate kind of identity for its perpetrators; it was something you did, not something which determined who you were.[40] As Ed Cohen states, "Since sodomy was never conceived of as the antithesis of any normative sexual standard, it was perceived to be a ubiquitous, nonprocreative possibility resulting from the sinfulness of human nature."[41] Indeed, there is evidence to suggest that, despite legislation introduced in 1533 by Henry VIII which declared sodomy a capital crime, sexual activity between males in Marlowe's time was fairly common and dealt with leniently by the authorities.[42] This much is evinced by cases such as that of Nicholas Udall, author of *Ralph Roister Doister* and headmaster at Eton, whose sentence for sodomizing two of his pupils was less than a year in prison, and whose career as a schoolmaster and author continued to flourish afterwards.[43]

---

[39] Plato, *The Symposium*, trans. W. Hamilton (London: Penguin, 1951). For Alcibiades and Socrates see 96–114.

[40] See Smith, *Homosexual Desire in Shakespeare's England*, 1–29, and DiGangi, *The Homoerotics of Early Modern Drama*, 1–28. In this chapter I use the term "homosexuality" to refer to male-male sexual practice rather than to a modern conceptual category.

[41] Ed Cohen, "Legislating the Norm: From Sodomy to Gross Indecency," *South Atlantic Quarterly* 88, no. 1 (1989): 183.

[42] Gill, introduction, 28.

[43] "Sodomy" is another theoretically loaded term. Ed Cohen uses it to refer to legal definitions of homosexual and other non-procreative sexual acts such as masturbation or heterosexual anal sex, and the practice of these. DiGangi, however, argues that "sodomy"

One might suspect from this that an audience might have reacted to a play incorporating an apparently sexual relationship between two men with no more shock than to one containing murder or any other crime or vice, but it is important to note that while homosexuality was not a constitutive category, and while the state was permissive in its approach to punitive action against it, homosexual sex was nonetheless unequivocally sinful. As such, some critics have insisted that the presence of a homosexual relationship in the play is an instance of Marlowe's attempt to court controversy, whether for sensation's sake or in order to make a coherent subversive statement on contemporary social strictures. Wilbur Sanders, in his polemical reading of the play, suggests that we may assume

> that there is a path leading directly from the weak be-minioned king of *The Massacre* to King Edward II, and that to see a common preoccupation with homosexual friendship in both plays is not a post-Freudian delusion, but the kind of thing a contemporary might have noticed ... It is thus, from an historical point of view, entirely possible that Marlowe was attracted to the reign of Edward by the opportunity it offered him to treat a forbidden sexual deviation.[44]

Implying that Marlowe has no artistic control over his impulses, Sanders asks "Does he, in short, use the homosexual motif, or does it use him?"[45] Rather than

---

is a political term that implies "homosexuality" in combination with subversion. He states that "'Sodomy' is not a politically neutral term: it always signifies social disorder of a frightening magnitude, and as such occupies one end on a spectrum of practices signified by the politically neutral term 'homoeroticism.'" "Marlowe, Queer Studies and Renaissance Homoeroticism," in *Marlowe, History and Sexuality: New Critical Essays on Christopher Marlowe*, ed. Paul Whitfield White (New York: AMS, 1998), 197. Alan Bray makes a similar argument, suggesting that sodomy was not just a sexual but "a political and a religious crime," and that the lack of distinction between the signs of male friendship and those of homosexual relationships meant that sodomy was a charge that could easily be brought against a political enemy; "[The accusation of sodomy] could turn what seemed like gifts into bribes and what seemed like patronage into the support of infamy; it revealed what they really were. If successful it turned all to ruin, and it could work its alchemy by a manipulation of the signs of friendship which it found so ready to hand." "Homosexuality and the Signs of Male Friendship in Elizabethan England," *History Workshop Journal* 29, no. 1 (1990): 13–14. See also Bredbeck, *Sodomy and Interpretation*, 3–30. In this chapter I have endeavoured to be mindful of these implications when using the term. On Nicholas Udall see Marie Rutkoski, "Breeching the Boy," 295, and Matthew Steggle, "Udall, Nicholas (1504–1556)," *Oxford Dictionary of National Biography* (Oxford: Oxford University Press, 2004); online ed., October 2006, <http://www.oxforddnb.com/view/article/27974> (accessed 16 July 2013).

[44] Sanders, *The Dramatist and the Received Idea*, 123. Sanders's perception of a path from *Massacre* to *Edward II* is a valid one: a number of similarities exist between the two plays and in particular between Edward and Henry III. Both kings keep favourites, and share strikingly similar dialogue; the anti-papal passages quoted earlier from both plays are a case in point, and Edward's exasperated outburst "Was ever king thus overruled as I?" (1. 4. 38) closely echoes Henry's "Ne'er was there king of France so yok'd as I" (21. 115).

[45] Ibid., 125.

imply an unhealthy and artistically redundant fascination with sexual deviance on Marlowe's part, Purvis Boyette credits the dramatist with a liberality that is ahead of his time, stating that the attitudes upheld in the play "make an enemy of every dogmatic moralist," and arguing that "[Marlowe's] strategy is to break, somewhat self-consciously, with morality, Christian or otherwise, and lead his audience dramatically into another, imagined world, different from the confining, though perhaps comforting, myths of the Elizabethan order."[46] Early modern sodomy then, is a curiously ambiguous concept. It is simultaneously an offence punishable by death and a largely permitted vice, an unspoken private pastime and a politically subversive act. This ambiguity is captured by David Riggs, who characterizes the "paradoxical status of Renaissance homosexuality" thus:

> The venerable custom of sleeping with a same-sex bedfellow, the exaltation of male friendship, the fear of being emasculated by heterosexual passion ... and the recovery of Greek and Roman gender systems, all served to legitimate homoerotic affection, especially in the universities. Love between men was intrinsic to the humanist educational programme. Yet the medieval-Christian impulse to demonize homosexual acts persisted regardless. The so-called buggers, pathics, ingles, cinaeduses, catamites, Ganymedes and sodomites who performed such acts were still regarded with horror and disgust.[47]

This early modern ambivalence regarding sodomy both as a practice and as a politically and religiously charged concept is reflected in the response of the play's characters to Edward and Gaveston's almost certainly sexual friendship. Isabella is the first to express a grievance about the erotic aspect of Edward and Gaveston's friendship, yet this grievance might be said to be more centred on Edward's infidelity and lack of attention bestowed on her than on the gender of his paramour. Similarly, it is unclear to what extent the nobles' grievances are predicated on the sexual nature of Edward's favouritism. Mortimer, in particular, does seem to express reservations at the nature of the king's preference for Gaveston: in response to Isabella's complaints he asks "is it not strange that he is thus bewitched?" (1. 2. 55), and he directs spiteful mockery at the distraught king when he is forced to agree to the banishment of his favourite, sneering that "The king is lovesick for his minion" (1. 4. 87). Lancaster expresses similar distaste for Edward's emotional attachment to his favourite:

> EDWARD: Ah, had some bloodless Fury rose from hell,
> And with my kingly sceptre struck me dead
> When I was forced to leave my Gaveston!
> LANCASTER: *Diablo!* what passions call you these?
> (1. 4. 315–18)

Yet, in the passage in which Mortimer Senior attempts to cool his nephew's rebellious fervour by contextualizing Edward's behaviour, Mortimer claims not to

---

[46] Boyette, "Wanton Humour and Wanton Poets," 33, 35.
[47] Riggs, *The World of Christopher Marlowe*, 74.

be concerned by Edward and Gaveston's private pastimes, but by the disruption of the order of the realm that is caused by the favourite's hold on the monarch:

> MORTIMER SENIOR: The mightiest kings have had their minions:
> Great Alexander loved Hephaestion;
> The conquering Hercules for Hylas wept;
> And for Patroclus stern Achilles drooped.
> And not kings only, but the wisest men:
> The Roman Tully loved Octavius,
> Grave Socrates, wild Alcibiades.
> Then let his grace, whose youth is flexible
> And promiseth as much as we can wish,
> Freely enjoy that vain light-headed earl,
> For riper years will wean him from such toys.
> MORTIMER JUNIOR: Uncle, his wanton humour grieves not me,
> But this I scorn – that one so basely born
> Should by his sovereign's favour grow so pert
> And riot it with the treasure of the realm
> While soldiers mutiny for want of pay.
> (1. 4. 390–405)

Mortimer Senior's liberal appraisal of the situation, and his invocation of the authority of classical precedent (mythical and historical) call to mind the kind of humanist attitude to homoeroticism which Riggs claims was prevalent in the universities. Furthermore, his suggestion that Edward's fascination with Gaveston is an ephemeral symptom of his youth implies the conception, discussed earlier, of homosexual practice as one among many vices, rather than something which defines an identity incompatible with monarchy. Mortimer's response indicates that he shares this view, but that his grievance is with poor leadership caused by Gaveston's distraction of Edward. In Brodwin's words, "Gaveston is not objected to because of his sex but because he is an irresponsible influence upon the king."[48] Boyette attributes a similar view to Marlowe himself, stating that "While [he] fails to stigmatize homosexuality, he sees Edward's impolitic favouritism to be a threat to the established order."[49] Indeed, Mortimer's concern at the negligent governance of the realm is illustrated by his reference to the lavishing of riches on Gaveston while soldiers starve, and later in the play when he and his co-conspirators confront the king with a conflated account of his political ineptitude (2. 2. 156–94).

It is telling, however, that Mortimer's response to his uncle mentions the lowness of Gaveston's birth before it does his influence over the king. This is typical of a number of exchanges in the play; Gaveston's social status is highlighted repeatedly by the barons throughout, a trend which is begun by Lancaster only one hundred lines into proceedings:

---

[48] Brodwin, "Marlowe's Culminating Treatment of Love," 140.
[49] Boyette, "Wanton Humour and Wanton Poets," 47.

> My lord, why do you thus incense your peers,
> That naturally would love and honour you
> But for that base and obscure Gaveston?
> (1. 1. 98–100)

References of this kind made by the faction of nobles continue to occur at a high frequency, often expressing indignation at the king's bestowal of favours upon one whose station is so far beneath his own.[50] There is some critical disagreement as to the extent to which Marlowe foregrounds the low social station of Edward's favourites. Gill suggests that he does so quite intentionally, arguing that "Gaveston and his two successors in Edward's favour could all claim higher birth than Marlowe has attributed to them, and the dependence of Spencer and Baldock on the Earl of Gloucester is entirely the dramatist's invention. In this way Marlowe develops a theme only latent in the histories."[51] Some more recent critics – whose stance is that the opposition of the nobles is predominantly a reaction to the king's status as a sodomite – have argued against this position, however. Emily Bartels, for example, states that "We are wrong to assume, as critics have, that the play has necessarily rewritten history to lower [Gaveston's] status and to exacerbate the problem of his rise, for it is only the discourse of the opposition that proffers that conclusion."[52] If it were the case that only the discourse of the opposition highlights the social inferiority of Gaveston, this would not alter the fact that social hierarchy is foregrounded as a theme considerably more in Marlowe's play than it is in his sources.[53] Yet it is misleading to claim that Gaveston's social status is an issue only addressed by the opposition; Gaveston himself scornfully acknowledges the reason for their animosity:

> Base leaden earls that glory in your birth,
> Go sit at home and eat your tenants' beef,
> And come not here to scoff at Gaveston,
> Whose mounting thoughts did never creep so low
> As to bestow a look on such as you.
> (2. 2. 74–8)

---

[50] Examples of this include the following: "We'ld hale him from the bosom of the king, / And at the court gate hang the peasant up" (1. 2. 29–30); "What man of noble birth can brook this sight? / *Quam male conveniunt!* / See what a scornful look the peasant casts" (1. 4. 12–14); "Then speak not for him; let the peasant go" (1. 4. 218).

[51] Gill, introduction, 21.

[52] Bartels, *Spectacles of Strangeness*, 164.

[53] Viviana Comensoli argues a similar course to Bartels, suggesting that the Mortimers' relegation of Gaveston and Edward's sodomy to a position of less importance than their general mistreatment of the realm is the result of a feeling that the social threat (if not the physical reality) of their sodomy has been abated by Gaveston's recent marriage, since "As long as heterosexuality is officially, if not privately, practiced sodomy is a containable threat." This argument seems to overlook the fact that Edward is married, and as such an official practiser of heterosexuality and a containable threat, throughout the play. See "Homophobia and the Regulation of Desire: A Psychoanalytic Reading of Marlowe's *Edward II*," *Journal of the History of Sexuality* 4, no. 2 (1993): 191.

While Gaveston clearly thinks himself his opponents' superior, he is well aware of the arbitrary code of hereditary nobility which dictates that they are his betters, a point he illustrates in his very first speech when he bids farewell to "base stooping to the lordly peers" (1. 1. 18). In Boyette's words, "The barons enjoy their wealth and place by accident of birth, a fortuity Gaveston disdains, since he must rise by other means. Full of self-interest, the barons hate Gaveston because the King has preferred him, taking from them that which is theirs by natural rights of lineage."[54] It would be to deny what is clearly a central theme of the play to suggest that only the sexual nature of Gaveston and Edward's relationship, and not the issue of a "night-grown mushroom" (1. 4. 284) overleaping his station through a monarch's favouritism, is at the centre of the conflict here. Yet, doubtless as a response to early twentieth-century readings of the play which subdued its sexual elements, much modern criticism has tended to focus discussion almost exclusively on sexuality in the play.[55] Clearly, social hierarchy and its disruption is central to *Edward II*, and cannot be overlooked in an account of the play.

This is not to say, as Logan does, that "no one in the play seems bothered by the specific sexual nature of Edward's and Gaveston's relationship."[56] The barons hate Gaveston because the king has preferred him above them, but this is not the only reason they hate him. The play's discourse of sexuality and sodomitical male friendship is as amplified from the sources as are problems of social climbing, and it is most likely impossible to understand these two themes of the play in isolation from one another. Rather, sexuality, friendship, social hierarchy and kingship form a nexus of anxieties in the play, converging and overlapping to form the competing world views which are at the heart of the play's irreconcilable conflict. In the remaining section of this chapter I will examine how Marlowe exploits the moral and thematic ambiguity of the play to interrogate competing conceptualizations of hierarchical order that are each understood as natural but which are nonetheless incompatible.

Unity, Hierarchy and Natural Orders

Edward II's discussion of social hierarchy is not limited entirely to the nobles' grievances with Gaveston and his responses to them, but pervades the entirety of the play. As early as the opening scene, we are introduced to hierarchical concerns when Gaveston encounters three poor men seeking his patronage whom he clearly

---

[54] Boyette, "Wanton Humour and Wanton Poets," 37.
[55] See, for example, Bartels, *Spectacles of Strangeness*, 143–72; Boyette, "Wanton Humour and Wanton Poets"; Comensoli, "Homophobia and the Regulation of Desire"; J. A. Porter, "Marlowe, Shakespeare, and the Canonization of Heterosexuality," *South Atlantic Quarterly* 88, no. 1 (1989); Albert Rouzie, "The Dangers of (D)alliance: Power, Homosexual Desire, and Homophobia in Marlowe's *Edward II*," *Genders* 21 (August 1995): 139–40; and Marie Rutkoski, "Breeching the Boy."
[56] Logan, *Shakespeare's Marlowe*, 95.

regards with distaste, declaring as they leave "These are not men for me" and going on to state his preference for the extravagances of court entertainment (1. 1. 49).[57] Upon the introduction of Spencer and Baldock the audience's attention is drawn to the social standing of the two new characters, initially by highlighting their need for a new patron after the death of the Earl of Gloucester, and subsequently by Spencer's distribution of advice to Baldock on how to win favour from his social superiors:

> Then, Baldock, you must cast the scholar off
> And learn to court it like a gentleman.
> 'Tis not a black coat and a little band,
> A velvet-caped cloak, faced before with serge,
> And smelling to a nosegay all the day,
> Or holding of a napkin in your hand,
> Or saying a long grace at a table's end,
> Or making low legs to a nobleman,
> Or looking downward with your eyelids close,
> And saying 'truly, an't please your honour,'
> Can get you any favour with great men.
> You must be proud, bold, pleasant, resolute –
> And now and then stab, as occasion serves.
> (2. 1. 31–43)

The subject is revived when Baldock meets with the king:

> EDWARD: Tell me, where wast thou born? What is thine arms?
> BALDOCK: My name is Baldock, and my gentry
>   I fetched from Oxford, not from heraldry.
> (2. 2. 241–3)

Baldock's declaration that his status as a gentleman comes not from birth but from his university education resonates both with Marlowe's own social position[58] and with Gaveston's disdain for the nobility arbitrarily glorying in their birth. The king himself joins in this discourse later in the same scene, when he declares that "The headstrong barons shall not limit me; / He that I list to favour shall be great" (2. 2. 261–2), a statement which, Claude J. Summers writes, attacks "the entire

---

[57] A contemporary audience is likely to have associated Gaveston's description of the "lascivious shows" he will stage for Edward with the Elizabethan court elite, if one accepts Harold Levin's statement that "Marlowe's anachronistic Gaveston, in anticipation of such entertainments as the Earl of Leicester gave for Queen Elizabeth at Kenilworth, becomes a lord of misrule, a master of the revels, as well as a stage manager of palace intrigue." *The Overreacher*, 114.

[58] Levin draws a parallel between Marlowe and Baldock, suggesting that it "is as if a painter, half in earnest and half in jest, had painted himself in the corner of some panoramic canvas." See *The Overreacher*, 127–8.

concept of nobility."⁵⁹ In each case, status is imagined as emanating from a source other than hereditary nobility: for Baldock and Spencer status is the product of merit or performance, while for Edward it is an honour which he, as absolute ruler, should be free to bestow arbitrarily.

A crucial aspect of *Edward II* is that its extensive treatment of hierarchy is inextricably bound up with images of nature, and of its disruption and subversion. The play abounds with animal imagery, in most cases employed (by both parties) comparatively in order to illustrate the hierarchical gulf between two characters. Edward repeatedly figures himself as a lion, king of beasts and a traditional symbol of royalty, in his exasperated condemnations of the barons' audacity, as in the following instance after they have openly criticized his conduct:

> Yet, shall the crowing of these cockerels
> Affright a lion? Edward, unfold thy paws
> And let their lives' blood slake thy fury's hunger.
> (2. 2. 202–4)

Later in the play, when Edward is encouraged to feel his grief less acutely by his jailor, Leicester, he responds in the same vein:

> The griefs of private men are soon allayed,
> But not of kings. The forest deer, being struck,
> Runs to an herb that closeth up the wounds;
> But when the imperial lion's flesh is gored,
> He rends and tears it with his wrathful paw,
> And highly scorning that the lowly earth
> Should drink his blood, mounts up into the air.
> (5. 1. 8–14)

The barons express their outrage at the station of Edward's choice of favourite using similar terms: Pembroke asks "Can kingly lions fawn on creeping ants?" (1. 4. 15), and even Gaveston employs the same rhetorical tactic to dismiss the chastisement of the three poor men:

> Ay, ay. These words of his move me as much
> As if a goose should play the porcupine,
> And dart her plumes, thinking to pierce my breast.
> (1. 1. 38–40)

This conceit assumes an ironic effect towards the end of the play, when Edward's representation of himself becomes gradually less puissant: first Edward becomes a "lamb, encompassèd by wolves" (5. 1. 41), a figuration which Mortimer reverses by referring to Edward as "an old wolf" (5. 2. 7), and later, when he is being shaved in puddle water and his degradation is almost complete, he muses that

---

⁵⁹ Claude J. Summers, "Sex, Politics and Self-Realization in *Edward II*," in *"A Poet and a Filthy Playmaker": New Essays on Christopher Marlowe*, ed. Kenneth Friedenreich, Roma Gill and Constance Brown Kuriyama (New York: AMS, 1988), 226.

> The wren may strive against the lion's strength,
> But all in vain; so vainly do I strive
> To seek for mercy at a tyrant's hand.
> (5. 3. 34–6)

His submission of the crown is prefigured by his submission of the figurative association with the regal lion to his opponents.[60]

These natural references spread further. When Edward demands to know the meaning of the emblems on the shields carried by Lancaster and Mortimer, Lancaster's explication – of a depiction of a fish rising out of the water only to be seized by a fowl – engages in a similar discourse to the instances quoted above, while Mortimer's uses a more botanical allegory:

> A lofty cedar tree fair flourishing,
> On whose top branches kingly eagles perch,
> And by the bark a canker creeps me up
> And gets unto the highest bough of all;
> The motto: *Æque tandem*.
> (2. 2.16–20)

Here the state is figured as a cedar tree, an imposing specimen at the top of the vegetable kingdom's hierarchical structure, with a creeping canker, undoubtedly representing Gaveston, working its way to the top and corrupting that work of nature as it goes.[61] The kingly eagles and the cankerworm, according to Mortimer's emblem, belong at the opposite ends of the tree that is their host, and when all is equal (*Æque tandem*), nature is corrupted. Similarly, Spencer, according to the nobles' herald, is "a putrifying branch / That deads the royal vine" (3. 1. 162–3), and Mortimer, at the height of his power, announces: "As for myself, I stand as Jove's huge tree, / And others are but shrubs compared to me" (5. 6. 11–12).

The play's hierarchical imagery is crowned by the numerous references to the sun, a traditional trope for sovereignty in early modern literature, and also foremost in the celestial world, as the ferocious lion and lofty cedar are in their own respective realms. As Deats states, reference to the sun "illumines the play's imagery, its

---

[60] See Levin, *The Overreacher*, 117.

[61] The cedar tree appears frequently in early modern literature as a byword for immensity, and, as in this case, at times as a trope for matters of state. Richard Edwards adopts the cedar to discuss the dangers of great power: "The higher that the cedar tree, unto the heauens do grow, / the more in daungers is the top, when sturdy windes gan blow: / Who iudges then in Princely throne, to be deuoide of hate, / Doth not yet know what heapes of ill, lyes his in suche estate." *The Paradise of Daintie Devices* (London: 1585), STC (2nd ed.) / 7520, Sig. L2. Thomas Lodge, like Marlowe's Mortimer, uses the image of the cedar beset by a canker to help depict an imperfect society: "I but thou wilte saye, that as the cleerest Christall hath his crack, the fairest day his clowde, the tallest Cedar his worme, the greenest Cicuta his poysen, so Cittyes cannot be without sinnes, nor monarchies without mischiefes." *Euphues Shadow, The Battaile of the Sences* (London: 1592), STC (2nd ed.) / 16656, Sig. B3.

rising and falling carefully co-ordinated with the ascensions and declensions of the leading historical players."[62] Again, this trope is employed primarily in a self-glorifying manner by Edward, but like those discussed above, it also serves his opponents, and eventually allows the king, in a moment of anagnorisis, to reflect on his own downfall. Those self-aggrandizing uses of the image by Edward tend to be related to his bestowing of favour, as in the scene in which he is temporarily reconciled with the nobles and offers a purifying embrace to Lancaster:

> Courageous Lancaster, embrace thy king,
> And as gross vapours perish by the sun,
> Even so let hatred with thy sovereign's smile:
> Live thou with me as my companion.
> (1. 4. 339–42)

The image recurs later, when he rewards Spencer Senior for his loyalty and provision of troops:

> Spencer, I here create thee Earl of Wiltshire,
> And daily will enrich thee with our favour
> That, as the sunshine, shall reflect o'er thee.
> (3. 1. 49–51)

Baldock employs the same rhetorical tactic later in the play when Edward is seized by the nobles, exclaiming: "We are deprived the sunshine of our life" (4. 7. 106). Just as Edward goes from regal lion to surrounded lamb, however, Marlowe also enacts what Cole calls an "inversion of the traditional sun-image used in Elizabethan poetic description of the state and function of kingship,"[63] when he has Edward forlornly ask

> But what are kings, when regiment is gone
> But perfect shadows in a sunshine day?
> (5. 1. 26–7)

The baronial faction turns the image against Edward and his favourite when Warwick taunts Gaveston with an inauspicious mythological analogy:

> Ignoble vassal, that like Phaeton
> Aspir'st unto the guidance of the sun.
> (1. 4. 16–17)

The political implications of Warwick's analogy are clear: Phaëthon's ill-prepared attempt to emulate his father's role as driver of the sun results in the scorching of the land. The concept of hierarchy, then, is figured in images of nature that, ranging from vegetation to the celestial sun, imply a unitary overarching natural order – a great chain of being. The application of images of natural order by

---

[62] Deats, "Marlowe's Fearful Symmetry," 257.
[63] Cole, *Suffering and Evil*, 175.

both factions has a similar function to Ferneze's attribution of his victory to the will of God; by figuring their own conception of social order in terms of natural cosmological order, each faction by definition asserts any subversion of it to be unnatural. Thus, the barons compare the king's favouring of a social inferior to perversions of nature such as lions fawning on ants, fish attempting to live out of water and mighty trees being scaled by cankers. Indeed, the peers are at times explicit in their suggestion of what is natural and what is not. In his above-quoted complaint, for example, Lancaster suggests that the unnatural behaviour of the king has alienated the barons, who "naturally would love and honour" him (1. 1. 99). Later, Warwick declares Edward's insistence upon his personal relationship with Gaveston being more important to him than the well-being of the realm to be a "desperate and unnatural resolution" (3. 2. 33). In turn, Edward's faction draws similar conclusions regarding the willingness of the nobles – "Inhuman creatures, nursed with tiger's milk" (5. 1. 71) – to confront their sovereign; Isabella, before she has decisively switched her allegiance and affection to Mortimer, laments the "Unnatural wars, where subjects brave their king" (3. 1. 86),[64] and is later described by her husband as "that unnatural queen, false Isabel" (5. 1. 17). The wavering Kent engages in this discourse of (un)naturalness whilst on either side of the divide, initially when defecting to Mortimer:

> Nature, yield to my country's cause in this.
> A brother – no, a butcher of thy friends –
> Proud Edward, dost thou banish me thy presence?
> But I'll to France and cheer the wrongèd queen,
> And certify what Edward's looseness is.
> Unnatural king, to slaughter noblemen
> And cherish flatterers.
> (4. 1. 3–9)

And later when reflecting on his own treachery:

> Rain showers of vengeance on my cursèd head,
> Thou God, to whom in justice it belongs
> To punish this unnatural revolt.
> (4. 6. 7–9)

Nature, then, is bound up in the politics of what is, contrary to a great deal of critical opinion, a deeply political play.[65] The emblematic natural imagery of the

---

[64] The sincerity of this lament is debateable if one accepts the position adopted by Summers and Anderson, which holds that Isabella's character does not make a seismic shift in the middle of the play but is consistently Machiavellian throughout. Notwithstanding, if this is the case then Isabella is adept enough a politician to adopt the appropriate rhetoric of Edward's faction.

[65] Until the late twentieth century it was a critical commonplace that the play is not primarily concerned with political issues. Statements such as the following are typical: "For Marlowe, the concept of England means little ... and he cared only for what happened to the individual human being. He was interested in Edward, not as embodying a suffering

play, exemplified by the scene in which Mortimer and Lancaster explicate the devices on their shields in the style of the emblem books that were in vogue at the time,[66] is highly suggestive of Elizabethan iconographical state propaganda.[67] Mark Thornton Burnett, while acknowledging that the play does not constitute a unilateral political allegory or analogy, nevertheless states that "the rhythms of the play articulate some of the political uncertainties for which the Elizabethan court was noted" and that it "bristles with sixteenth-century political preoccupations," to the extent that, in direct contradiction of the numerous early and mid-twentieth-century critics who argued that *Edward II* is primarily a personal play, "The state of England is *Edward II*'s essential subject."[68] Among the resonant contemporary issues identified by Burnett are the increased social mobility of the Elizabethan age and, in line with Berdan's unusually political early twentieth-century reading of the play,[69] the crisis facing a nation governed by an ageing heirless monarch whose most likely successor seemed to be James VI of Scotland, a head of state with a reputation for the irresponsible patronage of male favourites and a philosophy of absolutist monarchy.

In point of fact, the distinction made by critics between the personal and the political in *Edward II* is itself problematic. While Edward undoubtedly desires to abandon political responsibility in favour of frolicking in some "nook or corner" (1. 4. 72) with Gaveston, the fact of his kingship makes him one with the realm, and as such his every action is by necessity political.[70] This is not just a play about

---

England, but as a man, a man who had lost power," Leech, "Power and Suffering," 187; "Marlowe ... is not concerned with the state but, as always, with the individual; and, in this case, it is a poignant irony that the individual happens to be the head of state," Levin, *The Overreacher*, 110; "*Edward II* is narrowly personal: the people are small, and beyond them is nothing greater. England and the realm are sometimes mentioned, but they are not emotionally or dramatically involved," Steane, *Marlowe: A Critical Study*, 222; "Perhaps the most remarkable thing about Marlowe's *Edward II* is the fact that, although it has every appearance of being a play on a national and political theme, a play about kingship, it is yet an intensely personal play in which the public issues hardly arise," Sanders, *The Dramatist and the Received Idea*, 121.

[66] Manuel J. Gomez Lara, in "Ambiguous Devices: The Use of Dramatic Emblems in Marlowe's *Edward II* (1592)," *Sederi* 15 (2005), suggests that Marlowe makes use of the didactic quality of the emblem book in order to encourage the audience to consider contemporary political concerns: "the emblematic references seem to invite the spectators to detach themselves from the fictional plot and to evaluate the events as part of the complexities of state politics, including those which were a serious concern during the last decade of Elizabeth's reign" (111).

[67] See Mark Thornton Burnett, "*Edward II* and Elizabethan Politics," in *Marlowe, History and Sexuality: New Critical Essays on Christopher Marlowe*, ed. Paul Whitfield White (New York: AMS, 1998), 93.

[68] Ibid., 97, 104, 103.

[69] See Berdan, "Marlowe's *Edward II*."

[70] This statement takes on added significance if one considers Edward's actions to be sodomitical, since sodomy, as distinct from a physical homoerotic act, is itself a political concept. See DiGangi, "Marlowe, Queer Studies, and Renaissance Homoeroticism."

a man, or a man who happens to be a king, but a play about kingship. As Berdan writes, the "conception of a state distinct from the personality of the monarch ... was not generally understood."[71] This unity of king and realm, and the impact the actions of the former have on the latter, is something that the baronial faction, and even those closer to Edward, continually remind him of throughout the play; its rhetoric repeatedly collocates references to the king with mention of the realm. This feature of the play is typified by remarks made by Lancaster, who admonishes the king by demanding: "Learn then to rule us better and the realm" (1. 4. 39), and Mortimer, who, when speaking of the motives for allowing Gaveston's return to England, maintains "'Tis not for his sake, but for our avail – / Nay, for the realm's behoof and for the king's" (1. 4. 242–3). The arguably more genuine concern of Kent manifests itself in similar rhetoric, when he warns: "My lord, I see your love to Gaveston / Will be the ruin of the realm and you" (2. 2. 207–8).[72] Critics who suggest that Marlowe's interest in the play is purely personal would seem to be substituting him for Edward – Edward's interests are personal, but the play's are undoubtedly political. That is not to say, however, that Edward does not have a conception of what kingship is. Despite the barons' assertion that his responsibility to the realm obliges him to check his excesses, Edward clearly believes that there should exist no restrictions to his will, *because* he is king. Irving Ribner has argued that "there is not a single reference to the divine right of kings"[73] in the play, but it is clearly this doctrine that lies at the heart of Edward's conception of his own sovereignty. While the divine right of kings as a concept is largely associated with the Stuart dynasty, its tenets were current in Elizabethan culture and were spelled out in debates between supporters of absolutist monarchy and those of rule by consent. George Whetstone, in his 1586 work *The English Myrror*, argues that

> The dignitie Royall, is so greate and holy, as kings that are protectors and defenders of humane society, imitate the prouidence of God, whose office & action is to governe al things ... And he himselfe calleth them gods: figuring in that sacred name two hie charges, the one that kings crowned with so glorious a name, should imitate God, whose lieuetenants they are: in their religion, Justice and gouernement: the other that subiectes knowing the honour that God giueth unto kings, should adore and worship them with all possible reuerence.[74]

---

[71] Berdan, "Marlowe's *Edward II*," 200–201.

[72] Further examples of this pairing include: "KENT: Brother, in regard of thee and of thy land / Did they remove that flatterer from thy throne" (3. 2. 46–7); "MORTIMER: And for the open wrongs and injuries / Edward hath done to us, his queen and land" (4. 4. 20–21); "MORTIMER: Your king hath wronged the country and himself, / And we must seek to right it as we may" (4. 6. 67–8); "MORTIMER: 'Tis for your highness' good and for the realm's" (5. 4. 98).

[73] Ribner, "Marlowe's *Edward II* and the Tudor History Play," 249.

[74] George Whetstone, *The English Myrror* (London: 1586), STC (2nd ed.) / 2336, 201. The idea is developed later in the same passage: "Christian kings are nothing so seuere [as those of Persia, India, Ethiopia and ancient Rome] towards their subiectes, but Christian subiectes are farre lesse obedient to their kings: well, euill will fal upon his house that

Where the barons view the king as chief bureaucrat in an administrative system, and ultimately accountable for his actions, Edward sees himself, along the lines of Whetstone's argument, as existing on a higher plane: he associates himself, by virtue of rhetoric that aligns him with the celestial end of the cosmic hierarchy, with God, whose divine endorsement of his reign, he feels, entitles him to unmitigated autonomy. This is evident at the beginning of the play when Edward expresses bemusement at the complaints of the nobles, exclaiming to Lancaster "Beseems it thee to contradict thy king?" (1. 1. 91), then musing to himself "Am I a king and must be overruled?" (1. 1. 134). Towards the end of the play, Edward's supporters, at their arrests, insist that no amount of state politics stops a king from being a king, firstly when Spencer defies Mortimer's naming of him as a rebel by retorting "Rebel is he that fights against his prince; / So fought not they that fought in Edward's right" (4. 6. 71–2), and secondly when Kent is seized while attempting to reach Edward at his prison:

> GOURNEY: Bind him, and so convey him to the court.
> KENT: Where is the court but here? Here is the king,
>   And I will visit him.
> (5. 3. 58–60)

Kent's objection depicts sovereign power as abstract and locates it ever with the king, rather than with the material political machinery of the state.

Rather than conceiving of a unity between himself and the realm, Edward, in the manner of classically idealized friendship, instead sees himself as one with Gaveston. The play begins with a kind of unity between the two, with Gaveston reading aloud Edward's words from a letter, and this unity is more explicitly stressed by Edward at regular intervals throughout the play. When, upon their reunion in the first scene, Gaveston kneels to Edward, the king's response suggests not just a social equality between them but a shared identity: "Why shouldst thou kneel? Knowest thou not who I am? / Thy friend, thy self, another Gaveston!" (1. 1. 141–2). When the king appears to the nobles with Gaveston beside him at his throne, his response to their outrage makes mischievously ambiguous use of what is ostensibly the royal plural: "What, are you moved that Gaveston sits here? / It is our pleasure; we will have it so" (1. 4. 8–9), and the same concept arises when his wife attempts to convince him of the good will of the barons:

> ISABELLA: Sweet husband be content; they all love you.
> EDWARD: They love me not that hate my Gaveston.
> (2. 2. 36–7)

---

resisteth against the ordinance of the king, for he *that resisteth receiueth vnto hiselfe damnation*: Yea albeit the king bee a tyrant, so long as his commaundments are not to the dishonour of God. He that resisteth because the king is a tyrant encreaseth his sinnes, and doubleth Gods wrath, who sendeth Tyrants to punish the sinnes of the wicked ... By these and many other testimonyes it is apparant, that God setteth kings in their kingdomes, by they good or euill, and will not have them remoued at their subiectes pleasure" (202).

This rhetoric conforms to early modern conceptions of male friendship typified by writers such as Montaigne, who states: "In the friendship which I am talking about souls are mingled and confounded in so universal a blending that they efface the seam which joins them together so that it cannot be found."[75] This rhetoric of unity in idealized male friendship, or *amicitia*, reflects Edward's conception of his relationship with Gaveston. Indeed, just as Spencer does with the seizure of the monarch later in the play, Edward equates any attempt to break his bond with Gaveston with a disruption of nature, insisting that

> Ere my sweet Gaveston shall part from me,
> This isle shall fleet upon the ocean
> And wander to the unfrequented Inde.
> (1. 4. 48–50)

In the same way that the nobles see social hierarchy, and that he sees the divine sponsorship of his sovereignty, so Edward understands his bond with Gaveston as an aspect of nature. As has been noted by Laurie Shannon, there is a notable similarity between the unifying rhetoric of *amicitia* and that of the monarch's relationship to the state, the former evoking a single soul occupying two bodies, and the latter one person occupying both a personal body and a body politic.[76] Yet Edward cannot at the same time be one with Gaveston and one with the realm: while in early modern conceptions of kingship the interests of the state require a monarch to subordinate private interests to those of the commonweal (as exemplified by Elizabeth's "marriage" to England), friendship doctrine requires the full investment of one's identity in another individual. In Edward's case, one doctrine requires the maintenance of the state's social order, the other the dissolution of the hierarchical gulf between a monarch and one of his subjects. This conflict is not lost on early modern commentators on friendship; Angel Day's *The English Secretorie*, for example, states that "The limits of *Frienshippe* ... are streight, and there can be no Friend where an inequality remayneth. Twixt the party commanded & him that commaundeth, there is no societie, and therefore no *Friendship* where resteth a *Superiority*."[77] This sentiment is echoed by Francis Bacon, who argues that

> It is a Strange Thing to obserue, how high a Rate, Great Kings and Monarchs, do set vpon this *Fruit of Friendship*, wherof we speake: So great, as they purchase it, many times, at the hazard of their own Safety, and Greatnesse. For Princes, in regard of the distance of their Fortune, from that of their Subiects & Seruants, cannot gather this *Fruit*; Except (to make Themselues capable thereof) they raise

---

[75] Michel de Montaigne, *On Friendship*, trans. M. A. Screech (London: Penguin, 2004), 9.

[76] Laurie J. Shannon, "Monarchs, Minions, and 'Soveraigne' Friendship," *South Atlantic Quarterly* 198 (1998): 92.

[77] Cited in Shannon, "'Soveraigne' Friendship," 95.

some Persons, to be as it were Companions, and almost Equals to themselues, which many times sorteth to Inconuenience.[78]

Edward II, then, presents us with a world that is alive with mutually incompatible conceptions of world order that were current in Marlowe's time. John F. McElroy succinctly summarizes the atmosphere of incompatibility that dominates the play by writing that "division and dissonance, polarity and contrariety, far from being incidental by-products of the plot, are finally what the [first] scene, and the play as a whole, are all about."[79] The play is filled with contradictory ideas on the extent to which a monarch is also a person, on whether the aristocracy is obliged to practise unilateral allegiance to the monarch under any circumstances and on the nature of friendship and to whom it is available. In response to this ambiguity the play's characters attempt to impose reductive and unifying orders onto their own socio-political world views which present them as natural, and thus right. The blindness of each faction to the other's point of view, and the consequently disastrous outcomes of the play, however, suggest that these unifying world views are fantasies that cannot be fully realized, and that individual wills rule over collective ideals. This is not to say that *Edward II* is, as critics such as Steane and Sanders have suggested, a play about individual wills and desires and not about politics. It is rather a play that identifies state politics as an interminable battle of individual wills, and in doing so reflects the futility of appealing to ideas of order in an age of such acute political and religious uncertainty. So fundamental is the rift between the two factions that at times there is no recourse for them but to flatly contradict one another. Perhaps the essence of the play is summed up by the following banal exchange:

> WARWICK: St George for England and the barons' right.
> EDWARD: St George for England and King Edward's right.
> (3. 2. 35–6)

The play does admittedly offer – and it is probably unique amongst the Marlowe canon in this respect – at least a sense of resolution at its close. In the final scenes, the young King Edward becomes the play's single dominant voice, administering justice to the baronial faction and restoring the balance that has been upset since the triumph of Mortimer. Yet there is something unsatisfying about this resolution. Robert Logan, for instance, notes that the young Edward's rise allows Marlowe to drop the irreconcilable and challenging conflict of the rest of the play in favour of a more conventional and comfortable conflict between good (Edward III) and evil (Mortimer and Isabella), thus suppressing his own "will to play."[80] But while this resolution may seem to compromise the complexity of the play, the young king's

---

[78] Francis Bacon, "Of Friendship," in *Essays* (London: Oxford University Press, 1937), 108.
[79] McElroy, "Repetition, Contrariety, and Individualization in *Edward II*," 214.
[80] Logan, *Shakespeare's Marlowe*, 100.

closing lines – "And let these tears, distilling from mine eyes, / Be witness of my grief and innocency" (5. 6. 100–101) – convey a sense that it is, in any case, a fragile resolution. It is precisely his "innocency" (here denoting both his ignorance of the wrongs carried out by his erstwhile protectors and, more generally, his youthful inexperience) that allows the young Edward to act outside of the fractious division that dominates the rest of the play; because of it he is not implicated in the events that have passed, and he is not yet burdened by the weight of sovereignty and its associated *realpolitik*. But as Edward utters these lines his innocence is already evaporating; he speaks them, after all, while sharing a stage with the head of Mortimer, which has been severed at his own command. If the rest of this play and the rest of Marlowe's dramatic oeuvre are anything to go by, this moment of unity will be fleeting.

Afterword

The urge to unify, or the reductive endeavour to gain understanding or control of something that is mutable and multivalent, is, this study has shown, a consistent feature of Marlowe's drama. Whether manifested in imperial designs, in pursuit of knowledge, in the construction of self-serving world views or in the employment of religion to subdue the individual wills of the members of a populace, the sense of a struggle to master and reduce diversity and ambiguity is present throughout all of the plays studied in this book. As I have argued, these struggles undertaken in the plays engage with a discourse that pervaded the cultural climate in which Marlowe wrote. An age marked by its discord, the Renaissance in Europe, and specifically the 1580s and 1590s in England, gave rise to a number of cultural and political movements motivated by a unifying ethos: from occult philosophers attempting to formulate a synthesizing system of thought which could reconcile variant forms of Christianity and incorporate classical wisdom to cartographers striving to reduce an ever expanding world to a map, Elizabethans and their European counterparts struggled to make sense of a world which they had seen steadily dismantled since the onset of the Protestant Reformation.

As I have argued throughout this book, these struggles for unity, as represented in Marlowe's drama, are always either shown to be entirely in vain or exposed as fraudulent. Marlowe's play-worlds are consistently and profoundly ambiguous; we are never given the privilege of unobstructed access to a sense of right and wrong, nor are we allowed the benefit of characters that can be summarily dismissed from or embraced by our sympathy. They are also the worlds of competing individuals, in which any sense of collective interest is repeatedly undermined by personal greed. Fracture is evident throughout the Marlovian oeuvre, from the fabric of state down to the identity of the individual – there is no place for unity. Hence, Tamburlaine conquers the ancient world, but dies in the knowledge that the new one remains untouched by his feet – this at the end of an abortive struggle to distil his own identity into a unified warlike humour – and Faustus seeks universal knowledge that will allow him to know God, while his own persona and the world he occupies are split in two. Where there is unity in these plays, it is false: the imperial narratives connecting fledgling empires with their illustrious predecessors are satirized in *Dido, Queen of Carthage*, while the outward maintenance of unifying world views that are termed natural or religious is shown to have roots in self-seeking Machiavellianism in *The Jew of Malta*, *The Massacre at Paris* and *Edward II*.

This book, then, has attempted to demonstrate a cynical world view present throughout Marlowe's work, in which the concept of unity as a force for good is hopelessly reductive and in which unity as a political or religious concept is invariably a disguise for grimy individualist *realpolitik*. Yet, to consider Marlowe's plays as purely cynical would be reductive on our part as well. Where they demonstrate the triumph of individual greed over the common interest, they also show the resistance of diverse, distinct identities to artificially unifying narratives imposed from above. If Marlowe's characters are all as bad as each other, they are also all as good as each other, whether Christian, Muslim or Jew, and in these senses his work takes on a more radical appeal. Unity fails either because humanity is too inherently corrupt to welcome it or because it is an unwelcome concept in a world of limitless variety. As well as being true of each of Marlowe's plays individually, this can also be said about his dramatic oeuvre as a whole: it simultaneously invites mutually exclusive interpretations, a fact that is demonstrated by the diverse range of critical responses it has always provoked, and which it continues to provoke. Interpretations of Marlowe's plays continue to resist unification.

Bibliography

Adams, Joseph Q. "The *Massacre at Paris* Leaf." *The Library* 14 (1934): 447–69.

Altman, Joel. *The Tudor Play of Mind: Rhetorical Inquiry and the Development of Elizabethan Drama*. Berkeley: University of California Press, 1978.

Anderson, Kathleen. "'Stab as Occasion Serves': The Real Isabella in Marlowe's *Edward II*." *Renaissance Papers* (1992): 29–39.

Anon. *Arden of Feversham*. In *Minor Elizabethan Drama (1): Pre-Shakespearean Tragedies*. London: J. M. Dent & Sons, 1929.

———. *A Declaration of the Queenes Maiesties most gratious dealing with William Marsden and Robert Anderton, seminarie priests sithence the time of their iust condemnation, being conuicted according to the lawes, and of their obstinacie in refusing to acknowledge their duetie and allegeance to her Maiestie, 1586*. London: 1586. STC (2nd ed.) / 8157.

———. *Mar-Martine*. London: 1589. STC (2nd ed.) / 17461.

———. *A Myrror for Martinists, And all other Schismatiques, which in these dangerous daies doe breake the godlie vnitie, and disturbe the Christian peace of the Church*. London: 1590. STC (2nd ed.) / 23628.

Ardolino, Frank. "The 'Wrath of Frowning Jove': Fathers and Sons in Marlowe's Plays." *Journal of Evolutionary Psychology* 2 (1981): 83–100.

Aristotle. *Poetics*. Translated by Michael Heath. London: Penguin, 1996.

Averell, William. *A mervailous combat of contrarieties*. London: 1588. STC (2nd ed.) / 981.

Bacon, Francis. *Essays*. London: Oxford University Press, 1937.

Bale, John. *The Pageant of Popes, Contayning the lyues of all the Bishops of Rome, from the beginninge of them to the yeare of Grace 1555*. London: 1574. STC (2nd ed.) / 1304.

Barber, C. L. "The Death of Zenocrate: 'Conceiving and subduing both' in Marlowe's *Tamburlaine*." *Literature and Psychology* 16 (1966): 15–24.

Bartels, Emily C. *Spectacles of Strangeness: Imperialism, Alienation and Marlowe*. Philadelphia, PA: University of Philadelphia Press, 1993.

———. "Malta: *The Jew of Malta*, and the Fictions of Difference." In *Christopher Marlowe*, edited by Richard Wilson, 159–73. London: Longman, 1999.

Bartolovich, Crystal. "Putting Tamburlaine on a (Cognitive) Map." *Renaissance Drama* 27 (1997): 29–72.

Battenhouse, Roy W. "Tamburlaine, the 'Scourge of God.'" *PMLA* 56, no. 2 (June 1941): 337–48.

Bawcutt, N. W. "Machiavelli and Marlowe's *The Jew of Malta*." *Renaissance Drama* 3 (1970): 3–49.

Belsey, Catherine. *The Subject of Tragedy: Identity and Difference in Renaissance Drama*. London: Methuen, 1985.

Berdan, J. M. "Marlowe's *Edward II*." *Philological Quarterly* 3 (1924): 197–207.

Berek, Peter. "*Tamburlaine*'s Weak Sons: Imitation as Interpretation Before 1593." *Renaissance Drama* 13 (1982): 55–82.

Bevington, David. *From Mankind to Marlowe*. Cambridge, MA: Harvard University Press, 1962.

———. "*The Jew of Malta*." In *Marlowe: A Collection of Critical Essays*, edited by Clifford Leech, 144–58. Englewood Cliffs, NJ: Prentice Hall, 1964.

———. "Marlowe and God." *Explorations in Renaissance Culture* 17 (1991): 1–38.

Binding, Paul. *Imagined Corners: Exploring the World's First Atlas*. London: Review, 2003.

Boose, Linda E. "The Getting of a Lawful Race." In *Women, "Race," & Writing in the Early Modern Period*, edited by Margo Hendricks and Patricia Parker, 35–54. London: Routledge, 1994.

Bowers, Rick. "*The Massacre at Paris*: Marlowe's Messy Consensus Narrative." In *Marlowe, History and Sexuality: New Critical Essays on Christopher Marlowe*, edited by Paul Whitfield White, 131–42. New York: AMS Press, 1998.

Boyette, Purvis E. "Wanton Humour and Wanton Poets: Homosexuality in Marlowe's *Edward II*." *Tulane Studies in English* 22 (1977): 33–50.

Bray, Alan. "Homosexuality and the Signs of Male Friendship in Elizabethan England." *History Workshop Journal* 29 (1990): 1–19.

Bredbeck, Gregory W. *Sodomy and Interpretation: Marlowe to Milton*. Ithaca, NY: Cornell University Press, 1991.

Briggs, Julia. "Marlowe's *Massacre at Paris*: A Reconsideration." *The Review of English Studies* 34, no. 135 (1983): 257–78.

Brodwin, Leonora Leet. "*Edward II*: Marlowe's Culminating Treatment of Love." *English Literary History* 31, no. 2 (1964): 139–55.

Brooke, Nicholas. "The Moral Tragedy of Doctor Faustus." *The Cambridge Journal* 5 (1952): 662–87.

Brown, William J. "Marlowe's Debasement of Bajazet: Foxe's *Actes and Monuments* and *Tamburlaine*, Part I." *Renaissance Quarterly* 24, no. 1 (1971): 38–48.

Buckley, Emma. "'Live, false Aeneas!': Marlowe's *Dido, Queen of Carthage* and the Limits of Translation." *Classical Receptions Journal* 3, no. 2 (2011): 129–47.

Burnett, Mark Thornton. "*Edward II* and Elizabethan Politics." In *Marlowe, History and Sexuality: New Critical Essays on Christopher Marlowe*, edited by Paul Whitfield White, 91–107. New York: AMS, 1998.

———. "*Tamburlaine the Great, Parts One* and *Two*." In *The Cambridge Companion to Christopher Marlowe*, edited by Patrick Cheney, 127–43. Cambridge: Cambridge University Press, 2004.

Carter Hailey, Roger. "The Publication Date of Marlowe's *Massacre at Paris*, with a Note on the Collier Leaf." *Marlowe Studies: An Annual* 1 (2011): 25–40.

Cheney, Patrick. *Marlowe's Counterfeit Profession: Ovid, Spenser, Counter-Nationhood*. Toronto: University of Toronto Press, 1997.

Cohen, Ed. "Legislating the Norm: From Sodomy to Gross Indecency." *South Atlantic Quarterly* 88, no. 1 (1989): 181–217.

Cole, Douglas. *Suffering and Evil in the Plays of Christopher Marlowe*. Princeton, NJ: Princeton University Press, 1962.
Collinson, Patrick. "The Monarchical Republic of Queen Elizabeth I." In *Elizabethan Essays*, 31–58. London: The Hambledon Press, 1994.
Comensoli, Viviana. "Homophobia and the Regulation of Desire: A Psychoanalytic Reading of Marlowe's *Edward II*." *Journal of the History of Sexuality* 4, no. 2 (1993): 175–200.
Connolly, Annaliese. "Peele's David and Bethsabe: Reconsidering Biblical Drama of the Long 1590s." *Early Modern Literary Studies* Special Issue 16 (October 2007). <http://purl.oclc.org/emls/si-16/connpeel.htm>. Accessed 26 July 2013.
———. "*A Midsummer Night's Dream*: Shakespeare's Retrospective on Elizabeth I and the Iconography of Marriage." In *Goddesses and Queens: The Iconography of Elizabeth I*, edited by Annaliese Connolly and Lisa Hopkins, 136–53. Basingstoke: Palgrave, 2008.
Crowley, Timothy. "Arms and the Boy: Marlowe's Aeneas and the Parody of Imitation in Marlowe's *Dido, Queen of Carthage*." *English Literary Renaissance* 38, no. 3 (2008): 408–38.
de Montaigne, Michel. *On Friendship*. Translated by M. A. Screech. London: Penguin, 2004.
de Somogyi, Nick. *Shakespeare's Theatre of War*. Aldershot: Ashgate, 1998.
Deats, Sara Munson. "Marlowe's Fearful Symmetry in *Edward II*." In *"A Poet and a Filthy Playmaker": New Essays on Christopher Marlowe*, edited by Kenneth Friedenreich, Roma Gill and Constance B. Kuriyama, 241–62. New York: AMS, 1988.
———. *Sex, Gender, and Desire in the Plays of Christopher Marlowe*. London: Associated University Presses, 1997.
———. "The Subversion of Gender Hierarchies in *Dido, Queene of Carthage*." In *Marlowe, History and Sexuality: New Critical Essays on Christopher Marlowe*, edited by Paul Whitfield White, 163–78. New York: AMS Press, 1998.
———. "Marlowe's Interrogative Drama: *Dido*, *Tamburlaine*, *Faustus* and *Edward II*." In *Marlowe's Empery: Expanding His Critical Contexts*, edited by Sara Munson Deats and Robert Logan, 107–30. London: Associated University Presses, 2002.
———. "Mars or Gorgon?: *Tamburlaine* and *Henry V*." *Marlowe Studies: An Annual* 1 (2011): 99–124.
Deats, Sara Munson and Robert A. Logan, eds. *Placing the Plays of Christopher Marlowe: Fresh Cultural Contexts*. Aldershot: Ashgate, 2008.
DiGangi, Mario. *The Homoerotics of Early Modern Drama*. Cambridge: Cambridge University Press, 1997.
———. "Marlowe, Queer Studies and Renaissance Homoeroticism." In *Marlowe, History and Sexuality: New Critical Essays on Christopher Marlowe*, edited by Paul Whitfield White, 195–212. New York: AMS, 1998.
Dollimore, Jonathan. *Radical Tragedy: Religion, Ideology and Power in the Drama of Shakespeare and his Contemporaries*. 3rd ed. Basingstoke: Palgrave Macmillan, 2004.

Duxfield, Andrew. "Modern Problems of Editing: The Two Texts of Marlowe's *Doctor Faustus*." *Literature Compass* 2 (2005): 1–14.

Edwards, Richard. *The Paradise of Daintie Devices*. London: 1585. STC (2nd ed.) / 7520.

Eliot, T. S. *Elizabethan Dramatists*. London: Faber and Faber, 1963.

Ellis-Fermor, Una. *Christopher Marlowe*. London: Methuen, 1927.

Erne, Lukas. "Biography, Mythography, and Criticism: The Life and Works of Christopher Marlowe." *Modern Philology* 103, no. 1 (2005): 28–50.

Euclid. *The Elements of Geometrie*. London: 1570. STC (2nd ed.) / 10560.

Fanta, Christopher G. *Marlowe's "Agonists": An Approach to the Ambiguity of His Plays*. Cambridge, MA: Harvard University Press, 1970.

Farley-Hills, David L. "Was Marlowe's 'Malta' Malta?" *Journal of the Faculty of Arts, Royal University of Malta* 3, no. 1 (1965): 22–8.

Fehrenbach, R. J. "A Pre-1592 English Faust Book and the Date of *Doctor Faustus*." *Library: The Transactions of the Bibliographical Society* 2, no. 4 (2001): 327–35.

French, Peter. *John Dee: The World of an Elizabethan Magus*. London: Routledge & Kegan Paul, 1972.

French, William. "Double View in *Doctor Faustus*." *West Virginia University Philological Papers* 17 (1970): 3–15.

Gatti, Hilary. "Bruno and Marlowe: *Doctor Faustus*." In *Christopher Marlowe*, edited by Richard Wilson, 246–65. London: Longman, 1999.

Geoffrey of Monmouth. *History of the Kings of Britain*. Translated by Sebastian Evans, revised by Charles W. Dunn. London: J. M. Dent & Sons, 1963.

Gibbons, Brian. "'Unstable Proteus': *The Tragedy of Dido Queen of Carthage*." In *Christopher Marlowe*, edited by Brian Morris, 27–46. London: Ernest Benn Limited, 1968.

Gill, Roma. "Marlowe's Virgil: *Dido Queene of Carthage*." *Review of English Studies* 28, no. 110 (1977): 141–55.

Gillies, John. "*Tamburlaine* and Renaissance Geography." In *Early Modern English Drama: A Critical Companion*, edited by Garrett A. Sullivan Jr., Patrick Cheney and Andrew Hadfield, 35–49. Oxford: Oxford University Press, 2006.

Gilman, Ernest B. *The Curious Perspective: Literary and Pictorial Wit in the Seventeenth Century*. New Haven, CT: Yale University Press, 1978.

Godshalk, W. L. "Marlowe's *Dido, Queen of Carthage*." *English Literary History* 38, no. 1 (1971): 1–18.

Goldberg, Dena. "Whose God's on First? Special Providence in the Plays of Christopher Marlowe." *English Literary History* 60, no. 3 (1993): 569–87.

Gomez Lara, Manuel J. "Ambiguous Devices: The Use of Dramatic Emblems in Marlowe's *Edward II* (1592)." *Sederi* 15 (2005): 103–13.

Gosson, Stephen. *The Schoole of Abuse*. London: 1579. STC (2nd ed.) / 12097.

Grafton, Anthony. "Protestant versus Prophet: Isaac Casaubon on Hermes Trismegistus." *Journal of the Warburg and Courtauld Institutes* 46 (1983): 78–93.

Grande, Troni Y. *Marlovian Tragedy: The Play of Dilation*. London: Associated University Presses, 1999.
Greenblatt, Stephen. *Renaissance Self Fashioning: From More to Shakespeare*. Chicago: University of Chicago Press, 1980.
———. "Marlowe, Marx, and Anti-Semitism." In *Christopher Marlowe*, edited by Richard Wilson, 140–58. London: Longman, 1999.
Greenfield, Matthew. "Christopher Marlowe's Wound Knowledge." *PMLA* 119, no. 2 (2004): 233–46.
Greg, W. W. "The Damnation of Faustus." In *Marlowe: A Collection of Critical Essays*, edited by Clifford Leech, 92–107. Englewood Cliffs, NJ: Prentice Hall, 1964.
Guy, John. "The 1590s: The Second Reign of Elizabeth I?" In *The Reign of Elizabeth I: Court and Culture in the Last Decade*, edited by John Guy, 1–19. Cambridge: Cambridge University Press, 1995.
Hakluyt, Richard. *Voyages and Discoveries: The Principal Navigations, Voyages, Traffiques and Discoveries of the English Nation*, edited by Jack Beeching. London: Penguin, 1972.
Hammer, Paul E. J. *The Polarisation of Elizabethan Politics: The Political Career of Robert Devereux, 2nd Earl of Essex, 1585–1597*. Cambridge: Cambridge University Press, 1999.
Hariot, Thomas. *A briefe and true report of the new found land of Virginia*. London: 1590. STC (2nd ed.) / 12786.
Harlow, C. G. "A Source for Nashe's Terrors of the Night, and the Authorship of *1 Henry VI*." *Studies in English Literature, 1500–1900* 5, no. 1 (1965): 31–47.
———. "The Authorship of *1 Henry VI* (Continued)." *Studies in English Literature, 1500–1900* 5, no. 2 (1965): 269–81.
Harraway, Clare. *Re-Citing Marlowe: Approaches to the Drama*. Aldershot: Ashgate, 2000.
Hendricks, Margo. "Managing the Barbarian: *The Tragedy of Dido, Queen of Carthage*." *Renaissance Drama* 23 (1992): 165–88.
Hiscock, Andrew. *The Uses of This World: Thinking Space in Shakespeare, Marlowe, Cary and Jonson*. Cardiff: University of Wales Press, 2004.
Hitchcock, Robert. *The quintesence of wit being a corrant comfort of conceites, maximies, and poleticke deuises*. London: 1590. STC (2nd ed.) / 21744.
Hodgkins, Christopher. *Reforming Empire: Protestant Colonialism and Conscience in British Literature*. London: University of Missouri Press, 2002.
Honan, Park. *Christopher Marlowe: Poet and Spy*. Oxford: Oxford University Press, 2005.
Hopkins, Lisa. *Christopher Marlowe: A Literary Life*. Basingstoke: Palgrave, 2000.
———. "We Were the Trojans: British National Identities in 1633." *Renaissance Studies* 16, no. 1 (2002): 36–51.
———. *Christopher Marlowe: Renaissance Dramatist*. Edinburgh: Edinburgh University Press, 2008.
Hutchings, Mark. "Marlowe's Scourge of God." *Notes and Queries* 51, no. 3 (2004): 244–7.

Ide, Arata. "*The Jew of Malta* and the Diabolic Power of Theatrics." *Studies in English Literature 1500–1900* 46, no. 2 (2006): 257–79.

James, William. *A sermon preached at Paules Crosse the IX. of Nouember, 1589.* London: 1590. STC (2nd ed.) / 14464.

Jarman, Derek. *Queer Edward II*. London: British Film Institute, 1991.

Kirschbaum, Leo. "Marlowe's *Faustus*: A Reconsideration." *The Review of English Studies* 19 (1943): 225–41.

Klein, Bernhard. *Maps and the Writing of Space in Early Modern England*. Basingstoke: Palgrave Macmillan, 2001.

Knight, Sarah. "Flat Dichotomists and Learned Men: Ramism in Elizabethan Drama and Satire." In *Ramus, Pedagogy and the Liberal Arts: Ramism in Britain and the Wider World*, edited by Steven J. Reid and Emma Annete Wilson, 47–67. Farnham: Ashgate, 2011.

Knutson, Roslyn L. "Marlowe, Company Ownership, and the Role of Edward II." *Medieval & Renaissance Drama in England* 18 (2005): 37–46.

Kocher, Paul H. "François Hotman and Marlowe's *The Massacre at Paris*." *PMLA* 56, no. 2 (1941): 349–68.

———. "Marlowe's Art of War." *Studies in Philology* 39 (1942): 207–25.

———. "Contemporary Pamphlet Backgrounds for Marlowe's *Massacre at Paris*." *Modern Language Quarterly* 8, no. 2 (1947): 151–73.

———. "Contemporary Pamphlet Backgrounds for Marlowe's *Massacre at Paris*. Part Two." *Modern Language Quarterly* 8, no. 3 (1947): 309–18.

Leech, Clifford. "Marlowe's 'Edward II': Power and Suffering." *Critical Quarterly* 1 (1959): 181–96.

Lenker, Lagretta Tallent. "The Hopeless Daughter of a Hapless Jew: Father and Daughter in Marlowe's *The Jew of Malta*." In *Placing the Plays of Christopher Marlowe: Fresh Cultural Contexts*, edited by Sara Munson Deats and Robert Logan, 63–73. Aldershot: Ashgate, 2008.

Levin, Harold. *Christopher Marlowe: The Overreacher*. London: Faber and Faber, 1961.

Levin, Richard. "The Contemporary Perception of Marlowe's Tamburlaine." *Medieval and Renaissance Drama in England* 1 (1984): 51–70.

Lodge, Thomas. *Euphues Shadow, The Battaile of the Sences* (London: 1592), STC (2nd ed.) / 16656.

Logan, Robert A. "Violence, Terrorism, and War in Marlowe's *Tamburlaine* Plays." In *War and Words: Horror and Heroism in the Literature of Warfare*, edited by Sara Munson Deats, Lagretta Tallent Lenker and Merry G. Perry, 65–81. Lanham, MD: Lexington, 2004.

———. *Shakespeare's Marlowe: The Influence of Christopher Marlowe on Shakespeare's Artistry*. Aldershot: Ashgate, 2007.

Lunney, Ruth. *Marlowe and the Popular Tradition: Innovation in the English Drama Before 1595*. Manchester: Manchester University Press, 2002.

———. "Speaking to the Audience: Direct Address in the Plays of Marlowe and His Contemporaries." In *Christopher Marlowe the Craftsman: Lives, Stage, and Page*, edited by Sarah K. Scott and M. L. Stapleton, 109–22. Farnham: Ashgate, 2010.

Lupton, Julia Reinhard. "*The Jew of Malta.*" In *The Cambridge Companion to Christopher Marlowe*, edited by Patrick Cheney, 144–57. Cambridge: Cambridge University Press, 2004.

———. *Citizen-Saints: Shakespeare and Political Theology*. Chicago: The University of Chicago Press, 2005.

Machiavelli, Niccolò. *The Discourses*. Edited and translated by Bernard Crick. Harmondsworth: Penguin, 1970.

———. *The Prince*. Edited by Lucille Margaret Kekewich. Ware, Herts: Wordsworth Classics, 1997.

Mack, Peter. "Ramus and Ramism: Rhetoric and Dialectic." In *Ramus, Pedagogy and the Liberal Arts: Ramism in Britain and the Wider World*, edited by Steven J. Reid and Emma Annete Wilson, 7–23. Farnham: Ashgate, 2011.

Mackenzie, Clayton G. "*The Massacre at Paris* and the *Danse Macabre*." *Papers on Language and Literature* 43, no. 3 (2007): 311–34.

Mahood, M. M. *Poetry and Humanism*. New York: Norton, 1970.

Marlowe, Christopher. *Edward II*. Edited by Roma Gill. Oxford: Oxford University Press, 1967.

———. *Dido Queen of Carthage and The Massacre at Paris*. Edited by H. J. Oliver. London: Methuen, 1968.

———. *Tamburlaine*. Edited by J. S. Cunningham. Manchester: Manchester University Press, 1981.

———. *Doctor Faustus: A- and B-Texts (1604, 1616)*. Edited by David Bevington and Eric Rasmussen. Manchester: Manchester University Press, 1993.

———. *Edward II*. Edited by Charles R. Forker. Manchester: Manchester University Press, 1994.

———. *The Jew of Malta*. Edited by James R. Siemon. London: A & C Black, 1994.

———. *Doctor Faustus and Other Plays*. Edited by David Bevington and Eric Rasmussen. Oxford: Oxford University Press, 1998.

———. *The Complete Plays*. Edited by Mark Thornton Burnett. London: Everyman, 1999.

Maxwell, J. C. "The Sin of Faustus." *The Wind and the Rain* 4 (1947): 49–52.

McAdam, Ian. *The Irony of Identity: Self and Imagination in the Drama of Christopher Marlowe*. London: Associated University Presses, 1999.

McAlindon, Tom. "Classical Mythology and Christian Tradition in *Doctor Faustus*." *PMLA* 81, no. 3 (1996): 214–23.

McCullen, Joseph T. "Doctor Faustus and Renaissance Learning." *Modern Language Review* 51 (1956): 6–16.

McElroy, John F. "Repetition, Contrariety, and Individualization in *Edward II*." *Studies in English Literature, 1500–1900* 24 (1984): 205–24.

McIlwraith, A. K., ed. *Five Elizabethan Tragedies*. Oxford: Oxford University Press, 1938.

Mebane, John S. *Renaissance Magic & the Return of the Golden Age: The Occult Tradition in Marlowe, Jonson, and Shakespeare.* Lincoln: University of Nebraska Press, 1989.

Mills, L. J. "The Meaning of *Edward II.*" *Modern Philology* 32 (1934): 11–31.

Minshull, Catherine. "Marlowe's 'Sound Machevill.'" *Renaissance Drama* 13 (1982): 35–53.

Nashe, Thomas. *The Works of Thomas Nashe.* 5 vols. Edited by R. B. McKerrow. Oxford: Clarendon Press, 1958.

Nicholl, Charles. *The Reckoning: The Murder of Christopher Marlowe.* Rev. ed. London: Vintage, 2002.

Orgel, Stephen. *Impersonations: The Performance of Gender in Shakespeare's England.* Cambridge: Cambridge University Press, 1996.

Ornstein, Robert. "The Comic Synthesis in *Doctor Faustus.*" *English Literary History* 22, no. 3 (1955): 165–72.

Parker, John. *The Aesthetics of Antichrist: From Christian Drama to Christopher Marlowe.* London: Cornell University Press, 2007.

Patterson, Annabel. *Censorship and Interpretation: The Conditions of Writing and Reading in Early Modern England.* Madison: University of Wisconsin Press, 1984.

Pearce, T. M. "Tamburlaine's 'Discipline to His Three Sonnes': An Interpretation of *Tamburlaine Part II.*" *Modern Language Quarterly* 15 (1954): 18–27.

Peele, George. *David and Bethsabe.* In *Minor Elizabethan Drama (I): Pre-Shakespearean Tragedies.* London: J. M. Dent & Sons, 1929.

———. *The Battle of Alcazar.* In *The Stukeley Plays*, edited by Charles Edelman. Manchester: Manchester University Press, 2005.

Pincombe, Mike. *Elizabethan Humanism: Literature and Learning in the later Sixteenth Century.* London: Longman, 2001.

Plato. *The Symposium.* Translated by W. Hamilton. London: Penguin, 1951.

Poole, Kristen. "*Dr. Faustus* and Reformation Theology." In *Early Modern English Drama: A Critical Companion*, edited by Garrett A. Sullivan, Patrick Cheney and Andrew Hadfield, 96–107. Oxford: Oxford University Press, 2005.

———. "Garbled Martyrdom in Christopher Marlowe's *The Massacre at Paris.*" *Comparative Drama* 32, no. 1 (2008): 1–25.

Porter, J. A. "Marlowe, Shakespeare, and the Canonization of Heterosexuality." *South Atlantic Quarterly* 88, no. 1 (1989): 127–47.

Proser, Matthew. "*Dido Queene of Carthage* and the Evolution of Marlowe's Dramatic Style." In *"A Poet and a Filthy Playmaker": New Essays on Christopher Marlowe*, edited by Kenneth Friedenreich, Roma Gill and Constance B. Kuriyama, 83–99. New York: AMS, 1988.

Ribner, Irving. "Marlowe and Machiavelli." *Comparative Literature* 6, no. 4 (1954): 348–56.

———. "Marlowe's *Edward II* and the Tudor History Play." *English Literary History* 22, no. 4 (1955): 243–53.

Riggs, David. *The World of Christopher Marlowe.* London: Faber and Faber, 2004.

Roberts, Gareth. "Necromantic Books: Christopher Marlowe, Doctor Faustus and Agrippa of Nettesheim." In *Christopher Marlowe and English Renaissance Culture*, edited by Daryll Grantley and Peter Roberts, 148–69. Aldershot: Scolar Press, 1996.

———. "Marlowe and the Metaphysics of Magicians." In *Constructing Christopher Marlowe*, edited by J. A. Downie and J. T. Parnell, 55–73. Cambridge: Cambridge University Press, 2000.

Rouzie, Albert. "The Dangers of (D)alliance: Power, Homosexual Desire, and Homophobia in Marlowe's *Edward II*." *Genders* 21 (1995): 114–40.

Rutkoski, Marie. "Breeching the Boy in Marlowe's *Edward II*." *Studies in English Literature, 1500–1900* 46, no. 2 (2006): 281–304.

Sachs, Arieh. "The Religious Despair of Doctor Faustus." *Journal of English and Germanic Philology* 63 (1964): 625–47.

Sales, Roger. *Christopher Marlowe*. Basingstoke: Macmillan, 1991.

Sanders, Wilbur. *The Dramatist and the Received Idea: Studies in the Plays of Marlowe and Shakespeare*. Cambridge: Cambridge University Press, 1968.

Seaton, Ethel. "Marlowe's Map." In *Marlowe: A Collection of Critical Essays*, edited by Clifford Leech, 36–56. Englewood Cliffs, NJ: Prentice Hall, 1964.

Shakespeare, William. *The First Part of King Henry VI* (The Arden Shakespeare). Edited by Andrew S. Cairncross. London: Methuen, 1962.

Shannon, Laurie J. "Monarchs, Minions, and 'Soveraigne' Friendship." *South Atlantic Quarterly* 198 (1998): 91–112.

Shepard, Alan. *Marlowe's Soldiers: Rhetorics of Masculinity in the Age of the Armada*. Aldershot: Ashgate, 2002.

Shepherd, Simon. *Marlowe and the Politics of Elizabethan Theatre*. Hemel Hempstead: Harvester Wheatsheaf, 1986.

Sidney, Philip. *An Apology for Poetry*. Edited by Geoffrey Shepherd. London: Thomas Nelson and Sons, 1965.

Singer, Irving. "Erotic Transformations in the Legend of Dido and Aeneas." *Modern Language Notes* 90, no. 6 (1975): 767–83.

Smith, Bruce R. *Homosexual Desire in Shakespeare's England: A Cultural Poetics*. Chicago: University of Chicago Press, 1991.

Smith, Mary E. "Staging Marlowe's *Dido Queene of Carthage*." *Studies in English Literature, 1500–1900* 17, no. 2 (1977): 177–90.

Spence, Leslie. "Tamburlaine and Marlowe." *PMLA* 42, no. 3 (1927): 604–22.

Spenser, Edmund. *The Faerie Queene*. Edited by Thomas P. Roche Jr. with the assistance of C. Patrick O'Donnell Jr. London: Penguin, 1987.

Steane, J. B. *Marlowe: A Critical Study*. Cambridge: Cambridge University Press, 1964.

Steggle, Matthew. "Udall, Nicholas (1504–1556)." In *Oxford Dictionary of National Biography*. Oxford: Oxford University Press, 2004. Online ed. October 2006. <http://www.oxforddnb.com/view/article/27974>. Accessed 16 July 2013.

Stewart, Alan. "*Edward II* and Male Same-Sex desire." In *Early Modern English Drama: A Critical Companion*, edited by Garrett A. Sullivan Jr., Patrick Cheney and Andrew Hadfield, 82–95. Oxford: Oxford University Press, 2006.

Stubbes, Philip. *The Anatomie of Abuses*. London: 1583. STC (2nd ed.) / 23376.

Sullivan, Garrett A. Jr. "Space, Measurement and Stalking Tamburlaine." *Renaissance Drama* 28 (1997): 3–27.

———. "Geography and Identity in Marlowe." In *The Cambridge Companion to Christopher Marlowe*, edited by Patrick Cheney, 231–44. Cambridge: Cambridge University Press, 2004.

Summers, Claude J. "Isabella's Plea for Gaveston in Marlowe's *Edward II*." *Philological Quarterly* 52 (1973): 308–10.

———. "Sex, Politics and Self-Realization in *Edward II*." In *"A Poet and a Filthy Playmaker": New Essays on Christopher Marlowe*, edited by Kenneth Friedenreich, Roma Gill and Constance B. Kuriyama, 221–40. New York: AMS, 1988.

Taunton, Nina. *1590s Drama and Militarism: Portrayals of War in Marlowe, Chapman and Shakespeare's "Henry V."* Aldershot: Ashgate, 2001.

Thomas, Vivien and William Tydeman, eds. *Christopher Marlowe: The Plays and Their Sources*. London: Routledge, 1994.

Tillyard, E. M. W. *The Elizabethan World Picture*. London: Penguin, 1990.

Trismegistus, Hermes. *Hermes Mercurius Trismegistus his Divine pymander in seventeen books*. London: 1657. Wing / H1566.

Tromly, Fred B. *Playing With Desire: Christopher Marlowe and the Art of Tantalization*. Toronto: University of Toronto Press, 1998.

Uman, Deborah and Sara Morrison, eds. *Staging the Blazon in Early Modern English Theater*. Farnham: Ashgate, 2013.

Virgil. *The Aeneid: A New Prose Translation*. Translated by David West. London: Penguin, 1990.

Vitkus, Daniel. *Turning Turk: English Theater and the Multicultural Mediterranean, 1570–1630*. Basingstoke: Palgrave Macmillan, 2003.

———. "Turks and Jews in *The Jew of Malta*." In *Early Modern English Drama: A Critical Companion*, edited by Garrett A. Sullivan Jr., Patrick Cheney and Andrew Hadfield, 61–72. Oxford: Oxford University Press, 2006.

Waith, Eugene M. "Tamburlaine." In *Marlowe: A Collection of Critical Essays*, edited by Clifford Leech, 69–91. Englewood Cliffs, NJ: Prentice Hall, 1964.

Weiner, Carol Z. "The Beleaguered Isle: A Study of Elizabethan and Early Jacobean Anti-Catholicism." *Past and Present* 51 (1971): 27–62.

Whetstone, George. *The English Myrror*. London: 1586. STC (2nd ed.) / 2336.

Wiggins, Martin. "When Did Marlowe Write *Dido, Queen of Carthage*?" *Review of English Studies* 59, no. 241 (2008): 521–41.

Williams, Deanne. "Dido, Queen of England." *English Literary History* 73, no. 1 (2006): 31–59.

Wilson, Richard. "Another Country: Marlowe and the Go-Between." In *Renaissance Go-Betweens: Cultural Exchange in Early Modern Europe*, edited by Andreas Höfele and Werner von Koppenfels, 177–99. Berlin: Walter de Gruyter, 2005.

Wither, George. *An A. B. C. for Layemen*. London: 1585. STC (2nd ed.) / 25888.

Woolley, Benjamin. *The Queen's Conjuror: The Life and Magic of Dr Dee*. London: Flamingo, 2002.

Wraight, A. D. and Virginia F. Stern. *In Search of Christopher Marlowe*. London: Macdonald, 1965.

Yates, Frances. *The Occult Philosophy in the Elizabethan Age*. London: Routledge & Kegan Paul, 1979.

Index

Aeneid, The (Virgil) 13–15, 17n9, 22, 24, 26, 28, 30–32, 35–6
Agrippa, Heinrich Cornelius 78–80, 82, 86
ambiguity
    critics' identification of it in Marlowe's work 5–8
    in *Dido, Queen of Carthage* 14–28
    in *Doctor Faustus* 65–74, 76, 86–7
    in *Edward II* 117–35
    in *Jew of Malta, The* 90–100
    in *Tamburlaine* 47–63
    in the works collectively 147–8
Anatomie of Abuses, The (Stubbes) 119
Anderson, Kathleen 125n23, 140n64
Anderton, Robert 2n4
Annals of England, The (Stow) 126
Arden of Faversham (Anon.) 5
Ardolino, Frank 57
Aristotle 70–71, 113
Averell, William 2, 104

Bacon, Francis 144–5
Bacon, Roger 78
Bale, John 124n20
Barber, C. L. 43, 53, 60
Barclay, Alexander 46
Bartels, Emily 25–6, 34, 54n40, 96, 104, 134, 135n55
Bartolovich, Crystal 47
Battenhouse, Roy W. 53n37
Battle of Alcazar (Peele) 8
Bawcutt, N. W. 90
Beeching, Jack 33
Belsey, Catherine 9
Berdan, J. M. 117, 125n22, 127–8, 141–2
Bevington, David 68, 72, 78n23, 92n12, 98
Binding, Paul 45
Bowers, Rick 109, 111–12
Boyette, Purvis E. 128n37, 132–3, 135
Brant, Sebastian 46
Bray, Alan 131n43

Bredbeck, Gregory 21n19, 131n43
Brief and True Report (Hariot) 36
Briggs, Julia 109, 114
Brodwin, Leonora Leet 127, 128n37, 133
Brown, William J. 48
Bruno, Giordano 3, 78
Burnett, Mark Thornton 41–3, 108, 141

Cabala 78, 80, 82, 86–7
Cheney, Patrick 20n15
Chronicles (Holinshed) 33, 120, 125–6
Cohen, Ed 130
Cole, Douglas 22n21, 24, 91n7, 108, 128, 139
Comensoli, Viviana 134n53, 135n55
Corpus Hermeticum (Hermes Trismegistus) 79–85

David and Bethsabe (Peele) 8
Day, Angel 144
Deats, Sara Munson 6–7, 9, 17n9, 22, 24, 27, 49, 58n46, 117n1, 123n17, 138–9
Dee, John 3, 32–3, 65, 78–80, 82–3, 87
DiGangi, Mario 22n19, 130n40, 130n43, 141n70
discord 2–5, 11, 89, 98n31, 104, 147
Discourses on Livy (Machiavelli) 90, 105–6
Dollimore, Jonathan 7, 9, 86

Edwards, Richard 138n61
Elizabeth I 1–2, 4, 16, 32, 35–7, 80, 87, 124, 136n57, 144
Ellis-Fermor 9n28, 31n41, 43
English Myrror, The (Whetstone) 142–3
English Secretorie, The (Day) 144
Everyman 51n33, 71

Faerie Queene, The (Spenser) 5, 35n54
Fanta, Christopher G. 5–6, 59–60, 97
Ficino, Marsilio 80

French, Peter 79–82, 86n55
Friar Bacon and Friar Bungay (Greene) 78

Geoffrey of Monmouth 32–5
Gibbons, Brian 14n1, 16, 18, 28
Gill, Roma 21, 123, 128, 130n42, 134
Giorgi, Francesco 80, 82
Godshalk, William Leigh 18, 21
Goldberg, Dena 51n33, 54n40
Gorboduc (Sackville and Norton) 4
Gosson, Stephen 48, 95, 106
Grande, Troni Y. 32, 102, 109
Greenblatt, Stephen 9, 45–6, 54, 91, 94–5, 97
Greene, Robert 78
Greenfield, Matthew 50, 56–7
Greg, W. W. 68, 72n17
Guy, John 1, 3

Hakluyt, Richard 33, 36
Hariot, Thomas 36, 80–81
Hendricks, Margo 24–5, 30, 32–3, 35
Henry VI, Part One (Shakespeare) 4
Hermes Trismegistus 79–80, 82
Hermeticism 3, 8, 65, 78–87
Hiscock, Andrew 90, 105
Historia Regum Britanii (Geoffrey of Monmouth) 32–5
Hitchcock, Robert 2, 98n31, 104
Hodgkins, Christopher 36
Holinshed, Raphael 33, 120, 125–7
Hopkins, Lisa 10n28, 23n24, 32n44, 50n31, 54n40, 100, 127n30
Hutchings, Mark 53

imperialism 10, 13, 28–37

James, William 3
Jarman, Derek 127n30

Kirschbaum, Leo 67
Klein, Bernhard 45, 55
Knight, Sarah 113n67, 114
Kocher, Paul H. 48, 58n46, 107–9

Lara, Manuel J. Gomez 141n66
Leech, Clifford 118, 120, 125n22, 127–8, 140n65
Lenker, Lagretta Tallent 97n27

Levin, Harold 18n12, 31n41, 41, 42n6, 53n34, 91n9, 92, 95n19, 97n27, 99n33, 118n3, 123, 125n23, 128, 136n57, 136n58, 138n60, 141n65
Levin, Richard 8n22, 47–8
Lodge, Thomas 138n61
Logan, Robert A. 6n17, 49, 120n11, 135, 145
Lunney, Ruth 7, 94–5
Lupton, Julia Reinhard 90, 97–8, 102–3

Machiavelli, Niccolò 90–93, 105–7, 121n12
Machiavellianism 28, 89–93, 96, 105–8, 111, 118, 121, 126, 140n64, 147
Mack, Peter 113
magic 10, 68, 73, 75–87; *see also* Hermeticism
Mahood, M. M. 58n46
Marlowe, Christopher
    biography 9, 9n28
    works
        Dido, Queen of Carthage 3, 8, 10, 13–37, 118, 129, 147
            Aeneas's passivity 15–19
            ambiguity 14–28
            duty and desire 23–8
            frivolity of and conflict among Olympian gods 19–24
            mobility of Troy 28–31
            mytho-historical narratives 28–37
            performance by boys' company 22–3
            sexuality 19
        Doctor Faustus 3–4, 5, 8, 10, 65–87, 93, 113–15, 117, 124
            ambiguity 65–74, 76, 86–7
            genre 70–74
            Hermeticism 65, 78–87
            magic 73, 76–87
            unity/unification of knowledge 74–87
        Edward II 3, 8, 11, 111, 115, 117–47
            ambiguity 117–35
            Edward's murder 120n11
            Machiavellianism 121, 126
            natural order 137–40
            sexuality 127–35

social status 133–40
unity 142–6
Jew of Malta, The 3, 5, 8, 11, 89–107, 109–11, 114–15, 117, 140, 147
 ambiguity 90–100
 anti-Semitism 91, 93–4
 Knights of St John 95–6
 Machiavellianism 89–93, 105–7
 religion 98–107
 unity 89–90, 94, 98–107
Massacre at Paris, The 3, 8, 11, 89, 107–15, 117, 147
 critical history 107–9
 Machiavellianism 111
 Ramus's murder 113–14
 textual problems 107–8
 unity 109–15
'Passionate Shepherd to his Love, The' 20
Tamburlaine the Great, Parts One and Two 4, 8, 10, 39–63, 93, 120, 129
 ambiguity 47–63
 cartography 44–7
 language 40–41
 militarism 48–9
 murder of Calyphas 58–9
 physiology 55–9
 reduction 43–7
 relationship with Zenocrate 59–62
 religion 50–54
 Tamburlaine's appearance 42–3
 Tamburlaine's theatricality 43
Mar-Martine (Anon.) 104
Martin Marprelate controversy 2, 104
Maxwell, J. C. 69, 71, 72n17
McAdam, Ian 25, 123
McAlindon, Tom 73
McCullen, Joseph T. 67
McElroy, John F. 6n17, 145
Mills, L. J. 118n3, 119, 126–7, 129
Minshull, Catherine 90, 96, 106
Mirandola, Giovanni Pico Della 80, 82
Monas Hieroglyphica (Dee) 3, 82–3
Montaigne, Michel de 144
morality drama 7, 65, 71–4, 87

Norton, Thomas 4

Occulta Philosophia, De (Agrippa) 79, 86
'Of Friendship' (Bacon) 144–5
Oliver, H. J. 28, 107–8
On Friendship (Montaigne) 144
Organon, The (Aristotle) 113
Orgel, Stephen 120n11
Ornstein, Robert 67
Ortelius, Abraham 45
Ovid 22, 24

Pageant of Popes, The (Bale) 124n20
Pearce, T. M. 48
Peele, George 8
Pincombe, Mike 67
Plato 79–80, 82, 129–30
Poole, Kristen 6n17, 72, 112
Prince, The (Machiavelli) 90–93, 121n12
Principal Navigations, The (Hakluyt) 33, 36

realpolitik 11, 89–93, 105–7, 119, 146–8
Ribner, Irving 90, 128, 142
Riggs, David 10n28, 75, 77n22, 132–3
Roberts, Gareth 79n28, 86–7
Rutkoski, Marie 121, 131n43, 135n55

Sachs, Arieh 66–7, 69, 72n17, 85n51
Sackville, Thomas 4
Sales, Roger 62n51, 95, 96n25, 106n49
Sanders, Wilbur 91, 96n24, 108–9, 125n23, 131, 141n65, 145
Schoole of Abuse (Gosson) 95
sexuality 21, 117, 120n11, 127–35
Shakespeare, William 4, 6–7, 18, 59
Shepard, Alan 48–9, 58n46
Ship of Folys of the Worlde (Brant / Barclay) 46
Sidney, Philip 70–71
Siemon, James R. 92n11, 99
Singer, Irving 14, 18
Smith, Bruce R. 21n19, 130n40
Smith, Mary E. 22–3
Speed, John 55
Spence, Leslie 59
Steane, J. B. 14–15, 18, 21, 41, 54n40, 94, 97–8, 108, 118, 123, 128, 141n65, 145
Stow, John 126

Stubbes, Philip 118–19
Sullivan, Garret A. Jr. 45–6
Sullivan, J. S. 53
Summers, Claude J. 125, 136–7, 140n64
Symposium (Plato) 129–30

Taunton, Nina 48
Theatrum Orbis Terrarum (Ortelius) 45
Thomas, Vivien and William Tydeman 123
Tromly, Fred B. 15n6, 18n11, 23, 91n7, 96n24, 96n25, 97n28, 103n42

Udall, Nicholas 130
unity
    of Catholic church 4–5
    in *Doctor Faustus* 65, 74–87
    in *Edward II* 135, 142–6
    in Elizabethan society 1–3
    in *Jew of Malta, The* 89–90, 94, 98–107
    of knowledge 3–4, 8, 74–87
    in Marlowe's plays, collectively 10–11, 147–8

    in *Massacre at Paris, The* 109–15
    in *Tamburlaine the Great*, Parts One and Two 56
    tension with ambiguity of the plays 8–10
    in the work of Marlowe's contemporaries 4–5

Vanitate Scientiarum, De (Agrippa) 86
Virgil 13–15, 17, 19, 22, 24, 26, 28, 30–32, 35–6
Vitkus, Daniel, 49–51, 54, 62–3, 90, 91n9, 94, 99

Waith, Eugene M. 58
Weiner, Carol Z. 5
Whetstone, George 142–3
Willet, Andrew 102
Williams, Deanne 35
Wilson, Richard 90, 100
Wither, George 2–3, 104

Yates, Frances 65n2, 78, 80, 82, 86–7